Getting Incentives Right

Getting Incentives Right

Improving Torts, Contracts,
and Restitution

Robert D. Cooter and Ariel Porat

PRINCETON UNIVERSITY PRESS
Princeton and Oxford

Published by Princeton University Press, 41 William Street, Princeton, New Jersey 08540
In the United Kingdom: Princeton University Press, 6 Oxford Street, Woodstock,
    Oxfordshire OX20 1TW

press.princeton.edu

Library of Congress Cataloging-in-Publication Data

Cooter, Robert.
   Getting incentives right : improving torts, contracts, and restitution / Robert Cooter
and Ariel Porat.
      pages cm
   Includes bibliographical references and index.
   ISBN 978-0-691-15159-5 (hardcover : alk. paper) 1. Liability (Law)—United States.
2. Negligence—United States. 3. Torts—United States. 4. Contracts—United States.
5. Compensation (Law)—United States. 6. Restitution—United States. I. Porat, Ariel.
II. Title.
   KF1250.C67 2014
346.7302—dc23   2013027792

British Library Cataloging-in-Publication Data is available

This book has been composed in Minion Pro and Myriad Pro

Printed on acid-free paper. ∞

Printed in the United States of America

10 9 8 7 6 5 4 3 2 1

Contents

Acknowledgments

Many talented people contributed to this book, like a potluck dinner for chefs. Our teachers served up the first ideas. Over the years we mixed work and pleasure with colleagues in various universities who became our friends. Many commentators who knew the original papers on which the book is based helped us to keep the best and discard the rest. Others corrected errors and clumsiness in our arguments. It is hard to know where to start and stop acknowledging them. To avoid intellectual biography, we will mention those who directly helped us with the manuscript.

We thank our colleagues Ronen Avraham, Oren Bar-Gill, Omri Ben-Shahar, Eyal Benvenisti, Hanoch Dagan, Melvin Eisenberg, Ehud Guttel, Sharon Hannes, Alon Harel, Assaf Jacob, Roy Kreitner, Saul Levmore, Eric Posner, Cathy Sharkey, Alex Stein, Lior Strahilevitz, Stephen Sugarman, Avraham Tabbach, Ernest Weinrib, and Omri Yadlin. We also thank Chuck Myers from Princeton University Press, who worked with us on the book from its very early stages. His advice contributed a lot to the book's clarity and accessibility to a wide audience. Finally, we are very grateful to Vanessa Casado-Pérez and Omer Yehezkel for their superb research assistance; we were lucky to have those two very talented assistants on board. Ida Ng assisted in manuscript preparation.

Several of the topics developed in this book were initially published in the following law journal articles: Robert Cooter, *Prices and Sanctions*, 84 Columbia Law Review 1523 (1984); Robert Cooter & Ariel Porat, *Does Risk to Oneself Increase the Care Owed to Others? Law and Economics in Conflict*, 29 Journal of Legal Studies 19 (2000); Ariel Porat, *Symposium on the Restatement (Third) of Torts: Expanding Liability for Negligence Per Se*, 44 Wake Forest Law Review 979 (2009); Robert Cooter & Ariel Porat, *Total Liability for Excessive Harm*, 36 Journal of Legal Studies 63 (2007); Robert Cooter, *Unity in Tort, Contract, and Property: The Model of Precaution*, 73 California Law Review 1 (1985); Robert Cooter & Ariel Porat, *Anti Insurance*, 31 Journal of Legal Studies 203 (2002); Robert Cooter & Ariel Porat, *Decreasing Liability Contracts*, 33 Journal of Legal Studies 157 (2004); Ariel Porat, *Private Production of Public Goods: Liability for Unrequested Benefits*, 108 Michigan Law Review 189 (2009); Robert Cooter & Ariel Porat, *Liability Externalities and Mandatory Choices: Should Doctors Pay Less?*, 1 Tort Law Journal Issue 1, Article 2 (2006); Robert Cooter & Ariel Porat, *Should Courts Deduct Non-Legal Sanctions from Damages?*, 30 Journal of Legal Studies 401 (2001). We hope that the ideas in the book remain crisp and enticing to you, the readers, who will judge the feast better than its cooks.

Introduction

aw should promote the wellbeing of people. Tort law, which deals with accidents, should reduce their cost and frequency—an important matter, as accidents cause approximately 42 million hospital visits and 182 thousand deaths
per year in the United States.[1] Contract law, called upon in a range of activities
from renting an apartment to buying an oil field, should lubricate these transactions. Transactions based on contract law generate approximately fifteen tril-
lion dollars of national income annually in the United States.[2] Restitution law,
which mostly discourages people from using what belongs to others without
their consent, should encourage people to supply benefits for others that markets cannot provide.

In the law of torts, contracts, or restitution, the plaintiff in a suit is usually a
private legal person such as a citizen or corporation, not the state as in a criminal trial. The defendant is often a private legal person as well. For these reasons,
the law of torts, contracts, and restitution is called *private law*. By explaining
how private law reduces accident costs, lubricates bargains, and encourages
unrequested benefits, we will show three ways to improve the law of torts, contracts, and restitution. Before presenting our main claims, however, we briefly
summarize the received economic analysis of torts, contracts, and restitution.

Tort law creates incentives for manufacturers to design safer products, injurers and victims to take precautions, insurance companies to adjust their cov-
erage, governments to build safer roads, and so on. By imposing the cost of
accidents on the parties who can best avoid them, tort law can reduce the cost
of accidents to society. Unfortunately, when tort law or regulations fail to do so,
much money, time, and effort spent on preventing accidents are wasted. Thus,
investments in precaution are too high or too low when the negligent injurers'
liability does not correspond to the social harm that injurers cause. Indeed, we
spend too much money reducing a few small losses, as with some industrial
chemicals, but we do not spend enough reducing numerous large losses, as with
kerosene space heaters.[3] A better use of the same resources could provide more

---

[1] The three leading causes of accidental injury deaths are automobiles (more than 45,000 per
year), poisoning (more than 29,000 per year), and falls (more than 22,000 per year). U.S. Department of Health and Human Services, Centers for Disease Control and Prevention,
National Vital Statistics Reports, final data from 2007. Available at http://www.cdc.gov/nchs
/data/nvsr/nvsr58/nvsr58_19.pdf.

[2] Economic Report of the President, Table B-1. Gross domestic product, 1963–2011,
p. 316.

[3] *Id.*

safety at no more cost. "Inefficient expenditures" on safety sounds like dull accounting, but it is a matter of life and death. To make the world safer without wasting money, judges, legislators, and regulators need to improve tort law.

Tort law has two pervasive rules that provide incentives for actors to reduce the cost of accidents: strict liability and negligence. Under a rule of strict liability the actor is liable for any harm caused by his behavior, as long as the victim was not negligent. Under a rule of negligence the actor is liable only for harms caused by his *negligent* behavior—again, assuming the victim is not negligent.[4] Both rules can provide actors with efficient incentives to minimize social costs, but in different ways.

We begin with strict liability. Suppose an employer has to decide whether to install a safety device in the workplace to reduce risks to his employees. Assume the installation costs $9, and it reduces risks to employees by $10. A strict liability rule provides incentives for the employer to install the safety device that costs him $9 and avoids liability of $10. Installing the safety device is also socially efficient since society benefits from reducing a risk of $10 at a cost of $9.

Alternatively, suppose that the cost of installing the safety device is $11, rather than $10. A strict liability rule provides incentives for the employer *not* to install the safety device, since installation costs $11 and avoids liability of $10. Not installing the safety device is also socially efficient, since society suffers from reducing a risk of $10 at a cost of $11.

Interestingly, a negligence rule would provide the employer with the same incentives as a strict liability rule. Under a negligence rule, an actor is negligent and bears liability for the resulting harm if he fails to take precaution that costs less than the risk reduced by it. In the first version of our example, in which precaution costs $9 and reduces risk of $10, the employer who fails to install the safety device is negligent (9 < 10) and bears liability of $10, exactly as under a strict liability rule. As a result, he will take the precaution that efficiency requires. Conversely, in the second version of our example—precaution costs $11 and reduces risk of $10—the employer who fails to install the safety device is *not* negligent (11 > 10) and bears *no* liability. As a result, and as efficiency requires, he will *not* take the precaution. So both rules provide potential injurers such as the employer with efficient incentives to minimize social costs.

Contract law is the second large body of private law. Whereas accidents are sometimes a matter of life and health, contracts are mostly a matter of cooperation and money. Contracts help people to cooperate with each other and to achieve their goals, especially economic goals. Thus contracts create incentives for manufacturers to make quality products, consumers to rely on sellers' representations, employees to work productively, innovators to improve technology, divorcing spouses to care for their children, governments to take bids

---

[4] If the victim is negligent, the rules become more complex, but to simplify the exposition we proceed with the assumption that the victim is not negligent.

for procurement, and so on. Money pervades life more than accidents do, so contract disputes cause nine times more court filings than tort disputes in the state courts in the United States.[5]

To cooperate with each other, people should do what they say or compensate the victims of their broken promises. Contract law enables people to commit to keeping their promises by making them liable for breaking them. Whereas negligence is the dominant legal rule of tort law, the rule of strict liability dominates contract law. In case of a breach of contract, the promisor is typically liable for the promisee's losses regardless of whether or not the breach was negligent. While one liability rule dominates, contract law provides two fundamental remedies for broken contracts: damages and specific performance. With damages, the promisor who breaches the contract must compensate the promisee for the harm done. With specific performance, the promisee who suffers from a broken contract is entitled to a court order for the promisor to perform as promised. The Anglo-American legal systems describe damages as the primary remedy and specific performance as secondary, while the reverse is true in continental Europe. (In practice, the two legal systems provide similar remedies in similar situations.)

Here is how contract law achieves efficiency through the remedy of damages. Suppose that Builder promises to construct a house for Buyer. The house costs Builder $9 to construct, and it is worth $10 to Buyer. The price is $9.50, which Buyer pays Builder in advance. If Builder breaches the contract and fails to build the house, contract law allows Buyer to collect damages of $10, which is his value of the house. (We assume that Buyer suffers no additional losses.) Since Builder bears liability of $10 if she breaches the contract, she prefers to build the house at a cost of $9. This is socially efficient since performance increases social value by $1. Alternatively, suppose that performance costs $11, rather than $9. Since Builder bears liability of $10 if she breaches the contract, she prefers to breach instead of building the house at a cost of $11. This is socially efficient, since breaching saves social value of $1 that performance would destroy.

The remedy of damages for breach of contract creates incentives resembling strict liability in tort law. Contract law makes the promisor bear liability for losses ($10 in our example) and lets the promisor decide whether to breach (when performance costs are $11) or perform (when performance costs are $9). Similarly, strict liability in torts makes the injurer bear liability for losses ($10 in our example) and lets him decide whether to reduce the risk by taking precaution (when precaution costs $9) or not reduce the risk by omitting precaution (when precaution costs $11). Contract law aligns the promisor's incentives with the goal of promoting social efficiency, exactly as tort law does.

---

[5] ROBERT C. LaFOUNTAIN AND SHAUNA M. STRICKLAND, EXAMINING THE WORK OF STATE COURTS: AN ANALYSIS OF 2008 STATE COURT CASELOADS. Available at http://www.courtstatistics .org/other-pages/~/media/microsites/files/csp/ewsc-2008-online.ashx.

Unlike the remedy of damages for breach of contract, the remedy of specific performance can obstruct efficiency. Suppose the builder breaches the contract when construction costs $11 and the buyer is entitled to the remedy of specific performance. If the buyer insists that the builder construct the house, construction will destroy $1 in social value, because construction costs $11 and the house is worth $10. If builder and buyer are smart, however, they will renegotiate the contract. The builder will agree to pay, say, $10.50 to the buyer and the buyer will release the builder from the obligation to construct the house. Under this renegotiated contract, the builder and buyer each gain $.50 from not constructing the building. To gain $.50, the buyer will not insist on specific performance unless renegotiation fails with the breaching builder. Renegotiation is most likely to fail when negotiating is costly, in which case damages are a more efficient remedy than specific performance.

The law of restitution, which is also called the law of unjust enrichment, is the third body of private law. Whereas tort law allows victims to recover for harm that injurers caused them, the law of restitution allows benefactors to recover gains that their beneficiaries wrongfully obtained from them. Suppose that A digs and discovers a beautiful cave. The cave extends beneath both his land and B's land. A earns a great deal of money by charging tourists to tour the cave[6]—all without B knowing that part of the tour goes under her land. B is entitled to share the profits even though she suffered no harm from the unlawful use A has made of her land.

In this example, beneficiary A uses the property of benefactor B without the latter's consent. A most interesting part of restitution law concerns the opposite situation: benefactors can recover for benefits they voluntarily conferred upon beneficiaries without consent from the latter. Rescue cases are typical, as when a doctor gives first aid to an injured person in an emergency. Under restitution law, doctors can recover a modest amount of money for their services, even though their services were not "requested." It is easy to see how this rule promotes social welfare: it encourages benefactors (e.g., doctors) to create value for others (e.g., injured persons) when circumstances (e.g., emergencies) preclude a contractual transaction.

"Common fund" cases are another category in which restitution law allows benefactors to recover compensation for unrequested benefits. Take the case of an estate that is owed $100 by a recalcitrant debtor. Bringing a suit to recover $100 would cost $25. The net recovery of $75 would be split equally among the five heirs to the estate, so each heir would receive $15. Each heir's gain of $15 is less than the cost of $25 to bring suit. No heir will bring suit unless the other heirs share its costs. If the heirs cooperate, they may agree to share the suit's costs. However, one of the heirs may refuse to pay his share in the hope that the others will proceed without him and he can "free-ride" on

[6] *Edwards v. Lee* 96 S.W. 2d 1028 (1936).

their efforts. Given the possibility of free-riding, the heirs may be unable to cooperate. Restitution law provides a solution by allowing an heir who brings suit to recover a share of its costs from the other heirs, even though the others never agreed to pay anything to him. Here too restitution law promotes social welfare by making the beneficiaries compensate the benefactor who provided an unrequested benefit.

This book makes three central claims, each developed in a separate part and each related to a different branch of private law. All three claims have a common denominator: the desire to reform private law and to make it more effective in promoting social welfare.

Torts and Misalignments

The first claim relates to tort law. As explained, an actor is negligent if the costs of precaution he failed to take are lower than the risk that it would have reduced. Thus, in our previous example, if precaution (installing a safety device in the workplace) costs $9 and the risk of an accident to others (employees) is $10, the injurer (the employer) who failed to take precaution would be considered negligent and bear liability for the resulting harm. Expected liability of $10 would provide the injurer with efficient incentives to take precaution. In order to minimize social costs, the same risk of $10 that is used by courts to set the standard of care should also be used to set damages when liability is imposed. This is the *alignment principle*.[7] Misalignment occurs when some risks that courts considered in setting the standard of care are disregarded when courts impose liability for damages, or vice versa. To illustrate using our previous example, assume the employer is negligent (9 < 10), but liability is imposed for only half of the resulting harm (.5 × 10 = 5). The employer would prefer bearing liability of $5 rather than taking precaution that costs $9. Because of misalignment, the employer would not have efficient incentives.

So here is our first claim. *To achieve efficiency under negligence law, all foreseeable risks should be included when setting the standard of care and awarding damages* (unless there are compelling policy considerations to the contrary). In several important areas of law, however, *courts systematically misalign standards of care and liability for damages* by disregarding or miscalculating some risks. Courts either set the wrong standard of care or they award the wrong damages. Correcting misalignment would restore the law's social efficiency.

In part I of the book we identify misalignments in tort law that others have overlooked, and we explain how to eliminate them. Since these misalignments are embedded in the doctrines of negligence that most courts follow, these inefficiencies are systematic and endemic, not sporadic and episodic like other

---

[7] ARIEL PORAT, *Misalignments in Tort Law*, 121 YALE L.J. 82 (2011).

inefficiencies in tort law. The effects of misalignment are large and they urgently need measurement and study.

Chapter 1 ("Prices, Sanctions, and Discontinuities") explains an important feature of negligence law—its discontinuity. Under a negligence rule, a negligent injurer often bears liability for harms that he did not cause. Imagine that a statute or a court sets a reasonable driving speed, a driver who exceeds it by just one mile per hour hits a pedestrian, and the court imposes liability on the speeding driver. If the driver had been driving one mile per hour slower, perhaps he would still have had the accident, but the court would *not* have imposed liability. If so, a small increase in speed over the speed limit creates a sudden jump or discontinuity in expected liability.

In this example, slowing down by one mile per hour eliminates liability but not the accident. Therefore, the speeding driver, if liability is imposed, is liable for more harm than his negligence caused. Thus the discontinuity misaligns liability and the standard of care. The standard of care is set according to the actual harm caused by negligence (speeding), and liability for damages exceeds the actual harm caused by negligence. This misalignment overdeters injurers, and courts should correct it when they can.

Chapter 2 ("The Injurer's Self-Risk Puzzle") explains that when courts set the standard of care, they consider the risks the injurer created toward others but not the risks he created for himself. The negligent injurer ideally bears all risks, but courts take into account only some risks (risks to others) when setting the standard of care. To illustrate, imagine a driver who creates risk of $7 for himself and $8 for others, which the driver can eliminate by taking precautions that cost $10. The cost of precaution exceeds the risk to others ($10 > 8$), so the court imposes no liability. This is a mistake by the court. Since precaution costs less than the driver's risk to himself and others ($10 < 7 + 8$), the driver should be considered negligent and bear liability. In so far as possible, *all* risks should count when courts set the standard of care. The RESTATEMENT (THIRD) OF TORTS recently adopted the principle that an injurer's self-risk should be included when setting legal standards. It remains to be seen whether future courts will continue to ignore self-risk when setting legal standards of care, or, alternatively, follow the recommendation of the RESTATEMENT and this book.

Chapter 3 ("Negligence Per Se and Unaccounted Risks") identifies another misalignment that occurs when courts apply the doctrine of negligence per se. Negligence law ordinarily requires the injurer to take reasonable care. If, however, a statute requires the injurer to take a specified level of care, then failing to do so is negligence per se—the injurer is liable for violating the statute regardless of whether his care was reasonable or unreasonable. In order to recover damages under negligence per se, the victim must belong to the class of people protected by the statute. Assume that a statute obliges employers to install special railings along the stairs to provide safe conditions for disabled employees. Further assume that an employer breaches the statute, and an able-bodied employee falls on the stairs. A railing would have prevented the victim's fall. Under current law, the employee, whose injury was caused by the railing's absence, apparently cannot recover damages from the employer. The injured employee cannot recover because she is able-bodied, and the statute is interpreted as protecting only disabled employees.

This interpretation creates misalignment and inefficiency. Absent explicit evidence to the contrary, the best interpretation of the statute assumes that the legislature took all risks into account when it set the standard of care. The obligation to install railings is justified by the additional protection to everyone. Once the presence of disabled employees makes installing railings mandatory under the statute, liability should be imposed for all harms that materialize from failing to install railings. Able-bodied employees should recover for injuries that railings would have averted. Otherwise the employer will have too little incentive to install railings.

Chapter 4 ("Lapses and Substitution") touches on a special case where there is an alignment between the standard of care and damages, but both are inefficient. The chapter concerns lapses in attention or judgment that cause many accidents, especially road and medical injuries. Everyone lapses from time to time. To reduce the frequency of lapses, people can monitor their own behavior more carefully. Lapses can be morally innocent, as when an actor self-monitors to the best of his ability and still has bad luck. Alternatively, lapses can be morally culpable, as when an actor negligently monitors his own behavior. Tort law often holds actors liable for the harm caused by their lapses, regardless of whether the lapses are morally innocent or culpable. It costs almost nothing to take a careful look at the road before crossing or to avoid leaving a sponge in the patient's body during a medical operation. Courts, consequently, consider lapses as negligence that triggers liability.

However, the result of this typical interpretation of negligence doctrine is that courts impose liability for risks that reasonable precautions could *not* avoid. We argue that liability should ideally be imposed only for those lapses avoided by reasonable precaution. Other lapses should not trigger liability. Reasonable precaution against lapses should be a defense against liability for accidents caused by lapses. With a lapse defense, legality would follow morality more closely. In addition, a lapse defense sometimes increases the efficiency of the law.

To close part I, chapter 5 ("Total Liability for Excessive Harm") deals with situations in which negligence by some wrongdoers causes harm, but the victim cannot prove which wrongdoers were negligent. To illustrate, assume that five firms discharge pollution into a lake. The socially efficient level of discharge is 10 per firm. To achieve efficiency, a lawmaker sets the legal standard at 10 for each firm. Obeying the legal standard would result in total discharge of 50. Unfortunately, the actual discharge totals 60. The courts know that the actual discharge of 60 exceeds the legal discharge of 50, but no one can prove how much each firm discharged. The courts cannot impose liability on any firm under the standard negligence rule, because the victim cannot prove that a specific injurer caused his harm. The standard of care is efficient, but liability of 0 for its violation is inefficient. Consequently, the standard of care misaligns with damages.

We analyze various solutions, such as proportionate liability, that seem appealing, and then show that they fail to provide efficient incentives. Instead, we propose a novel solution that will work, which we call *total liability for excessive harm*. If each polluter is liable for the total excess harm (10) caused by all polluters, then each polluter will respond by discharging at the efficient level. Excess harm will disappear, pollution will fall to the efficient level (50), and none of the five firms will have to pay damages.

Contracts and Victims' Incentives

Part II of the book turns to contracts, the area of law where we make our second claim. In a contract between two people, the law misaligns their incentives unless they make a novel contract that we call "anti-insurance" with a third party. Misalignment occurs because efficient incentives for the promisor undermine efficient incentives for the promisee. As explained above, the damages remedy incentivizes the promisor to breach the contract when performance is inefficient and to perform the contract when performance is efficient. As long as the promisor compensates the promisee for all the latter's losses, the promisor's incentives to breach and perform would be efficient and align with the goal of promoting social welfare. In contrast to these efficient incentives for the promisor, however, contract law provides inefficient incentives to the promisee. Once the promisee realizes that he will be fully compensated for all his losses from breach, he may over-rely on the promise and undercooperate with the promisor. This problem is acute when over-reliance and undercooperation are unverifiable in court.

As an illustration, suppose a builder contracts to construct an addition to a restaurant. The builder encounters difficulties in getting permits from the municipality, and the delay jeopardizes his chances of completing construction on time. The restaurateur could help to get the permits but fails to do so. The restaurateur could also postpone some orders of perishable food yet makes a large order for the scheduled opening of the addition anyway. In brief, the restaurateur undercooperates with the builder and over-relies on the builder's promise. After the fact, however, it is hard for courts to verify that the restaurateur's reliance and cooperation were unreasonable. When cooperation and reliance are unverifiable, contract terms promising efficient cooperation and reliance are unenforceable.

The second claim in this book is that contract law should respond more to the promisee's incentives, especially in regard to the problems of undercooperation and over-reliance. In three chapters, we explain the problem of promisee's incentives, and we offer possible solutions. Anti-insurance is a market innovation that clarifies the incentive problem and solves it in principle.

Chapter 6 ("Unity in the Law of Tort and Contracts") analyzes the problem of providing efficient incentives for the promisor and promisee simultaneously. This problem in contract law is much the same as the problem in tort law of providing efficient incentives for the injurer and victim in an accident. However, tort law often explicitly considers the victim's incentives, whereas contract law seldom explicitly considers the promisee's incentives. Perhaps the presence of a contract explains the difference. With a contract, the parties can attend to the victim's incentives through the contract's terms.

Chapter 7 ("Anti-Insurance") proposes novel terms that perfectly solve the incentive problem for promisor and promisee in a contract, even if their behavior is unverifiable.

Here is the basic idea. Breach of contract by the promisor poses a risk of loss to the promisee. The promisor can reduce this risk by taking precautions to avoid breaching, and the promisee can reduce this risk by cooperating more and relying less. Perfect incentives for the promisor and promisee require each of them to bear the cost of breach, so each of them balances the cost of breach against the cost of reducing it. In brief, perfect bilateral incentives require promisor's liability of 100 percent of the harm from breach and promisee's compensation of 0 percent. To achieve this result, promisee and promisor can sign a contract with a third party called the "anti-insurer," who buys the promisee's right to compensation for breach. The promisee gains the sale price of the liability right. If a breach materializes, promisor pays compensation of 100 percent to the anti-insurer. The promisee who assigned the right to the promisor receives no compensation for the promisor's breach. With anti-insurance, promisor's liability for breach is 100 percent and promisee's compensation is 0 percent, as required for efficient incentives. Anti-insurance, like most voluntary contracts, is attractive in principle to all parties because everyone benefits.

Anti-insurance is partly an explanatory device—by understanding anti-insurance, you understand the tension between the promisor's and promisee's incentives—and partly a practical proposal for future implementation in markets. However, markets currently generate few contracts resembling anti-insurance. As standard insurance too took a very long time to develop and come into widespread use, perhaps in time a functional market for anti-insurance will emerge. In the interim, because anti-insurance is so rare, the doctrines of contract law should provide some other solution to create efficient incentives for promisor and promisee.

Chapter 8 ("Decreasing Liability Contracts and the Assistant Interest") offers such a solution for a certain kind of contract. This chapter explains that reducing liability below full compensation improves the promisee's incentives and worsens the promisor's incentives. In certain kinds of contracts, reducing liability below full compensation improves the promisee's incentives by *more* than it worsens the promisor's incentives. In these contracts, reinterpreting legal doctrine to reduce damages or stipulating lower damages in the contract improves the contract overall.

This is typically true when the promisor performs a contract in phases, as in constructing a building or participating in a joint venture to develop a new product. In a decreasing liability contract, the promisor's liability decreases as he completes each successive phase of the contract. The promisor is liable for full compensation at the beginning of the contract, and he is subsequently liable for a lower and lower share of the loss. Specifically, the promisor is liable for full compensation minus his expenditure on the contract's phases up to the time of breach. This liability schedule allocates enough losses from breach—but not more than necessary—to make the promisor want to complete the contract and provides that the promisee shall bear the remaining losses. The remaining losses encourage the promisee to cooperate and restrain reliance. In phased contracts, decreasing liability with partial performance provides better incentives than retaining full liability until performance is complete.

Restitution and Positive Externalities

While parts I and II concern losses, part III concerns benefits. Arguably, just as injurers and promisors should pay for harming others, so benefactors should be paid for benefiting others. The law, however, treats benefactors very differently from injurers and promise-breakers. Tort law and contract law both require that injurers and promisors pay for the harms that they cause (or wrongfully cause) to others, whereas the law seldom entitles benefactors to be paid for benefits that they confer to others without a contract ("unrequested benefits").

The third claim in this book is that the law should compensate for unrequested benefits more often in order to induce people to provide more of them. The proposal in chapter 9 ("A Public Goods Theory of Restitution") requires recipients to compensate benefactors for unrequested benefits in more circumstances than under current law. Specifically, a duty of restitution should apply when benefactors cannot exclude beneficiaries from receiving benefits that are indisputable and measurable. When the benefactor cannot exclude others from benefiting, the beneficiaries often refuse to reimburse the benefactor for the cost of the good. They "free-ride" by enjoying benefits without paying the costs, so private markets undersupply the good. For example, removing pollution from a stream benefits all downstream property owners. In some circumstances, the upstream property owner who removes pollution from a stream should be able to collect a share of the costs from downstream property owners. Otherwise, the stream will remain polluted.

In economics, "public goods" have the characteristic of "nonexclusion." Thus, when an upstream owner abates pollution, a downstream owner who refuses to share in the abatement costs cannot be excluded from the benefits of clean water. Nonexclusion and the related free-rider problem lead to a general undersupply of public goods. One remedy for the undersupply of public goods by private markets is for the state to collect taxes and supply public goods. The state supply of public goods, however, needs supplementing, especially for local public goods. According to chapter 9, the courts should expand the duty of restitution to encompass the unrequested supply of some local public goods.

Some activities convey both uncompensated benefits and risks of harm to others. If actors internalize negative externalities and not positive externalities, they will engage in too little of the activity. Tort liability can make actors internalize the risk of accidental harm that their activities impose on others, while at the same time the actors externalize some of the benefits. For instance, negligent medical treatment sometimes harms patients, and tort liability can make doctors internalize this risk. However, doctors usually convey greater benefits than the fees paid by their patients. Uncompensated benefits that doctors convey to patients are positive externalities. If doctors internalize the risk of negligent treatment and externalize much of the benefit from successful treatment, then doctors often have an incentive to take excessive care. They engage in "defensive medicine," such as favoring treatments with low liability risk for doctors even though the chosen treatments are worse for patients than alternative treatments with high liability risk.

Tort theorists often think that the ideal assignment of liability is to internalize the harm from accidents. Instead, chapter 10 ("Liability Externalities and Mandatory Choices") focuses on adjusting liability for accidents in light of effects on others besides the accidental harm to victims. Notably, doctoring brings patients much greater benefits than the fees that patients pay doctors. Therefore, if a doctor's negligence breaks a patient's leg, the ideal liability is less than the harm to the patient because a lower level of liability encourages more doctoring, which has external benefits. Conversely, driving causes pollution and congestion, which harms others aside from accidents. If a driver's negligence breaks a pedestrian's leg, the ideal liability is more than the harm to the pedestrian. A higher level of liability discourages driving, which has external costs. This contrast between doctoring and driving shows the difference between actual and ideal law. According to actual law, a doctor who negligently breaks a patient's leg has the same liability as a driver who negligently breaks a pedestrian's leg. Ideally, however, the doctor's liability should be less than the driver's liability.

The ideal liability for an accident is the *net* harm from the activity that caused the accident: the harm to victims minus the activity's external benefits. By following the net harm principle, courts would reduce liability for accidents from activities with beneficial externalities and increase liability for accidents with harmful externalities. Courts cannot, and should not, consider every type of benefit and harm when deciding a case in private law. In specific circumstances, however, courts can and should adjust damages in light of external effects. In particular, if a doctor negligently increased a particular risk to the patient and caused him harm, but at the same time decreased another risk for the same patient, liability should be reduced to account for both increased and decreased risk.

Chapter 11 ("The Relationship between Nonlegal Sanctions and Damages"), the book's last chapter, deals with positive externalities caused by nonlegal sanctions. The same act often triggers legal and nonlegal sanctions. For example, a judge finds a seller of televisions liable for breach of contract (legal sanction), and some buyers boycott the seller (nonlegal sanction). Or a judge finds the owner-operator of a limousine liable for an accident, and some customers transfer their business elsewhere. Chapter 11 asks whether courts should take nonlegal sanctions into account when awarding damages. Specifically, should courts deduct the nonlegal sanction from the damages that the defendant owes to the victim in a civil suit?

All benefits and costs to society count when creating efficient incentives. As explained, efficient incentives for injurers usually require setting liability equal to the net harm done to others. The net harm equals the actual harm minus the benefits to others. Nonlegal sanctions often transfer benefits from the injurer or the breaching party to its competitors, and nonlegal sanctions often create social benefits for the public by deterring injurers or telling potential victims whom to avoid. Thus, after the court finds breach of contract by the television seller or liability for an accident by the limousine owner-operator, some customers may transfer their business elsewhere. The court, when calculating liability for damages, should take into consideration the benefits transferred or created for others by the nonlegal sanction and deduct accordingly from the victim's actual harm. If the injurer causes harm of 100 and triggers a nonlegal sanction that benefits others by 40, the injurer's liability should equal 60. Deducting the benefits of nonlegal sanctions from compensatory damages typically improves incentives for both injurers and victims. Situations involving nonlegal sanctions arise frequently in a wide range of cases, and when deciding these cases, courts should ideally apply the net harm principle to set damages.

This book has three main claims: misalignments in tort law should be removed; in contract law, promisee's incentives should be improved; and the law should recognize some right of compensation for those who produce unrequested benefits. All three claims could be summarized in one short sentence: private law could, and should, promote social welfare better. To substantiate these three claims, we take the reader on a tour of economic analysis in private law. As with holidays, we hope that the journey is as attractive as its destination.

Torts and Misalignments

Courts typically determine tort liability in two stages. First the court decides whether the defendant behaved wrongfully and caused the harm suffered by the plaintiff. If the court decides affirmatively, it proceeds to the second stage and decides on the amount of damages to award. When negligence is alleged in the first stage, courts often apply the Learned Hand formula to determine whether or not the defendant was in fact negligent. Under this formula, a defendant is considered negligent, and therefore liable for the harm his negligence caused, if and only if the cost of precautions that he failed to take was lower than the expected harm that those precautions would have reduced. In algebraic terms, the injurer is considered negligent if and only if $B < PL$, when B stands for the burden of precaution, P for the probability of harm, and L for the loss.[1]

The Hand formula provides injurers with an incentive to take precautions when, and only when, precautions cost less than the expected harm reduced by them. The injurer realizes that if $B < PL$, not taking precautions will cost him PL in expected terms, and he will prefer to spend B on precautions so as to avoid liability. If, instead, $B > PL$, the injurer will not be considered negligent and therefore will not take precautions. The Hand formula thus provides injurers with an incentive to achieve the goal of economic efficiency.

One important point should be noted: to realize the economic goal, the negligent injurer should compensate the victim for the amount of the entire harm, no more and, more importantly, no less. Thus, the same PL that defines the injurer as negligent will also delineate his liability: any harm that materialized from the risk PL will trigger liability L. (For the sake of simplicity, we ignore cases in which the victim is contributorily negligent.)

Sometimes liability for less than the entire harm would suffice to produce efficient incentives for the injurer. Thus, if B is much lower than PL ($B \ll PL$), liability for less than the entire harm would provide the injurer with incentive

---

[1] *United States v. Carroll Towing Co.* 159 F.2d 169, 173 (2d Cir. 1947) (developing the Learned Hand formula); RICHARD A. POSNER, THE ECONOMIC ANALYSIS OF LAW 167–71 (2003) (explaining the correct use of the negligence rule according to the Hand formula).

to take precautions. But negligence law strives for a uniform rule that applies universally to all cases in the same manner and requires as little information as possible for its application. Therefore, to create efficient incentives under *all* circumstances, the rule of negligence is that as long as B < PL, the negligent injurer who failed to take precautions will bear liability for the entire harm. Only such a rule will, at least in theory, provide efficient incentives in *all* circumstances, regardless of B's magnitude in any given case. *Negligence law thus aligns the standard of care with compensable harms.*

To be sure, in some cases injurers are exempt from liability, in full or part, even if negligent. Most of these cases do not breach the alignment principle. Unforeseeable harms are not compensated,[2] and unforeseeable plaintiffs cannot recover for their losses.[3] However, unforeseeable harms and plaintiffs are also not taken into account by courts when they set the standard of care, and therefore no misalignment arises. In other cases, certain types of harms are not compensated and certain types of plaintiffs cannot recover, for reasons related to proximate cause ("scope of liability"[4]) or duty of care[5] that mandate no compensation. In general, these are cases in which policy considerations exclude liability even if the harm in question was caused by wrongdoing.[6]

This part of the book identifies previously unnoticed misalignments that policy considerations mostly cannot explain or justify.[7] We analyze those misalignments and suggest how courts could ameliorate them.

We start this part (in chapter 1) by identifying a misalignment between the standard of care and damages due to a court's lack of information regarding causation. Ideally, under negligence law, an injurer who fails to satisfy the standard of care is liable for the harm caused by his negligence, no less and no more. Thus an injurer who was slightly negligent should *not* bear liability for any harm caused by his *behavior*, but only for the harm caused by his *slight deviation* from the standard of care. Courts, however, often lack the information to distinguish the harm caused by the injurer's behavior and the incremental harm caused by his deviation from the standard of care. Consequently, courts often impose liability on the slightly negligent injurer for *all* harms caused by his behavior. This creates discontinuity in liability: if the injurer satisfies the standard of care he bears no liability, but if he deviates even slightly from that standard he is liable for much more than the harm caused by his negligence.

---

[2] RESTATEMENT (THIRD) OF TORTS: LIABILITY FOR PHYSICAL AND EMOTIONAL HARM § 3 cmt. g (2010).

[3] See, e.g., *Palsgraf v. Long Island R.R. Co.* 162 N.E. 99 (N.Y. 1928).

[4] Section 29 of the RESTATEMENT (THIRD) OF TORTS: LIABILITY FOR PHYSICAL AND EMOTIONAL HARM (2010) adopted the term "scope of liability" to refer to what is commonly known as "proximate cause."

[5] See *id.* § 7.

[6] *Id.* § 7 cmt. a.

[7] ARIEL PORAT, *Misalignments in Tort Law,* 121 YALE L.J. 82 (2011).

This discontinuity in liability under negligence law creates a misalignment, as we explain, and may result in overdeterrence.

We also explain that incomplete information sometimes makes courts impose liability for less than the harm caused by the injurer's negligence, not for more of it. This kind of misalignment may result in underdeterrence. We analyze these misalignments and suggest how they could be mitigated.

The second misalignment we identify is due to courts' ignorance of the injurer's self-risk when they set the standard of care (chapter 2). In setting the standard of care, courts consider the risks the injurer created toward others, and, unfortunately, systematically exclude the risks the injurer created for himself. Thus courts set the standard of care for driving in light of the danger to others, without considering the danger to the driver. As a result, legal standards are systematically set too low, even though damages may be set optimally. This misalignment is different from others that we identify. With other misalignments the standard of care is set at the optimal level and damages are set too high or too low, but the opposite is true in this misalignment. Courts should cure this misalignment by including the injurer's self-risk in the cluster of risks considered by courts when they set the standard of care.

A third misalignment concerns cases of "negligence per se." Statutes often require injurers to take specific care that especially benefits a class of people. Breaching the statute typically constitutes "negligence per se." When the injurer's breach of the statute harms people, courts systematically compensate the victims explicitly targeted by the legislation and not other victims. Chapter 3 explains that this creates a misalignment. When a statute sets the standard of care, it should be interpreted—as long as there is no clear evidence to the contrary—as taking into account risks to *all* people affected by the statute, not only those explicitly referenced in it. Therefore, compensating only the latter group of victims creates a misalignment: while the (statutory) standard of care is set in light of risks to everyone affected by it, damages are awarded for harms suffered by only some of them. This misalignment underdeters injurers and undermines the goal of protecting those victims explicitly referenced in the statute.

Chapter 4 deals with lapses of attention, for example by a driver or a doctor. Should a lapse of attention always be considered negligence, and trigger liability for the resulting harm? Under current tort law the answer is yes, but we show it should be no. Many lapses of attention could not be prevented by reasonable care. By imposing liability and awarding damages for all lapses, current law sets both the standard of care and damages too high. Thus, with lapses of attention, the standard of care and damages align at an inefficient level. We stress the point that while misalignments are generally inefficient, sometimes an alignment at the wrong level is as problematic as misalignment. The problem can be cured at least partially if courts will allow a "lapse defense" that we describe.

Finally, chapter 5 analyzes situations when several injurers cause harm, and the court can verify the total harm caused by all injurers, but cannot verify the degree of harm caused by each injurer. For instance, these could be the applicable circumstances when several factories emit the same pollutant into a lake. Under these conditions, the victims cannot recover damages under a traditional negligence rule because they cannot prove that a particular injurer caused a particular harm. Damages are effectively zero, even though the standard of care for each injurer may be optimal. Courts lack the information to correct this misalignment. We propose a novel form of the negligence rule to solve this problem. Under our proposal, each injurer bears liability equal to the difference between the actual total harm caused by all injurers and the optimal total harm. "Excessive harm" is our phrase for the difference between the actual total harm and the optimal total harm. Liability for excessive harm causes all of the injurers to satisfy the legal standard of care, so none of them are liable for any of the harm that materializes.

Prices, Sanctions,
and Discontinuities

A city reduces parking congestion in the downtown by maintaining a parking lot where cars pay by the hour. A rational driver will stay parked so long as an extra hour is worth more to him than the price. As soon as staying another hour is worth less than the price, the driver will leave the parking lot. This example suggests that a price is usually a payment of money that is required in order to do what is permitted. A price allows the individual to choose what to do as long as he pays it. The rational individual equates his marginal benefit to the price. A fall in price increases demand (downward sloping demand curve).

To reduce parking congestion further, the city imposes a two-hour parking limit on downtown streets with a high fine for overstaying. This example suggests that a monetary sanction is a cost imposed for doing what is forbidden. If a sanction is attached to forbidden activities, there is a jump or discontinuity in the actor's costs at the partition between permitted and forbidden activities. Parking is free for two hours, so drivers will often stay for a second hour even when the extra hour has little value to them. However, rational drivers will be careful not to stay beyond two hours when costs jump up. For most people, the cost of overstaying easily exceeds the benefit. They are not on the margin where the cost of overstaying equals the benefit, so they do not respond to moderate changes in the sanction or the frequency of its application.

The price at the parking lot nudges customers to move along. The sanction for overstaying on the street compels drivers to do so. Prices nudge and sanctions compel. Is liability for causing an accident like a price or like a sanction? What about liability for breaking a contract? The law of torts and contracts sometimes nudges and sometimes compels, and economics explains why.

A. Distinguishing Prices from Sanctions

Unlike a price for permitted conduct, a sanction jumps up at the legal standard separating permitted and forbidden behavior. In a graph of liability costs, the jump is a discontinuity. The presence or absence of discontinuities is decisive for distinguishing between prices and sanctions in liability law, as some examples show.

Example 1: Leak. A firm hires a caterer to make a gala breakfast for 1,500 guests. The firm supplies the caterer with 500 liters of milk and 50 kilos of chocolate. The caterer supplies a vat and labor for making hot chocolate. The vat has a valve manufactured from the best available technology, but it cracks very occasionally when heated. After turning on the heat in the vat, the caterer goes to work in another room, and the valve immediately cracks. The caterer returns ten minutes later and half of the hot chocolate has gone down the drain.

With the valve cracked, the loss from the vat increased continuously with each second that the caterer was in another room rather than tending the vat. Figure 1.1 illustrates this graphically, with the vertical axis representing the loss and the horizontal axis representing the length of time that the vat was left unattended. The curve begins at the graph's origin (0,0) and increases continuously until the vat is drained.

In example 1, a rule of strict liability might hold the caterer liable for the entire loss from leaving the vat unattended. Alternatively, a negligence rule might hold the caterer liable for a fraction of the loss. If leaving the vat unattended for five minutes was reasonable, then the caterer's negligence did not cause the loss in the first five minutes. If leaving the vat unattended for *more* than five minutes was *un*reasonable, then the caterer's negligence caused the loss in the last five minutes. Under this application of the negligence rule, the caterer would be liable for half of the total loss.

In this scenario, the rational caterer's liability is twice as great under strict liability as under a negligence rule. Will a rule of strict liability cause the rational caterer to leave the vat unattended for longer than a rule of negligence? If you think the answer is "Yes," then you just made the most fundamental mistake in economics—confusing total and marginal values.

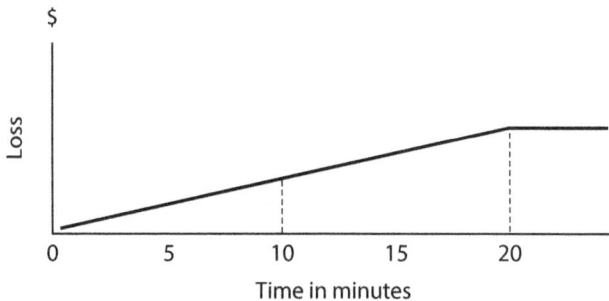

FIGURE 1.1. Natural Continuity

Assume that a rule of strict liability would cause a rational caterer to leave the vat unattended for seven minutes. So would a rule of negligence. Both rules induce the same behavior because the *incremental* liability from leaving the vat unattended for additional minutes after the seventh minute is the same under both rules. The rational caterer decides how long to leave the vat unattended by comparing the incremental loss and the opportunity cost of spending time watching the vat.[1] A modest change in either one would cause a rational caterer to change how long he attends to the vat. The caterer is on the margin where even small changes in incremental costs cause changes in behavior.

Unlike example 1, the loss function in example 2 is naturally discontinuous.

Example 2: Boil. A firm hires a caterer to make a gala breakfast for 1,500 guests. The firm supplies the caterer with 500 liters of milk and 50 kilos of chocolate. The caterer supplies a vat and labor for making hot chocolate. The caterer pours the milk and chocolate into the vat and turns the dial to heat the vat. The caterer wants to heat the milk quickly to save time. The caterer negligently turns the dial too far, the vat heats to 110 degrees centigrade, and the milk boils and spoils.

Any temperature of 100 degrees or more would spoil the milk, and any temperature below 100 degrees would not spoil it. Harm is nil as the temperature rises to the boiling point and then the whole vat is abruptly ruined. In figure 1.2, with the vertical axis representing the loss and the horizontal axis representing the vat's temperature, the loss curve begins at the graph's origin (0,0) and remains 0 until the temperature reaches 100 degrees, but then the loss instantaneously jumps up to vat's entire value.

The caterer's overheating the milk caused its ruin, so the caterer is liable under a rule of strict liability. Overheating the milk was also negligent, and negligence caused the ruin, so the caterer is also liable under a negligence rule. Since liability is the same under both rules, so are the injurer's incentives. With either liability rule, a rational caterer would presumably aim to heat the milk a little below 100 degrees in order to leave a margin of error. A modest change in the amount of liability—say from 100 percent to 75 percent of the value of the vat—would have little or no effect on the rational caterer's precaution. The caterer is not on the margin where a small change in costs causes significant changes in behavior.

---

[1] The *expected harm* from leaving the vat unattended equals the probability of leaving the tap open multiplied by the resulting harm h, which we write $H = ph$. The harm h is an increasing function of the length of time that the vat is left unattended, which we write $h = h(t)$. The opportunity cost of attending to the vat is also an increasing function of t, which we write $c = c(t)$. Assume the minimum of expected harm and lost opportunity, $ph(t) - c(t)$, occurs at $t = 7$.

The liability rule maps the harm h into liability according to the function $L = L(h(t))$. Thus the rational caterer chooses t to minimize $pL(h(t)) - c(t)$. For a rule of strict liability, $L(t)' = 1$ for all t. For a rule of negligence, $L(t)' = 1$ for all $t \geq 5$. In both cases, the minimum occurs when $t = 7$.

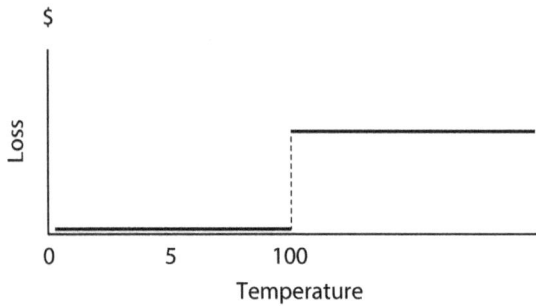

FIGURE 1.2. Natural Discontinuity

B. Tort Law

In example 2 discontinuity in nature causes discontinuity in liability. In many torts cases like example 3, however, a rule of negligence causes discontinuity in liability when nature is continuous.

> *Example 3: Probabilistic Cause.* A firm hires a caterer to make a gala breakfast for 1,500 guests. The firm supplies the caterer with 500 liters of milk and 50 kilos of chocolate. The caterer supplies a vat and labor for making hot chocolate. The vat has a poorly maintained valve with a probability of cracking from heat equal to 3 in 1,000. With proper maintenance, the probability of cracking would be 1 in 1,000. The valve cracks as soon as the heat is turned on. The caterer immediately sees the crack but cannot save the hot chocolate.

The caterer is liable under a rule of strict liability because he owns the vat whose faulty valve caused the loss of hot chocolate. In contrast, liability under a negligence rule is unclear. Did the caterer's negligence cause *this* accident? The caterer's negligent maintenance of the valve increased the probability of its failure from 1 in 1,000 to 3 in 1,000. Presumably no one can tell whether this valve failure is one of 2 in 1,000 failures that reasonable maintenance would prevent, or *the* 1 in 1,000 incidence of failure that reasonable maintenance would *not* prevent. The plaintiff can prove that the defendant's negligence increased the probability of harm, but can he prove that the defendant's negligence caused *this* accident?

Perhaps the court decides that increasing harm's probability is not a proof of harm's cause. In that case, the caterer is not liable, which undermines the caterer's incentives for care. Or perhaps the court decides that increasing harm's probability is proof of harm's cause by a preponderance of the evidence. If the caterer had taken reasonable care in maintaining the valve, then two out of three accidents that occur could have been avoided. Perhaps this fact amounts to proof by the preponderance of the evidence. If so, the caterer will be liable for the valve failures that maintenance would have avoided, and he will also be liable for those that maintenance would not have avoided.

Liability for unavoidable harm causes a jump or discontinuity in the caterer's cost from not maintaining the valve. To see why, assume that the probability of valve failure increases continuously with the age of the valve, and reasonable maintenance of the vat requires replacing the valve annually. Replacing the valve more often would cost more than the accidents avoided by doing so, and replacing the valve less often would cost less than the accidents avoided by doing so. Under a rule of strict liability, the caterer's expected liability increases continuously as the delay between valve changes lengthens. A rational caterer would balance the cost of replacing the valve more often against the resulting savings in liability. By assumption, their marginal values equate at annual replacement of the valve. A small increase in liability results in a small increase in precaution, just like a small decrease in the market price of a good results in a small increase in its consumption. Liability resembles a price for catering.

Under a negligence rule, however, the caterer's liability jumps up at the legal standard of annual replacement. If the replacement rate falls a little below the legal standard, he immediately bears liability for accidents, including those that annual replacement would prevent and those that annual replacement would *not* prevent. If the replacement rate increases to the legal standard, he immediately avoids liability for accidents, including preventable and unpreventable accidents. To allow a margin of error, the caterer will probably replace the valve more than once per year. The caterer is not on the margin where a small change in liability causes significant changes in behavior. Liability resembles a sanction for failing to replace the valve annually.

In example 3, one interpretation of the causation requirement for negligence results in no liability for exposing others to risk. The injurer externalizes risk because it is unpriced. The other interpretation results in a sanction for failing to satisfy the legal standard. The legal rule of negligence induces a discontinuity, even though nature is continuous. Instead of an all-or-nothing approach, the court could divide costs according to probability. An example discussed for decades by economists illustrates such situations.[2]

Example 4: Sparks. A railroad locomotive emits sparks that sometimes set fire to fields beside the tracks. Reasonable care requires installing a spark arrester, which cuts the emission of sparks and the resulting fires by 60 percent. It is impossible to distinguish between fires that a spark arrester would have prevented and fires caused by sparks that would have passed through a spark arrester. A farmer sues the railroad for destruction of crops worth

---

[2] The example first appears in ARTHUR C. PIGOU, THE ECONOMICS OF WELFARE (4th ed., 1932), and famously reappears in RONALD H. COASE, *The Problem of Social Cost*, 3 J. L. & ECON. 1, 29-35 (1960).

$10,000 caused by a fire from a locomotive without a spark arrester. The farmer can prove that the probability that the railroad's negligence caused the fire is .6. The farmer cannot prove that the railroad's negligence caused this fire. The court decides that the railroad's negligence was more likely than not the cause of the fire and awards the farmer $10,000 in damages.

The injurer's negligence in example 4 caused harm of $10,000 with a probability of 60 percent. That is all that anyone knows or can know. However, the court holds the injurer liable for $10,000. In the long run when many such cases occur, injurers will be held liable for more than the *actual* harm that they cause. Therefore, once the railroad fails to comply with the legal standard, it is liable not only for harms caused by its negligence, but also for harms that would have occurred anyway. The railroad faces 67 percent more liability than the expected harm caused by its negligence.[3] Liability for not installing a spark arrester is a sanction to deter wrongdoing, not a price to internalize the harm caused by negligence.

Alternatively, a small change in the facts will make the injurer liable for fewer fires than its negligence actually causes. If the probability that the railroad's negligence caused the fire is 30 percent, the court might decide that the farmer has not proved causation by the preponderance of the evidence, so the railroad is not liable. The railroad will be held liable for 0 percent of the fires, although it causes 30 percent of them in the long run. The railroad pays no price and bears no sanction in tort law for not installing a spark arrester.

Instead of an all-or-nothing approach, the court might reduce the damages according to the strength of the probabilistic evidence. Thus, the court might award damages of $6,000 if the spark arrester traps 60 percent of the sparks, and the court might award damages of $3,000 if the spark arrester traps 30 percent of the sparks.

Legal doctrine seldom allows probabilistic damages,[4] although courts sometimes act as if they were allowed.[5] With probabilistic recoveries, the railroad's expected liability equals the expected harm caused by its negligence and the discontinuity disappears. Liability for not installing a spark arrester is a price, not a sanction.

This problem pervades liability for automobile accidents.

Example 5: Driving. A driver fails to stop her car and hits a pedestrian crossing the street. The driver was traveling at 46 mph at the time of the accident. Given the risks of driving, the reasonable speed to drive was 45 mph. The court applying a negligence rule imposes liability on the driver for the harm

---

[3] 100:60=167 percent

[4] ARIEL PORAT & ALEX STEIN, TORT LIABILITY UNDER UNCERTAINTY 57-83 (2001).

[5] SAUL LEVMORE, *Probabilistic Recoveries, Restitution, and Recurring Wrongs*, 19 J. LEGAL STUD. 691, 705-710 (1990).

suffered by the pedestrian. Did the court impose a sanction on the driver or charge her a price?

A court imposing liability in example 5 may reason that since speeding is the cause of the accident, the negligent driver should bear liability. If the driver drives 45 mph or slower, she will *never* bear liability for harms that slower driving will prevent; if, however, she drives 46 mph or faster she will bear liability for *all* harms that slower driving will prevent. There is a discontinuity in liability, so liability resembles a sanction.

Alternatively, the court may reason that the negligent driver is liable only for the incremental harm, namely the harm caused by her *negligent* behavior, and not for the harm that would have been caused even if she had driven reasonably. Under prevailing negligence law and causation principles, liability should be imposed only for harms *caused* by the injurer's *negligence*. Therefore, in example 5, reasoning compatible with prices better reflects the law than reasoning compatible with sanctions.

With a small change, example 5 (driving) can be converted to a probabilistic cause case, with discontinuity in liability. Assume that if the driver in example 5 had been traveling at 45 mph instead of 46 mph, the driver's probability of hitting the pedestrian, as determined by traffic authorities, would have fallen by 50 percent. Following prevailing practice, the court needs to know whether or not the accident would have occurred but for the driver's negligence, but the information is inconclusive. Either the court finds the driver not liable, an outcome that extracts no price from the driver for imposing negligent risk on others, or else the court finds the driver fully liable, in which case the court imposes a sanction.

The discontinuity problem pervades tort liability, as we show by some more examples.[6] Example 6 illustrates discontinuity in a common medical malpractice case.

Example 6: Gout and Perfect Causal Attribution. A patient's big toe has gout (a painful, inflammatory arthritis). The doctor prescribes a powerful drug and tells him to stop drinking alcoholic beverages. The doctor prescribes the wrong drug for this type of gout and the patient continues drinking alcohol. Before these problems are detected and resolved, the patient's toe suffers permanent harm that makes walking painful. The patient sues the doctor and the court finds that compensation for permanent harm to the joint equals $10,000. It divides the permanent harm into four components: The mistaken prescription by the doctor caused $6,000; the interaction between drinking and the mistaken prescription caused $1,000; the patient's drinking

---

[6] Punitive damages would magnify the discontinuity even further. For an insightful analysis of punitive damages, see CATHERINE SHARKEY, *Punitive Damages as Societal Damages*, 113 YALE LAW JOURNAL 347 (2003).

caused $2,000; and $1,000 in harm would have occurred if the doctor had prescribed the right drug and the patient had stopped drinking. The court concludes that the doctor is liable to the patient for $7,000.

In example 6, the harm of $6,000 caused by the doctor's negligence alone, which we denote H_I, would have been avoided if the doctor had prescribed correctly. The harm of $1,000 caused by the interaction between the doctor's negligence and the patient's negligence, which we denote H_{IV}, would have been avoided if the doctor had prescribed correctly or the patient had stopped drinking. The harm of $2,000 caused by the patient's negligence alone, which we denote H_V, would have been avoided if the patient had stopped drinking. The unavoidable harm of $1,000, which we denote H_0, would have occurred even if the doctor had prescribed correctly and the patient had stopped drinking. The total harm H is given by the equation

$$H = H_0 + H_I + H_V + H_{IV}.$$

The mathematics behind this concept can be expressed more rigorously, though this is not essential for our purposes.[7] In example 6, the doctor is liable for the harm that his reasonable care would have avoided, $H_I + H_{IV}$. He is not liable for the unavoidable harm H_0 or the harm that could have been avoided only by the victim's reasonable care H_V.[8] Since the doctor pays only for harms caused by his negligence, there is no discontinuity, and the doctor's liability resembles a price rather than a sanction.

In reality, however, courts observe the victim's actual harm H and guess about its components. Courts often cannot disentangle the harm avoidable by the injurer, the harm avoidable by the victim, and the unavoidable harm. In these circumstances, the courts face a difficult problem of whether or not the plaintiff has proved that the defendant's fault caused the harm. The court must often choose between deciding that the injurer is not liable because causation is unproved, or holding the injurer liable for the victim's *actual* harm, as in the next example.

---

[7] The 1st and 2nd order terms in a Taylor expansion for the harm $H(x,y)$ can be written

$$H(x,y) \approx [H(x^*,y^*)] + [(x^* - x)H_1 + \frac{1}{2}(x^* - x)^2 H_{11}] + [(y^* - y)H_2 + \frac{1}{2}(y^* - y)^2 H_{22}]$$
$$+ [(x^* - x)(y^* - y)H_{12}].$$

To get the equation in the text, define the terms in square brackets as H_0, H_I, H_V, and H_{IV} respectively.

[8] The injurer could have avoided causing any harm by refusing to see the patient. In general, acting negligently presupposes engaging in an activity. Our analysis focuses on the decision to take care, not the decision to engage in an activity. To adjust the mathematics, let z denote the injurer's activity level and write total harm as $H(x,y,z)$, where $H(x,y,0) = 0$.

Example 7: Gout and Imperfect Causal Attribution. The same facts are true as in Example 6, except the court cannot distinguish harm of $10,000 into its four causes. Recognizing that the doctor's fault caused most of the harm, the court holds the doctor liable for the patient's actual harm of $10,000.

In example 7, the doctor is liable for $H_0 + H_I + H_V + H_{IV}$. Perhaps the court in example 7 knows that the doctor's fault increased the probability of permanent harm, but the court does not know how much harm the doctor's reasonable care would have avoided in this case. Perfect causal attribution is often impossible because the connection between fault and harm is probabilistic. Imposing liability on the negligent doctor for all harms including those not caused by him creates discontinuity—his expected liability jumps up when his care falls below the legal standard. Therefore, the doctor's liability in example 7 resembles a sanction rather than a price.[9]

C. Contract Law

The same problem of causation and discontinuity arises in contracts, but it has a different basis in legal doctrine. Example 8 adapts the facts in a contracts case to parallel example 6.

Example 8: Breach and Perfect Causal Attribution. A general contractor wins the bid to build a bridge. He promises to pay $1,000 per day for late completion. The general contractor delivers the bridge 10 days late and pays $10,000. The general contractor sues the subcontractor for $10,000, alleging that the subcontractor caused the general contractor's delay. At trial, the court divides the causes of delay into four components. One day of delay was due to bad weather, with harm $H_0 = \$1,000$. The contract explicitly states that bad weather excuses the subcontractor's nondelivery. Six days of delay were caused by the subcontractor's tardiness, with harm $H_I = \$6,000$. The general contractor promised to supply a cement mixer for the subcontractor's use. Two days of delay were caused by the general contractor's failure to supply a cement mixer to the subcontractor, with harm $H_V = \$2,000$. The general contractor was obligated to maintain the cement mixer in good repair and the subcontractor was obligated to inform the general contractor immediately if

---

[9] For former discussions of the discontinuity argument under a negligence rule, see ROBERT COOTER, *Economic Analysis of Punitive Damages*, 56 S. CAL. L. REV. 79 (1982); ROBERT COOTER, *Punitive Damages for Deterrence: When and How Much?* 40 ALABAMA L. REV. 1143 (1989); MARK F. GRADY, *A New Positive Economic Theory of Negligence*, 92 YALE L.J. 799 (1983); MARCEL KAHAN, *Causation and Incentives to Take Care under the Negligence Rule*, 18 J. LEGAL STUD. 427 (1989); RICHARD CRASWELL & JOHN E. CALFEE, *Deterrence and Uncertain Legal Standards*, 2 J. L. ECON. & ORG. 279, 295-7 (1986); JASON S. JOHNSTON, *Punitive Liability: A New Paradigm of Efficiency in Tort Law*, 87 COLUM. L. REV. 1385, 1393 (1987).

the machine broke. Both parties breached their obligation, and the cement mixer was idle for 1 day, with harm of $H_{IV} = \$1,000$. The court concludes that the subcontractor is liable to the general contractor for $7,000.

The court holds the subcontractor liable for the harm $H_I + H_{IV}$ caused by his breach, not the harm $H_0 + H_V$ caused by the weather and the general contractor. Applying law and the terms of the contract, the court attributes damages perfectly according to their cause. Liability in example 8 resembles a price, not a sanction.

In a more realistic case represented by example 9, the court cannot attribute damages perfectly according to their cause.

Example 9: Breach and Imperfect Causal Attribution. The same facts pertain as in example 8, except the general contractor promises to pay $10,000 for completing the bridge late by one to ten days. The court concludes that four factors each caused the contractor's loss—the bad weather, the subcontractor's disorganization, the general contractor's failure to supply a cement mixer in good repair, and the subcontractor's failure to report when the cement mixer broke. Any one of them would have caused delay of at least one day and liability of $10,000. The court concludes that the subcontractor is liable for $10,000.

With imperfect causal attribution in example 9, the court concludes that the subcontractor is liable for the harm that occurred *when* she breached, and consequently applies a sanction for that breach.

Now we can explain how the law of torts and contracts uses prices and sanctions as incentives. Prices and sanctions are two fundamentally different ways to incentivize precaution. A negligence rule prices unreasonable precaution by holding the injurer liable for the harm *caused* by it, and nothing more. With continuous natural costs, liability falls to zero as the injurer's precaution rises toward the reasonable level. With perfect causal attribution, negligence rules in tort law impose prices.

This is true for all forms of the negligence rule—negligence with a defense of contributory or comparative negligence and strict liability with a defense of contributory or comparative negligence. For any form of the negligence rule, one of the parties can escape liability by conforming to the legal standard. Thus the injurer can escape liability by conforming to the legal standard imposed by a rule of (simple) negligence, and the victim can escape liability by conforming to the legal standard imposed by a rule of strict liability with a defense of contributory negligence. The accidental harm borne by this party falls toward zero as his precaution rises to the legal standard.

Alternatively, the law sanctions unreasonable precaution by holding the injurer liable for the harm that occurs *when* he is negligent, which includes some or all of the unavoidable harm and the harm that the victim causes. With continuous natural costs, liability falls with precaution until it approaches the legal standard and then liability jumps down to zero. The jump equals harm that the injurer's negligence did not cause or some fraction thereof.[10]

D. A Normative Theory of Lawmaking

The difference in incentives is important for lawmakers deciding whether to price or sanction behavior. If officials always possessed perfect information, socially desirable behavior could be induced by either prices or sanctions. Officials could either charge the price that exactly internalizes costs and induces individuals to take socially efficient precaution, or officials could create a legal standard backed by a sufficient sanction to induce conformity by most people. Regardless of the approach, individuals would respond by choosing the efficient level of precaution.

In reality, however, lawmakers and officials who administer the law often make mistakes because they lack information. The behavioral consequences of mistakes differ depending on whether the law creates a sanction or a price. A normative theory for choosing between sanctions and prices can be based upon the propensity of lawmakers to make mistakes, which depends in part upon the cost of information to them.

If lawmakers can obtain accurate information on externalities, then behavior can be priced at its external cost. For efficiency the price must fully reflect the external harm caused by the behavior. Since behavior is more elastic with respect to prices than sanctions, using prices to create efficient incentives requires accurate assessment of external costs. Inaccurate setting or collection of prices will distort the behavior of many people. However, pricing behavior does not require setting a legal standard, so lawmakers need not compute the socially optimal behavior.

In contrast, if lawmakers can identify the efficient precaution level, then the legal standard can be equated with it. Since behavior is less elastic with respect to sanctions than prices, using sanctions to create efficient incentives does not require accurate magnitudes of sanctions. Mistakes in computing the level of the sanction or its application will have little influence on behavior because

---

[10] Of course, it is possible to expand the definition of a price to cover sanctions by defining a sanction as a discontinuous price, or to expand the definition of a sanction to cover prices by defining a price as a continuous sanction. However, the important point is not to argue about names but to understand the differences in the behavior caused by prices and sanctions.

For the argument that "liability rules" are prices, and "property rules" are sanctions, see RICHARD CRASWELL, *Property Rules and Liability Rules in Unconscionability and Related Doctrines*, 60 U. CHI. L. REV. 1, 3 (1993); for the argument that tort law should be regulated by prices and criminal law by sanctions, see JOHN C. COFFEE, JR., *Does Unlawful Mean Criminal: Reflections on the Disappearing Tort/Crime Distinction in American Law*, 71 B. U. L. REV. 193 (1987).

most people will conform in spite of these mistakes. However, lawmakers who create an obligation backed by a sanction must be certain that the legal standard is right. Most people will conform to an obligation backed by a sanction even if the standard is too high or too low.

These observations lead to a simple decision rule for lawmakers: if obtaining accurate information about external costs is cheaper for officials than obtaining accurate information about socially optimal behavior, then they should control the activity by pricing it. If the converse is true, then they should control the activity by sanctioning it.[11]

It may seem paradoxical that lawmakers could have information about socially optimal behavior and not have information about external costs. Isn't the latter needed to compute the former? Community standards resolve this apparent paradox. A community standard represents a consensus among private individuals about reasonable behavior. In many circumstances, government officials can observe the community standard, but not the costs and benefits that private individuals took into account when arriving at it. If—but only if—the community's judgment is sound, then officials can achieve optimality by adopting the community standard as the legal standard and attaching a sanction to it, even though officials lack information about the underlying social costs.

To illustrate, suppose that everyone in a community is exposed to the risk of accidents of a certain type, and everyone can take precautions against them. Over time, the community may develop a negligence standard that reflects its judgment about balancing the costs and benefits of precaution. If an accident occurs and the victim sues, then a court can accurately identify the community standard of negligence by hearing testimony from third parties. However, the victim may exaggerate the seriousness of his injury in order to increase his recovery, thus preventing the court from assessing the cost accurately.

The preceding example concerns a standard of the general public. Specialized communities may also have standards. For example, an accountant who plans to work in a town for many years will have a stronger incentive to maintain a good reputation by avoiding mistakes than an accountant whose aim is to turn a quick profit and leave town. This is an application of the well-known result in game theory that cheating in one-shot games can be reduced or eliminated by replacing the one-shot game with a sequence of repeated games. The practices of the accountant of good repute may be taken as evidence of the

---

[11] This proposition is similar to the claim in the pollution literature that quantitative restrictions are preferable to pollution taxes when authorities know the optimal quantity of pollution but do not know the tax price which would achieve it. It has been suggested that this situation might occur when, for example, smoke reaches an emergency level. Conversely, tax prices should be used when authorities know the external cost of pollution, but not the optimal quantity. See WILLIAM J. BAUMOL & WALLACE E. OATES, THE THEORY OF ENVIRONMENTAL POLICY (1988); MARTIN L. WEITZMAN, *Prices vs. Quantities*, 41 REV. ECON. STUD. 477 (1974).

standards that the court should apply to all accountants.[12] The importance of reputation may overcome market failures that would otherwise prevent accountants from adopting the most efficient standards. Thus, a community standard will be efficient in general when most of its members gain from having the reputation of taking precautions whose costs are commensurate with the resulting reduction in accidents.

In driving, community standards tend toward efficiency because of symmetry: anyone can be either a victim or an injurer in an automobile accident. Symmetry facilitates a consensus about reasonable care because each person must consider both the costs and the benefits of precaution. In the case of accountants, cultivation of a good reputation to ensure long-term client retention, not symmetry, tends to create a standard of reasonable care. In either case, whether the standard results from symmetry or reputation, a court may deduce that the community standard is optimal by examining the institutional structure that created it.

In some circumstances, however, lawmakers may be unable to observe the community standard, or there may be a special interest standard instead of a community standard, or the problem may be so novel that no standard has arisen. Without a community standard to guide them, officials who attempt to control behavior through sanctions must assess the socially optimal level of behavior themselves. This assessment requires information about benefits and costs that may be difficult to obtain. If officials obtain the necessary information and create an optimal legal standard, then private persons will be required to obey the legal standard upon pain of suffering the sanction attached to it. Private persons will not need to assess the socially optimal behavior—the officials will have done that for them. An advantage of an obligation backed by a sanction, as opposed to a price, is that the computation is made once by officials rather than many times by individuals, thus reducing the costs of decision-making.

Suppose that scientists prove that an ingredient widely used in cooking is carcinogenic. The legislature, using the scientists' results, balances benefits against costs, and determines that humans should never consume the ingredient. If the legislature outlaws the ingredient, private individuals must abstain from using the ingredient. If the ingredient is not banned, private individuals must decide whether to use it. To decide, they would have to collect information and replicate some aspects of the legislature's decision process. Thus a legislative ban on the ingredient reduces the cost of decision-making for the community as a whole.

In reality, such decisions are difficult for officials to make, especially when the affected individuals are heterogeneous. To illustrate, if pollution has many sources and many victims, it will be excessive in the absence of government

---

[12] Things become more complicated when reputational sanctions—or, more generally, nonlegal sanctions—combine with legal sanctions. See *infra* chapter 10.

intervention.[13] If officials try to prescribe efficient pollution standards, they must know the abatement costs and the external harm for every source of pollution. It is impossible for officials to possess that much information, as the recent history of the Environmental Protection Agency has demonstrated. Obligations backed by sanctions will not succeed unless individual differences in compliance costs are comparatively small or receive no social weight.

When individual differences in compliance costs are important, relying upon prices instead of sanctions reduces the amount of information that officials need. Assigning the correct price to an activity only requires officials to compute the external cost, as opposed to balancing the costs and benefits. For example, if government creates pollution rights and encourages their exchange in a market, polluters will abate until the abatement cost at the margin equals the price of pollution rights. Thus, the market in pollution rights will reveal the marginal abatement cost of polluters without officials having to know anything about abatement technology.

Once the market reveals marginal abatement costs, officials can compare these costs to their computation of the external harm from pollution. If the external harm caused by pollution exceeds the marginal abatement cost, then efficiency requires further abatement, so government should buy back some pollution rights to reduce their number. If the relative magnitudes are reversed, government should create and distribute additional pollution rights.[14] These observations lead to the conventional conclusion that controlling pollution through prices requires less information than controlling it through obligations backed by sanctions.[15]

E. Conclusion

The distribution of information about social costs suggests two different ways for the law to create optimal incentives to reduce social costs. The first way is to impose a legal standard backed by a sanction. If private persons are good

---

[13] This assumes that the existence of many polluters and pollutees will prevent a solution through private negotiation.

[14] Pollution taxes, rather than a market in pollution rights, can achieve the same result while providing revenues to the government. Assuming transaction costs are minimal, the only difference between a pollution tax and a government auction of pollution rights is that the government chooses the price and the market chooses the quantity with taxes, while the opposite is true with an auction. See ROBERT COOTER, *The Cost of Coase*, 11 J. LEGAL STUD. 1 (1982). Both approaches raise revenues for the government by correcting distortions in the allocation of resources rather than by creating such distortions. The revenues raised by nondistorting taxes can be substituted for the revenues raised by distorting taxes such as income tax, thus increasing efficiency. On the other hand, the government can allocate ownership of pollution rights to individuals, rather than operate a government auction, in which case the government will not derive revenues from pollution control.

[15] This is the familiar Pigouvian tax solution to pollution. See W. BAUMOL & W. OATES, *supra* note 11.

observers of social costs and benefits, then a community standard may reflect a consensus about efficient behavior. Raising the community standard to the level of law can create optimal incentives. Alternatively, if officials can observe benefits and costs more accurately than private persons, then the legislature can impose a legal standard by fiat that creates optimal incentives. Whether legal standards originate in community standards or legislative fiat, liability often produces a discontinuity in costs at the legal standard, which resembles a sanction. The second way to create optimal incentives for controlling social costs is to price them. If private persons can assess the benefits from their own acts and officials can assess the external costs, then optimal incentives can be created by imposing liability equal to the externality.[16] When external costs vary continuously with the injurer's behavior, liability equal to the externality resembles a market price.

---

[16] To exhaust the logical possibilities, we add: if private persons can assess the costs of their own acts and officials can assess the external benefits, then optimal incentives can be created by official subsidies.

The Injurer's Self-Risk Puzzle

In economics, "joint product" refers to two goods unavoidably bundled in a production process, like wool and mutton from raising sheep. Similarly, "joint risk" refers to an activity that unavoidably bundles risks to the actor (self-risk) and nonactors (other-risk). For example, driving a car imposes joint risk on the driver and other people. Safety standards should balance the burden of precaution against reduction in all risks, including self-risk and other-risk. Unfortunately, courts often decide liability based on the injurer's risk to others and not the risk to himself. These legal decisions make no sense morally or economically. These decisions cause less compensation of victims, less precaution by injurers, and more accidents. The new RESTATEMENT (THIRD) OF TORTS: LIABILITY FOR PHYSICAL AND EMOTIONAL HARM acknowledges that all risks should be considered in setting the standard of care, both risks to others and risks to oneself, referring to the argument we have made on this matter.[1] It is too early to predict whether courts will follow the RESTATEMENT's rule.

This chapter explains why courts should determine liability by reference to the risk the injurer imposes on others and himself. We begin with an example.

> *Example 1:* Getting into his car, John discovers that the buckle on his seat belt is broken. Buckling it is impossible. No statute requires drivers to wear seat belts. The speed limit is 30 miles per hour. Time is very valuable to John this morning, so he decides to drive unbuckled. John drives 30 miles per hour, his car skids, and he hits Tony's parked car. If John had driven 25 miles per hour, he would have avoided hitting Tony's car. Considering John's risk to other people and himself, the reasonable speed to drive was 25 miles per hour. Considering only John's risk to other people, the reasonable speed to drive was 30 miles per hour. The rule of law is negligence. In a suit for damages by Tony, should the court find John liable? Should the court admit evidence on the broken seat belt?

---

[1] RESTATEMENT (THIRD) OF TORTS: LIABILITY FOR PHYSICAL AND EMOTIONAL HARM § 3, cmt. b (and Reporter's Note, cmt. b) (2010). The RESTATEMENT also refers in this context to KENNETH W. SIMONS, *The Puzzling Doctrine of Contributory Negligence*, 16 CARDOZO L. REV. 1693, 1725-28 (1995), who argued that all risks should count in determining whether the victim was contributorily negligent.

In cases like this one, most courts would find the defendant not liable. Courts would arrive at this decision by considering the injurer's risk to others and ignoring the injurer's risk to himself. The intuition behind such decisions is that the duties one person owes to another depend on the other person's risk, not his own risk. In this chapter we show that this intuition is wrong, from both efficiency and nonefficiency perspectives. We also show that in example 1, courts should admit evidence on the broken seat belt when they determine whether John was negligent.

A. Applying the Hand Rule

Under negligence law the injurer is considered negligent when he poses unreasonable risks to other people to whom he owes a duty of care. The materialization of the unreasonable risk satisfies the proximate cause requirement that triggers tort liability for the resulting harm. A crucial question for courts that apply negligence law is whether the injurer was negligent or not. To answer this question courts across the United States apply the Hand rule, named after Judge Learned Hand, who was the first to formulate it in algebraic terms. The Hand Rule, or the Hand Formula, was later adopted by the RESTATEMENT (SECOND) OF TORTS and recently by the RESTATEMENT (THIRD) OF TORTS: LIABILITY FOR PHYSICAL AND EMOTIONAL HARM.[2] According to the Hand Rule, the injurer is considered negligent if he failed to take precautions, when taking precautions incurs lower costs than the expected damage that would have been reduced by those precautions. In formal terms the Hand Formula directs courts to determine liability by comparing the burden of precaution (B) with expected damages (PL), when L stands for harm and P for the probability of its occurrence. If $B < PL$ the injurer is found negligent, and if $B > PL$ he is not found negligent. Under the best interpretation, these variables refer to marginal values. Consequently, the injurer is considered negligent when his marginal costs of precaution fall short of the marginal reduction in the expected damages.

Now we explain why the Hand Formula should balance precautions against *all* risks that would have been reduced by the precautions, including the injurer's self-risk. We call it the economic application of the Hand Formula, and contrast it with the traditional or prevailing law application of that Formula, which ignores the injurer's self-risk. We return to example 1 and ascribe numbers to this example in table 2.1. According to the first column of numbers in table 2.1, slowing down from 30 mph to 25 mph costs John 100 in lost time. If John is unbuckled as in example 1, then slowing down reduces the expected cost of the joint risk to himself and others, each by 75. Thus, if the seat belt is unbuckled, the cost of precaution (100) is less than its social benefit (150), so

---

[2] RESTATEMENT (THIRD) OF TORTS: LIABILITY FOR PHYSICAL AND EMOTIONAL HARM, § 3 (2010).

efficiency requires John to slow down. Since the burden of precaution (100) is less than the reduction in joint risk (150), an economic application of the Hand Rule concludes that the driver should be held liable for proceeding at 30 mph. If he is held liable for driving 30 mph, he clearly minimizes his costs by driving 25 mph. Thus the economic interpretation of the Hand Rule provides incentives for efficient behavior.

Courts that follow the prevailing law application of the Hand Formula and compare the burden of precaution and the reduction of risk to others, however, would reach a different result. According to table 2.1, the burden of precaution (100) exceeds the risk to others (75), so such a court would presumably find John not negligent. If the court finds John non-negligent, then slowing down from 30 mph to 25 mph costs John 100 in lost time while it saves him 75 in risk to himself, so he will *not* slow down. Under a prevailing law application of the Hand Formula, self-interest motivates John to drive 30 mph in a situation where efficiency requires a speed of 25 mph.

Risks to others and to the injurer should be taken into account by the Hand Formula. Courts should estimate the magnitude of the injurer's self-risk. Consequently, in example 1, the court should admit evidence on the broken seat belt because John has increased the risk to himself by driving unbuckled. If John had been buckled, his risk would have probably been lower, and maybe the total risks reduced by slowing down would have been lower than 100. In this alternative set of circumstances, John should not have been considered negligent for driving 30 miles per hour.

Notice that the joint risk is 150 in table 2.1, whereas the other-risk is 75. When joint risk is symmetrical between injurer and victim, as in many collisions, prevailing law underestimates the benefits of precaution by 50 percent. In asymmetrical accidents, however, prevailing law tends to underestimate the benefits of precaution, though the degree of underestimate can vary from 0 percent to 100 percent.

This example considers only two levels of precaution (driving 25 or 30 miles per hour), so precaution is treated as binary. This example illustrates three generalizations about binary precaution: (i) The traditional application of the Hand Rule finds "no liability" whenever the burden of precaution is more than the reduction in risk to others ($B > PL_o$). (ii) Given no liability, the injurer takes no precaution when the burden is more than the reduction in risk to himself ($B > PL_s$).

Table 2.1.
Numerical example of joint risks, seatbelt unbuckled

	Cost to John from lost time	Risk to self	Risk to others	Social costs
Drive 25	100	0	0	100
Drive 30	0	75	75	150

(iii) Minimizing social costs requires taking precaution whenever the burden is less than the sum of the reduction in risk to self and others ($B < PL_s + PL_o$). In summary, the traditional application of the Hand Rule creates inefficient incentives for the injurer to take no precaution whenever the burden is more than self-risk and also more than other-risk, and the burden is less than the sum of self-risk and other-risk. If one of these conditions is relaxed, however, the injurer may take efficient precaution even under the traditional Hand Rule. In any case, the economic Hand Rule completely solves this problem.

Instead of being binary, precaution often takes several different values or changes continuously, as with driving speed. Given continuous precaution the traditional Hand Rule inevitably results in setting the standard of precaution too low. The standard is inevitably too low because the marginal cost of a little more precaution, which should be balanced against the marginal benefit to self and others, is only balanced against the marginal benefit to others. With continuous variables, setting the standard of care too low typically results in insufficient precaution by potential injurers. Thus the conditions for the failure of the traditional Hand Rule are simpler and more general when precaution is continuous rather than binary. As in the binary case, the economic Hand Rule completely solves this problem.

B. Prevailing Law Critiqued

By ignoring the effect of an injurer's precaution on self-risk, American common law systematically fails to analyze accurately the problem of joint risks. The RESTATEMENT (SECOND) OF TORTS adopts this inefficient approach. Article 291 states as follows:

> Where an act is one which a reasonable man would recognize as involving a risk of harm to *another*, the risk is unreasonable and the act is negligent if the risk is of such magnitude as to outweigh what the law regards as the utility of the act or of the particular manner in which it is done. (emphasis added)

Article 293 adds:

> In determining the magnitude of the risk for the purpose of determining whether the actor is negligent, the following factors are important:
> . . . (b) the extent of the chance that the actor's conduct will cause an invasion of any interest of the *other* or of one of a class of which the *other* is a member. . . . (emphasis added)

Risk to oneself is not mentioned in the latter articles of the RESTATEMENT (SECOND) OF TORTS.[3] In the new RESTATEMENT (THIRD) OF TORTS: LIABILITY

---

[3] See also RESTATEMENT (SECOND) OF TORTS, §§ 298, 300 (1965).

FOR PHYSICAL AND EMOTIONAL HARM, however, the reporters noted that all risks should be taken into account by courts in determining whether the injurer was negligent, including the risks to the injurer.[4] It is yet to be seen whether courts will follow the new RESTATEMENT on the self-risk issue.

By its wording, the Hand Rule is not limited to others' risks. It may encompass the actor's risk to himself. Thus the Hand Rule can receive an economic interpretation that encompasses social risks. Judges since Learned Hand, however, have systematically ignored the injurer's risk to himself in applying the rule. Instead, judges (and scholars) systematically define "negligence" in terms of creating unreasonable risks toward *others*.[5]

The complexity of facts obscures this conclusion about the well-known *U.S. v. Carroll Towing Co.* case,[6] which established the Hand Rule among American judges. A prior decision of Judge Hand, *Conway v. O'Brien*,[7] which was given seven years earlier and used the same formula without the algebraic terms, is simpler and clearer. In *Conway* the plaintiff was injured in a road accident while a passenger in the defendant's car. Under the statute prevailing at the time, the driver was liable toward his guest-passenger only if he had been grossly negligent in causing the accident. The specific question posed by the court was whether or not the defendant's driving was grossly negligent. Judge Hand formulated the standard of care as follows:

> The degree of care demanded of a person by an occasion is the resultant of three factors: the likelihood that his conduct *will injure others*, taken with

---

[4] RESTATEMENT (THIRD) OF TORTS: LIABILITY FOR PHYSICAL AND EMOTIONAL HARM § 3, cmt. b (and Reporter's Note, cmt. b) (2010).

[5] E.g., W.L. PROSSER & W.P. KEETON, TORTS (5th ed., 1984) § 31, at 169: "[Negligence] has been defined as . . . conduct 'which falls below the standard established by law for the protection of others against unreasonable risk of harm'"; PROSSER, *id.*: "The essence of negligence is . . . behavior which should be recognized as involving unreasonable danger to others"; PROSSER, *id.*, § 65, at 453: "Negligence as it is commonly understood is conduct which creates an undue risk of harm to others. Contributory negligence is conduct which involves an undue risk of harm to the actor himself"; ERNEST WEINRIB, THE IDEA OF PRIVATE LAW (1995) 147: "The standard [of reasonable care] is breached by action that creates a risk that no reasonable person would impose upon others. . . . Through the notion of risk, what one person does can be regarded from the standpoint of what another person might suffer"; P. CANE, ATIYAH'S ACCIDENTS, COMPENSATION AND THE LAW 46 (2006): "The allegation in a negligence action is basically that the defendant paid insufficient attention to the interests of others in deciding how to behave, and has pursued his or her own objectives at the risk of injuring other people or damaging their property"; CANE, *id.*, at 46: "People may drive their cars at a 'reasonable' speed because the gain to them and the public from being allowed so to drive is at least worth the risk of the harm such driving may cause; but people are not allowed to drive at an 'excessive' speed because the additional gain that it brings to them does not outweigh the additional risk that it imposes on others."

[6] 159 F. 2d 169 (1947).

[7] 111 F. 2d 611 (1940).

the seriousness of the injury if it happens, and balanced against the interest which he must sacrifice to avoid the risk.[8] (emphasis added)

Applying this test, Judge Hand concluded that the defendant was not grossly negligent.[9] Judge Hand seems unaware that minimizing social costs in these circumstances involves balancing the burden of precaution against the reduction in self-risk and other-risk. Had Judge Hand weighed the driver's self-imposed risk together with passengers' risks, he might have reached a different conclusion.

Like Judge Hand, courts applying the Hand Rule in subsequent cases fail to understand the nature of joint risks. A case decided by Judge Posner, *Brotherhood Shipping Co., Ltd. v. St Paul Fire & Marine Insurance Co.*,[10] illustrates this point. In this case a ship owner brought a suit against the City of Milwaukee for damages resulting from a collision between the ship and the slip in which it was berthed at the time of the accident. The slip was also damaged, and therefore a counterclaim was brought by the City to recover its damages from the ship owner. Since this case appealed a motion for summary judgment dismissing the ship owner's claim, the court had to decide whether "viewing the evidence . . . as favorable to the shipowner . . . [the court] can say that no reasonable trier of fact could conclude that the city had been even a little bit negligent."[11]

The design and maintenance of the slip presumably affects the risk to ships (other-risk) and the slip (self-risk). An economic application of the Hand Rule should balance the City's burden of precaution and the resulting reduction in joint risk. The risk to the slip was large, as indicated by the damages that actually materialized. When Judge Posner compared the burden of precaution that the city could have taken to the resulting reduction in risk, his discussion does not mention the risk to the slip.[12] Perhaps Judge Posner was unaware of the potential importance of self-risk in this case, or perhaps Judge Posner responded to the arguments of attorneys who never raised the issue of self-risk. In any event, after discussing other-risk and not self-risk, Judge Posner concluded that the City's alleged negligence must be tried in the District Court. If the District Court decides the case by ignoring the risk to the City's slip, it will presumably set the legal standard too low for economic efficiency.

---

[8] *Id.*, at 612.

[9] The U.S. Supreme Court thought otherwise, and the case was reversed and the question of gross negligence was retried. See *Conway v. O'Brien* 312 U.S. 492 (1941).

[10] 985 F. 2d 323 (1993).

[11] *Id.*, at 324.

[12] "Evaluating these facts with the aid of the Hand formula, we note first that L in the formula—the magnitude or gravity of the loss that an accident that the precautions the defendant failed to take would have averted could be expected to inflict—was substantial. The ships that dock at the Port of Milwaukee are expensive machines carrying expensive goods. Moreover, an accident to such a ship, even while the ship is berthed, could endanger human life. . . . The ship could have sunk, like the E.M. Ford, in which event the loss might easily have exceeded $5 million. . . ." *Id.*, at 329.

C. The "Net Burden" Approach

As explained, courts show no awareness that minimizing social cost requires the legal standard of care to respond to the injurer's risk to himself. If judges reflected upon the effect of self-risk on the legal standard, or if lawyers argued this point to judges, perhaps the practice of courts would change. Adjusting the "burden" in the Hand Rule provides a natural way to make the change. We state abstractly the nature of the adjustment and then discuss a case that seems to show the judge making just this adjustment.

As explained, the economic Hand Rule balances the burden of precaution to the injurer and the reduction in expected accident costs to the injurer and the victim. If the former is lower than the latter, the injurer who failed to take precautions is considered negligent. In algebraic terms, under the economic Hand Rule the injurer is negligent if: $B < pL_s + pL_o$. But the formula can also be written as: $B - pL_s < pL_o$. As this construction makes clear, the injurer is negligent if the burden of precaution minus reduction in self-risk is lower than reduction of other-risk. The term "burden of precaution minus reduction in self-risk" subtracts the injurer's benefit from the injurer's burden, thus equaling the "net burden." The "net burden" interpretation of the Hand Rule fully encompasses social costs.

According to the net burden interpretation, the Hand Rule concerns the net costs of precaution, not the gross costs. If precautions benefited the injurer in any way, those benefits are subtracted from the gross costs of precaution, and only the difference is compared to the expected damages of others. Applying this approach to our previous example in table 2.1, the court would define John's net precaution costs as $100 - 75 = 25$. His precaution costs are only 25 according to this reasoning, whereas this precaution creates benefits of 75 to others, so failing to take precaution is negligent. The net burden approach creates incentives for efficient behavior.

With rare exceptions, however, courts follow the gross burden approach when interpreting the Hand Rule. Courts sometimes mention that precaution reduces the benefit of the activity to the injurer. When more precaution reduces the benefit from the activity, courts may take this reduction into account when setting the negligence standard. Conversely, though, courts do not mention that precaution increases the *safety* of the activity for the injurer.

A federal district court case, *Johnson v. City of Milwaukee*,[13] departs from this pattern by following a special version of the "net burden" approach. In *Johnson* the court used the Hand Rule to determine whether an off-duty police officer who shot a suspect while trying to arrest him infringed the victim's Fourth Amendment right against "unreasonable search and seizure." Specifically, the court considered the question whether reasonableness required the off-duty

---

[13] 1999 U.S. Dist. 41 F. Supp. 2d 917 (1999).

police officer to wait until on-duty help arrived, instead of using force immediately. The court concluded that the police officer behaved unreasonably under the circumstances. The court reasoned, *inter alia*, that had the police officer waited for back-up, he could have reduced the risks to the suspect, the community in general, and himself. In the court's words:

> Brown [the police-officer] could have taken precautions which would have increased both Johnson's safety and *his own*. . . .
>
> In this case the possibility of harm to individuals or the community if Officer Brown had waited for back-up, used verbal control or ordered Johnson to the ground before frisking him was nonexistent. If Brown had waited for back-up or put Johnson on the ground, *his own safety* and Johnson's would have been enhanced. . . .
>
> The discharge of a firearm could have caused great harm—even death— to *the officer* or the suspect. In sum, a reasonable jury considering the officer's conduct in light of the Hand formula could conclude that the burden of precautions was less than the probability of an accident times the potential loss and that Brown's actions were therefore unreasonable. (emphasis added)

When a police officer arrests a dangerous criminal, the risks to the officer and to the criminal connect in an obvious way. In the typical case, the officer can reduce the risk to himself by increasing the risk to the criminal. When the officer's risk and the criminal's risk trade off, an increase in the officer's own risk *is* the burden of reducing the criminal's risk. When an increase in self-risk *is* the burden of precaution, any use of the Hand Rule inevitably focuses on the net burden. The court in *Johnson* inevitably focused on the net burden because the central question was whether or not a tradeoff existed between self-risk and other-risk.

D. The Pervasiveness of Joint Risks

The following four paradigmatic examples, based on real cases, illustrate some forms of joint risk that pervade law.

Collisions. In any road accident, the injurer's precaution affects the risk to himself and others. Ignoring self-risk leads to suboptimal standards of care. Besides road accidents, this holds true in other collisions such as marine accidents, as illustrated by the preceding discussion of the *Brotherhood* case.[14]

---

[14] For cases representing the *collision* case, in which courts probably ignored the risk to the injurer, and could have reached different outcomes if they had not ignored it, see, e.g., *Barnes v. Charles W. Thames, Fireman's Fund Insurance Co.* 578 So. 2d 1155 (1991), *Blair v. Tynes* 610 So. 2d 956 (1992).

The failure to protect others from criminals. A criminal attacks and injures an employee in the workplace. The victim sues her employer for failing to protect her from criminals. In considering the question of liability under negligence law, courts should weigh the employer's precautions against the reduction in everyone's risk at work. "Everyone's risk" includes the risk to the property and persons of the employees and the employer. To illustrate concretely, a bank robbery risks harm to people and a large loss of money, whereas robbery of a grocery store risks harm to people and the loss of comparatively little money. Consequently, economic efficiency requires a bank to take more precaution against robberies than a grocery store.[15] In general, a company's duty of care to protect against criminals should increase to the extent that criminals impose risks on the company as well as others.[16]

Maintenance of property. A guest in a house who falls on the stairs sues the homeowner. In considering the homeowner's liability under negligence law, courts should consider the cost and benefits of maintaining the stairs. The benefits include the reduction in risk to guests and the owner. Insofar as the owner uses the stairs more frequently than guests, the reduction in risk to the owner should affect the legal standard of care owed to guests more than the risk to guests. In any case, taking the owner's risks into account will increase the precautions required by the law.[17]

Abatement of a nuisance. A neighbor seeks to enjoin an adjacent property owner whose activity causes smoke, sparks, noise, odors, effluent, or floods. If an injunction is issued, the property owner will have to abate the nuisance or abandon the activity. Following *Spur v. Del Webb*[18] and *Boomer v. Atlantic Cement*,[19] the court balances the benefits and costs of abating, abandoning, or allowing the harm to continue. Besides benefiting the victim, abating will presumably reduce the smoke, sparks, noise, bad odors, effluent, or floods that the injurer afflicts upon himself. In weighing the benefits of abating, the court must consider the benefits to injurer and victims.

---

[15] For cases representing the failure to protect others from criminals, in which courts probably ignored the risk to the defendant, see, e.g., *McCarty v. Pheasant Run, Inc.* 826 F. 2d 1554 (1987), *Madden v. C & K Barbecue Carryout, Inc.* 758 S.W. 2d 59 (1988), *Doe v. Dominion Bank of Washington, N.A.* 963 F. 2d 1552 (1992).

[16] A decision of the Israel Supreme Court, based upon our argument, is illustrative of this category of cases. In *Valas v. Egged* 55 (5) P.D. 826, 844 (2001) (Hebrew), criminals attacked a passenger at the central bus station. The passenger sued the bus company for his bodily injury under negligence law. The district court dismissed the claim, but the Supreme Court remanded it for further hearings, instructing the district court, that in considering whether the bus company was negligent in failing to post guards at the station, not only reduction of risks to passengers using the station should be taken into account, but also reduction of risks to the bus company property.

[17] For maintaining property and similar acts, in which courts probably ignored the risk to the defendant, see, e.g., *Lirette v. State Farm Insurance Co.* 581 So. 2d 265 (1991), *Eaton v. McLain* 891 S.W. 2d 587 (1994).

[18] 494 P. 2d 700 (1972).

[19] 257 N.E. 2d 870 (1970).

E. Qualification: Self-Risk and Other Risks Are Not Joint

Risks to others and self-risk are often separate, not joint. In such cases the economic application of the Hand Rule is more complicated. To explain these cases, we use a second example that is the same as the first,[20] except that the seat belt is *not* broken. With the facts changed in this way the injurer can take precaution that reduces the risk to himself without affecting the risk to others. Specifically, buckling the seat belt in example 2 reduces the risk to John without affecting the risk to Tony, whereas slowing down reduces the risk to John and Tony.

> *Example 2:* Getting into his car, John is in a hurry and he carelessly does not buckle his seat belt. No statute requires drivers to wear seat belts, but considering John's risk to himself, John was *un*reasonable not to buckle his seat belt. The speed limit is 30 miles per hour. Time is very valuable to John, so he drives 30 miles per hour, his car skids, and he hits Tony's parked car. If John had driven 25 miles per hour, he would have avoided hitting Tony's car. Given the *un*buckled seat belt, and considering John's risk both to himself and to Tony's car, the reasonable speed to drive was 25 miles per hour. Considering only the risk to Tony's car, the reasonable speed to drive was 30 miles per hour. If the seat belt had been *buckled*, once again considering John's risk both to himself and to Tony's car, the reasonable speed to drive was 30 miles per hour. The rule of law is negligence. In a suit for damages by Tony, should the court find John liable?

Applying conventional causation principles to example 2, even a court that is willing to follow the economic application of the Hand Rule should find John not liable. The reasonable behavior for John in example 2 is to buckle his seat belt and drive at the 30 mph speed limit. If, contrary to fact, John had buckled his seat belt, he would not have driven any *slower* than he actually drove. The outcome, but for the unbuckled seat belt, would have been identical; John would have skidded into Tony's car. Consequently, John's unreasonable behavior was *not* the "but-for" cause of Tony's harm. A court applying conventional causation principles would conclude that the unbuckled seat belt did not *cause* the injury, so John is not liable. As we will show, no liability provides efficient incentive to John to buckle his seat belt and drive at 30 mph, as required by efficiency. Indeed, the law could give additional incentives for drivers to buckle their seat belts by holding them negligent for not slowing down when driving unbuckled. But typically, from an efficiency perspective, there is no advantage in imposing liability when self-interest already compels socially efficient behavior.

Note that a judge who attempts to minimize social costs and follow the economic application of the Hand Rule is likely to make an error in applying the Rule. The mistake arises from a false comparison between example 1 and example 2. In the first example, John does not buckle his seat belt because he

---

[20] *Supra* text following note 1.

Table 2.2.
Numerical example of joint risks, seatbelt buckled

	Cost to John from lost time	Risk to self	Risk to others	Social costs
Drive 25	100	0	0	100
Drive 30 (buckled)	0	0	75	75

cannot. In the second example, John does not buckle his seat belt because he is unreasonable. If efficiency requires holding John liable in the first example, the judge might reason, then *a fortiori* efficiency must require liability in the second example. This reasoning, however, is wrong. Correct reasoning asserts that minimizing social costs requires the driver in example 1 to slow down, and liability creates an incentive to slow down. In contrast, minimizing social costs in example 2 requires the driver to buckle his seat belt and not slow down, and no liability provides these incentives.

To illustrate the latter point we extend the numerical illustration we used for example 1 to example 2. Whereas table 2.1 shows costs when John drives with his seat belt unbuckled, table 2.2 shows costs when John drives with his seat belt buckled. For simplicity, we assume that buckling the seat belt is costless and completely eliminates the additional risk to the driver from higher speed. Table 2.2 shows that social costs fall to their minimum of 75 when John buckles and drives at the speed limit. Provided John can buckle his seat belt, this is the first-best outcome. In example 2, no liability for driving 30 mph provides an incentive for John to buckle his seat belt and drive at that speed. Specifically, under no liability, John can drive 30 mph buckled and bear costs of 0, or John can drive 25 buckled or unbuckled and bear costs of 100.

F. Objections

Several objections could be raised against the self-risk argument, but we find none of them persuasive.

1. SELF-RISK AND PRECAUTIONS ARE INCOMMENSURABLE

One possible objection to the self-risk argument is that the burden of precaution and the reduction in risk are incomparable. Thus, the burden is often monetary in nature and the risk is often nonmonetary. If valid, this objection would undermine all negligence law, since courts often determine negligence by comparing monetary costs of precaution with risks to people's life and limbs. In this regard the self-risk argument does not require courts to do anything different in nature from what they currently do.

More interestingly, on many occasions reduction in self-risk is monetary and can be compared easily with precaution. Take the example of *Doe v. Dominion Bank of Washington, N.A.*[21] In this case criminals attacked a bank employee at the workplace and inflicted harm upon her. The employee sued the bank for negligent failure to post guards at the bank to protect its employees. Under the economic Hand Rule that we propose, the reduction in the bank's self-risk from guards should have been considered in determining whether the bank was negligent. Reduction in the bank's self-risk can be very easily translated into money. For example, if the bank had posted guards, the bank's insurance-against-robbery premiums might have decreased. Alternatively, the bank might have spent less on other precautionary measures against robbery, such as safes and alarms. The *net burden* of the bank in posting guards is not the money paid to the guards, but instead that sum of money minus the bank's savings either in insurance premiums or in costs incurred for other precautionary measures.

2. THE SELF-RISK ARGUMENT IS PATERNALISTIC AND ANTI-LIBERAL

In setting the standard of care, is including the injurer's risk to himself paternalistic? People are pushed to reduce self-created risks by threatening them with liability. But the rationale for taking self-risk into account is not the notion that people should reduce their risks to themselves, but, rather, that they should reduce risks to others when mandated by efficiency. Efficiency requires that an injurer reduce risks to others when the risk exceeds the injurer's *net* burden, as distinguished from gross burden. While a legal approach that takes the injurer's self-risk into account would indeed boost the incentive for potential injurers to reduce the risks to themselves, this is not the justification for doing so.

Similarly, it might be argued that considering the injurer's self-risk in setting the standard of care is anti-liberal because it results in sanctioning the injurer for assuming a risk and thereby restricts his available choices and the scope of his autonomy. However, taking self-risk into consideration in the application of the Hand Formula yields no greater an infringement on injurers' autonomy qualitatively than does the traditional application of the formula. Negligence law—by all accounts, efficiency and corrective justice alike—is based on the idea that people's autonomy should be restricted only when they create *unreasonable* risk for others. The reasonableness of a risk is determined by the magnitude of the risk, on the one hand, and the magnitude of the burden of reducing it, on the other.[22] The greater the burden, the more adverse the impact on the

---

[21] 963 F. 2d 1552 (1992).

[22] For the view that only risks, and not burdens, should count in defining "unreasonable risks," see WEINRIB, *supra* note 5, at 147-52, who argues that negligence should be determined only according to the risks created by the injurer, without consideration of the burden imposed upon him to reduce those risks.

actor's autonomy if liability is imposed, and vice versa.[23] Since the magnitude of the burden is indicative of the effect of liability on the actor's autonomy, it is crucial to define it accurately, and the injurer's self-risk does precisely that. Specifically, the greater the self-risk, the lesser the (net) burden on the injurer in taking precautions, and the smaller the infringement on the injurer's autonomy.

3. IMPLEMENTATION PROBLEMS

Perhaps many people underestimate their self-risk because they don't care about it. If so, is it wrong to assume that self-risk has objective value that should matter to courts? Maybe the driver in example 1 who failed to buckle his seat belt did not care about his self-risk, or truly estimated it at much less than its objective value (which is assumed in the example to be 75). This underestimation is not necessarily the result of lack of information or cognitive biases: it could be the result of the different views people have with respect to their own safety.[24] Naturally, an injurer would have good reasons to convince courts that his self-risk was considered by him to be very low: the lower the value assigned to self-risk, the lower the likelihood that the court would find the injurer negligent. In sum—so the implementation objection goes—since it is hard to verify the real value of self-risk to the injurer, maybe the best strategy is to stay with the traditional Hand Rule, which relieves courts from the task of considering the injurer's self-risk.

This objection is based on a wrong understanding of the way negligence law is implemented by courts. Ideally, at least from an efficiency point of view, courts should consider negligence according to the values injurers and victims ascribe to precautions and harms, respectively. But in our nonideal world, courts facing scarce or uncertain information seek to use objective criteria to evaluate both precautions and harms. Most noneconomic theories also favor objective criteria to determine negligence, not subjective criteria. For exactly the same reasons, self-risk should be estimated objectively. The fact that some injurers would truly estimate their self-risk below its objective value should be irrelevant for courts. It would be irrelevant in just the same way as it would be irrelevant for a court to determine whether a driver who rushed home at a very

---

[23] *Cf.* Gregory C. Keating, *Reasonableness and Rationality in Negligence Theory*, 48 Stan. L. Rev. 311, 349 (1996) ("The enhanced freedom of action injurers gain from imposing risks must be balanced against the loss of security those risks impose on victims. Conversely, the lost freedom of action that injurers suffer when they are forced to take precautions must be balanced against the benefits those precautions afford the property and physical integrity of victims.").

[24] See Leo Katz, *What to Compensate? Some Surprisingly Unappreciated Reasons Why the Problem Is So Hard*, 40 San Diego L. Rev. 1345, 1356-7 (note 10) (2003). Katz presents our argument on self-risk as the "Cooter-Porat Paradox." According to Katz it is a paradox, because on the one hand we may be right, but on the other hand we may be wrong because self-risk is not necessarily considered a bad thing for some actors. Katz suggests that maybe for this reason courts chose to ignore self-risk. He argues that this "paradox" is part of a more general problem which he calls "The Raw Utility Problem."

high speed and hit a pedestrian loved the thrill of fast driving or simply wanted to arrive home in time to kiss his kids before they went to bed.

The current application of the Hand Rule would have been equivalent to the economic Hand Rule only if self-risk was always or widely considered by injurers as zero. While injurers have an incentive to downplay their self-risk, there is no reason to assume that most of them consistently disregard their self-risk in this way.

G. Conclusion

As interpreted by courts, the Hand Rule, which formulates and critiques the duty of care that people owe to others, balances the injurer's burden of precaution and the victim's reduction in risk. Efficiency, however, requires using the Hand Rule to minimize total social costs, which mandates balancing the burden of precaution against the reduction in risk to everyone. In cases where precaution reduces joint risk (risk to oneself and others), the legal interpretation underestimates the reduction in risk relative to the economic interpretation, often by 50 percent. The consequence is a lower legal standard of care than required to minimize social costs.

We recommend that courts reconceptualize the Hand Rule so that risk to oneself increases the care owed to others. In order to take account of self-risk, courts must determine its extent. In the absence of a countersuit, courts do not ordinarily inquire into the extent to which an accident exposed the defendant to risk. The application of the economic Hand Rule requires changing this practice. Perhaps the easiest way to make the change is to interpret the injurer's "burden" of care as the "net burden," by which we mean the injurer's burden of care minus the reduction in injurer's risk.

If courts make this change, they will create a new problem. If courts consider the defendant's self-risk, defendants will have an incentive to understate it. By understating self-risk, defendants can hope to lower the legal standard of care applied to their behavior. Courts have means to correct this bias, but even if the correction fails, understating self-risk leads to better results than the current practice of computing the legal standard as if self-risk were zero.

Besides applying the Hand Rule, courts also determine negligence by applying a community standard of care. An unanswered question is whether or not community standards take account of joint risk, as required for efficiency, or whether communities, like courts, restrict attention to other-risk. Answering this question requires a theory of the evolution of social norms that we will not attempt to construct here.

Critics of the economic analysis of law may offer a variety of reasons to dismiss our conclusions. Our rejoinder is that careful consideration of our arguments should show that the objections are unfounded. Most negligence theories recognize the relevance of the injurer's interests when determining his responsibility toward others. Any theory recognizing the injurer's burden as relevant to his responsibility must acknowledge that reducing self-risk reduces the injurer's "real" burden, which we call the net burden. Our argument, consequently, refines the explanation of the injurer's burden. Everyone who accepts the relevance of the injurer's burden to the legal standard should welcome our clarification of its real extent.

Negligence Per Se
and Unaccounted Risks

W hen a statute imposes a duty of care, courts presume that its breach is "negligence per se."[1] If the breach causes harm, courts allow recovery of damages by some victims and not others, or courts allow recovery for some injuries and not others. Unfortunately, courts often draw the wrong boundary. An example adapted from the new RESTATEMENT (THIRD) OF TORTS: LIABILITY FOR PHYSICAL AND EMOTIONAL HARM illustrates the problem:[2]

> *Example 1: The Stairway Railing.* A statute requires employers to install railings alongside stairways at the workplace if they have five or more disabled employees. An employer who has five disabled employees fails to install such railings, and an *able-bodied* employee is injured in a fall that would have been prevented by a railing. Should the employer be found liable for the employee's injury under the doctrine of negligence per se?

In this example, the statute refers to disabled employees and remains silent about able-bodied employees. Can able-bodied employees recover damages for the harm caused by violating the statute? According to the new RESTATEMENT, the answer is "No." This answer can give an employer an incentive not to install railings that cost less than the accidents that they prevent. Consequently, we say that the answer should be "Yes."

---

[1] In order to prove negligence per se, the plaintiff has to prove that the defendant violated the statute. The plaintiff who alleges common law negligence by the defendant must prove that the defendant's behavior was unreasonable, whereas the doctrine of negligence per se presumes that violating the statutory standard of care is unreasonable. In some jurisdictions the defendant could raise a defense that his behavior, although it violated the statute, was in fact reasonable. See DAN B. DOBBS, THE LAW OF TORTS § 140, at 329-331(2000).

[2] Here is the example exactly as it appears in RESTATEMENT (THIRD) OF TORTS: LIABILITY FOR PHYSICAL AND EMOTIONAL HARM § 14 cmt. g (2010): "[I]f a statute designed to prevent falls by persons with disabilities requires elaborate railings on the side of stairways, and if a person who is able-bodied is then injured in a fall that such a railing, if present, would have prevented, this fall can be seen as not the type of accident the statute is considering."

Here is another example based on an actual case:

Example 2: The School-Zone Speed Limit. A statute imposes a speed limit of 25 mph in a neighborhood, except near schools where the speed limit is 15 mph. A car traveling 25 mph in a school zone hits a pedestrian, who would not have been hit if the car were travelling 15 mph. The injured pedestrian is an adult who did not know that he was walking in a school zone. Should the driver be liable to the pedestrian under negligence per se?

In the case on which example 2 is based, the court said, "No."[3] This answer can give drivers an incentive to speed in school zones where slowing down costs drivers less than the resulting reduction in accident costs. Consequently, we say that the answer should be "Yes."

When a legislature enacts a safety statute, the lawmakers have some risks in the foreground of their minds. Other risks are in the background. Failing to install railings increases both risks—the foreground risk to the disabled and the background risk to able-bodied people in example 1, and the foreground risk to children and the background risk to adult pedestrians in example 2.

Violation of the statute creates liability for foreground risks. What about liability for background risks? To make the safest society at the least cost, injurers should be liable for *all* foreseeable harms caused by their violation of safety standards, including foreground and background harms. Making injurers liable for *some* of the foreseeable harms—the foreground harm and not the background harm—distorts their safety incentives and increases accidents. Exempting injurers from liability for the background risks would often frustrate the legislature's aim to reduce foreground risks. These conclusions follow from the principle that safety standards should balance the cost of precaution and the resulting reduction in *all* foreseeable risks. The preceding chapter explains the mistake when courts balance the cost of taking precaution against the risk to others but not against the risk to the injurer himself. Similarly, this chapter explains the mistake when courts impose liability for foreground harm but not for background harm caused by the same wrongdoing.

[3] See *Grant v. McKiernan* 60 S.E.2d 794 (Ga. Ct. App. 1950). In this case, a thirty-five-year-old woman was injured in a car accident near a school when the driver had exceeded the school-zone speed limit. The court held that the woman was not included in the class of people to be protected by the special speed limit in a school zone but that children and others on their way to and from the school would be. In contrast, see *Whitley Construction Co. v. Price* 79 S.E.2d 416 (Ga. Ct. App. 1953), where the plaintiff was injured while sitting as a passenger in a trolley that stopped at a bus stop for the purpose of picking up passengers, including school children. The defendant had exceeded the speed limit in a school zone and collided with the trolley, resulting in the plaintiff's injury. The court found for the plaintiff, stating that speed limitations in school zones are set for the protection of all persons using the highway within such zones.

A. Negligence Per Se

A breach of a statutory duty that causes harm often results in injurer's tort liability under the doctrine of negligence per se. Under this doctrine, not all victims can recover and not all negligent injuries are compensable. For the tort suit to succeed, the victim must fall within the class of persons protected by the statute and the injury must be the type that the statute was intended to prevent.[4] These two conditions, which we call the "liability limitations," generate controversy and litigation because they are vague. It is often unclear which victims or which injuries the legislature intended to cover by the statute.

In example 1 (The Stairway Railing), courts applying the negligence per se doctrine would probably not impose liability on the defendant. The legislature apparently designed the statute to protect disabled people, not able-bodied employees like the plaintiff.[5] However, this reasoning and its conclusion are often wrong, especially if the enacting legislature aimed to make people as well off as possible.

To see why, assign numbers to example 1. Assume that the average cost of installing railings is 80, and installing them reduces risks to able-bodied employees by 30. Under these conditions, in the absence of disabled employees, installing railings is not cost-justified (30 < 80). Assume that when five disabled employees are present at the workplace, railings reduce risk to them by 60. Under these conditions, installing railings is cost-justified (30 + 60 > 80).

---

[4] RESTATEMENT (THIRD) OF TORTS: LIABILITY FOR PHYSICAL AND EMOTIONAL HARM § 14 (2010).

[5] See *Anderson v. Turton Dev., Inc.* 483 S.E.2d 597 (Ga. Ct. App. 1997), where the court rejected appellant's claim that the negligent design of the handicap ramp, which was the cause of appellant's fall, constituted a violation of the Georgia Handicap Act because appellant was not handicapped or elderly, but finding appellee liable for appellant's damages on grounds of common-law negligence. In *Carman v. Dunaway Timber Co.* 949 S.W.2d 569 (Ky. 1997), the court refused to define appellee's violation of the safety act as negligence per se because the purpose of the act was to protect employees only, and appellant did not belong to this group.

But there are also examples in which courts interpreted the relevant statute as encompassing a very broad range of victims, even though a narrower reading could have been given. In *Cappa v. Oscar C. Holmes, Inc.* 102 Cal. Rptr. 207 (Ct. App. 1972), for example, a boy was injured while crossing an area of a parking lot being constructed by the defendant. The trial court ruled in favor of the boy, basing the defendant's liability on a breach of the duty imposed by the Construction Safety Orders. The appellate court affirmed, noting that although it has been held that safety orders are primarily intended for the benefit and protection of workmen, as long as a safety order does not indicate to the contrary, persons consensually on the premises to which the safety order applies also fall within its protection. In *Porter v. Montgomery Ward & Co.* 313 P.2d 854 (Cal. 1957), a woman fell on a stairway in a department store and sued the store owner for compensation for her injury. She based her claim on a breach of a safety order issued by the Division of Industrial Safety, according to which a center handrail should have been installed along the stairway. The court dismissed the defendant's argument that the plaintiff was not a member of the class for whose protection the order was designed. It held that the safety orders and the provisions of the California Labor Code were intended not only to protect employees but also to safeguard the public generally against injury or loss of life.

The presence of able-bodied and disabled employees justifies the expenditure on railings. Note that installing railings for disabled employees alone is not cost-justified (60 < 80). Imposing liability only with regard to the disabled employees would result in deficient incentives for the employer to take precautions. He will prefer liability of 60 to spending 80 on railings, even though railings reduce the expected harm by 90.

Why, then, do courts disallow recovery by able-bodied people in cases like example 1? They focus on the risks in the forefront of the minds of the lawmakers and disregard the background risks. By doing so, they ignore the possibility that the legislature was responding to the aggregate of both foreground and background risk.[6]

The same argument applies to example 2 concerning the school-zone speed limit. In example 2, some courts might find no liability because the victim, who was not a child, does not fall within the class of persons protected by the statute. This decision is especially likely if the accident did not occur during school hours and no pupils were on the street. Other courts, however, might hesitate to reach this conclusion.[7] A court might conclude that the rationale for the lower speed limit is the density of pedestrians in a school zone, including children and adults, regardless of whether they are walking to or from school.

In any case, liability should be imposed in example 2 for the same reason as in example 1. The lower speed limit reduces risk to everyone, pupils and others alike. Aggregate risk is the reason for the 15 mph speed limit, not just risk to pupils. Perhaps the reduction in the risk to others alone or to pupils alone does not warrant a 15 mph speed limit. Let us assume the cost of slowing down from 25 mph to 15 mph is 80, the reduction of risk to pupils (foreground risk) is 60, and the reduction of risk to nonpupils (background risk) is 30. If the driver bears liability only toward pupils, he will prefer to drive faster and bear liability of 60 toward pupils, instead of slowing down at a cost of 80, even though slowing down reduces expected harm by 90.

In general, a standard is economically justified by the totality of its foreground and background effects. Consequently, when interpreting the statute,

---

[6] Compare example 1 to an analogous case where a statute obliges employers to hire someone trained in first aid for each workplace where the number of employees exceeds 100. Suppose now that in a specific workplace the number of employees is 100 and no one trained in first aid is provided. At a certain point of time, the 101st employee is hired, but nevertheless the employer fails to provide someone trained in first aid, and one of the first 100 employees suffers harm which could have been prevented if someone trained in first aid had been present at the workplace. Would the employer be released from liability, since the 101st employee, but not the plaintiff, was the reason the employer's statutory duty arose? The answer is of course "no." The reason the duty arises is the presence of all 101 employees at the workplace, regardless of the order in which they were hired. The fact that before the 101st employee was hired there was no duty to provide someone trained in first aid is irrelevant to the question of whether the employer is liable under negligence per se.

[7] Compare *Grant* 60 S.E. 2d 794, *supra* note 3, with *Whitley Constr. Co.* 79 S.E. 2d 416, *supra* note 3.

the court should not automatically conclude that it only protects referenced people. In most circumstances, the best interpretation is that the standard protects everyone—disabled and able-bodied, pupils and nonpupils. In that case, both types of victims should recover under negligence per se when breach of a statute harms them.

B. The Problem of Unaccounted Risks

The Hand Rule explained in the preceding chapter precisely shows how unaccounted risks can be a problem. According to the Hand Rule, courts will find an injurer to be negligent if he has failed to take precautions that cost less than the expected damages that the precautions would have avoided. In the notation used by Judge Hand, B denotes the burden of precaution, L denotes the harm caused by failing to take the burden of precaution, and P denotes the probability of its occurrence. If $B < PL$ the injurer is found negligent, and if $B \geq PL$ he is not found negligent. The boundary between negligence and non-negligence is the point where the burden of precaution equals expected damages: $B = PL$. Under the best interpretation, these variables refer to marginal values. Consequently, the boundary is where the marginal costs of precaution fall short of the marginal reduction in the expected harm.

The preceding chapter explained a mistake courts persistently make in interpreting PL. We distinguished the harm L caused by the injurer into harm to others L_o and harm to himself L_s. Minimizing social costs requires locating the boundary between negligence and non-negligence at the point where the burden equals the sum of the reduction in risk to self and others: $B = PL_s + PL_o$. Courts, however, usually locate the boundary at the point where the burden equals the reduction in risk to others: $B = PL_o$. Consequently, courts set the standard of care too low.

The problem with negligence per se, however, concerns the scope of liability, not the standard of care. Distinguish the harm L caused by the injurer's wrongdoing into two different classes: foreground L_f and background L_b. When injurers breach statutory duties, courts allow victims in the foreground to recover L_f, and courts often disallow victims in the background to recover L_b. The negligent injurer consequently expects liability of $P_f L_f$, whereas he causes expected harm of $P_f L_f + P_b L_b$. If the expected liability $P_f L_f$ is less than the legal burden of care B, then potential injurers would rather be liable than careful. If the burden is also less than the expected harm $P_f L_f + P_b L_b$, then efficiency requires potential injurers to be careful and not liable. Disallowing recovery by victims of background harms creates deficient incentives for care when $P_f L_f < B < P_f L_f + P_b L_b$.

Example 1 satisfies these conditions because the expected liability of $P_f L_f$ to the disabled costs 60, the burden B of installing the railing costs 80, and the expected harm to disabled and able-bodied victims equals 90. Absent liability toward able-bodied employees, a self-interested, rational, wealth-maximizing employer might prefer not to spend 80 on railings, and instead choose to shoulder liability of 60 toward disabled plaintiffs. This would reduce the protection of disabled employees sought by the statute and it would be socially inefficient.

As we noted, excluding background risk under negligence per se causes inadequate protection for the foreground class of people. Although disabled employees will be compensated if injured, most victims of bodily injury would presumably prefer not being injured to suffering an injury and receiving damages. Thus the primary goal of the statute must be the installation of railings when socially efficient, not ensuring compensation for injuries due to their absence.

Disallowing one class of victims from recovering damages for the harm caused by the injurer's negligence generally reduces the injurer's incentive to satisfy the legal standard. In many cases he will cease satisfying it. Sometimes, however, the injurer will satisfy the legal standard anyway. In example 1, if the risk to disabled employees were 100 rather than 60, the employer would have sufficient incentive to install a railing even without being liable to her able-bodied employees (since 100 > 80). But we (or the courts) do not really know what the numbers are, and there is always the possibility that they could indeed work out similarly to the numbers in example 1.[8] Furthermore, there are definite advantages to a uniform doctrine of negligence (or negligence per se) that can be applied to all cases, regardless of the numbers. This is precisely how the general doctrine of negligence works: the injurer bears liability for risks he or she could have reasonably prevented, even if lower liability would provide adequate incentives for precaution.[9]

C. Common Law Negligence

When the traffic code says that the speed limit is 15 mph near schools, it may be interpreted as imposing a duty owed to everyone or a duty owed only to children. Courts sometimes prefer the latter interpretation, but we have given

---

[8] Injurers will satisfy the legal standard when they are liable for at least the harm caused by their omitted precaution. Thus a defendant who exposed people to a carcinogen may be held liable for 100 percent of the cancers that they develop, even though exposure to the chemical was the cause of 60 percent of these cancers, and the other 40 percent of the claimants would have gotten cancer without the defendant's negligence. This is the famous "discontinuity" discussed in chapter 1 *supra*.

[9] Thus, a liability threat equivalent to costs of precaution plus would be sufficient to create efficient incentives. Accordingly, if costs of precaution are 2 and expected harm is 100, liability of 2 percent of harm plus 1 would be sufficient to incentivize the injurer to take the precautions. In some circumstances, however, the lawmakers intend to restrict legal protection to one class of people and deny it to others. For example, special interests may confine the benefits of a statute to organized groups or the friends of politicians. Or the plaintiff's bar may induce lawmakers to impose a legal duty in order to generate more fees from lawsuits, not to protect the victims of harm. In these cases, the lawmakers' intent conflicts with the best economic interpretation of the statute.

good reasons why the former interpretation is better. The common law poses the same issue. Instead of a traffic code, assume that there is a rule of reason that drivers should not exceed 15 mph near schools. When interpreting this common law duty of care, courts have to ask about its scope. Does the rule of reason about driving near schools impose a duty that is owed to everyone or only to children?

An injurer is liable for harms that materialize from the risks that define his behavior as negligent, but not for harms that materialized from risks that did not define his behavior as negligent.[10] This is the "wrongful risk limitation" on liability. (Liability is also limited by other legal doctrines, notably "duty of care," "proximate cause," and "public policy."[11]) Unfortunately, courts often misapply the wrongful risk limitation and arrive at inefficient results, for much the same reason as with the doctrine of negligence per se.

To show why, consider a doctor who must decide whether to deliver a baby vaginally or by C-section. (We mutate this example throughout the book to illustrate different considerations affecting a doctor's liability for bad results.)

Example 3: Delivering a Baby. A doctor delivered a baby vaginally, even though the large size of the baby warranted a C-section. A knot of the umbilical cord caused the baby's death. Prior to delivery, nothing indicated unusual risk relating to the umbilical cord. Compared to C-section, however, vaginal delivery generally increases the risk of death by a knot in the umbilical cord. In this case, a C-section would have saved the baby's life. The parents bring a wrongful death action against the doctor for her negligent failure to deliver by C-section. Should she be held liable?[12]

A court will probably find no liability by reasoning as follows. The vaginal delivery imposed a wrongful risk to deliver an oversize baby, but the wrongful risk did not materialize. Vaginal delivery also imposed a risk from a knot in the umbilical cord that materialized, but this risk is not wrongful. Since the non-wrongful risk materialized, the doctor is not liable. According to this reasoning, it is not enough for liability that the plaintiff's harm would not have occurred but for the injurer's negligence. Also, continuing along this line of reasoning, it is not enough for liability that the doctor's negligence increased the foreseeable risks to the class of persons to whom the victim belongs. For liability, the materialized risk must be one in light of which the doctor's act is defined as negligent. In common law negligence cases like example 3, however, courts tend to

---

[10] See RESTATEMENT (THIRD) OF TORTS: LIABILITY FOR PHYSICAL AND EMOTIONAL HARM § 29 cmt. d. (2010); DOBBS, *supra* note 1, § 187 n.1; W. PAGE KEETON ET AL., PROSSER AND KEETON ON THE LAW OF TORTS 273 (W. Page Keeton et al. eds., 5th ed. 1984); ERNEST J. WEINRIB, *Correlativity, Personality, and the Emerging Consensus on Corrective Justice,* 2 THEORETICAL INQUIRIES L. 107 (2001).

[11] See RESTATEMENT (THIRD) OF TORTS: LIABILITY FOR PHYSICAL AND EMOTIONAL HARM §§ 7 & 29 (2010).

[12] This example is based on an Israeli Supreme Court decision that dismissed a suit for lack of proximate cause. C.A. 2717/02 *Plonit v. Bnei Zion Med. Ctr. Haifa* (2003) Isr.S.C. 58(1) 516.

define foreground risks created by the injurer as wrongful and impose liability accordingly, while ignoring background risks.

This approach is wrong in common law negligence for the same reason that it is wrong in negligence per se. As in negligence per se cases, common law should recognize liability when *any* foreseeable risk that was increased by the injurer's negligence materialized into harm, regardless of whether it was in the foreground or the background. In example 3 vaginal delivery increased the background risk of death by a knot in the umbilical cord. The doctor's negligence in delivering vaginally should establish liability for the baby's death from a knot in the umbilical.

The Hand Rule definition of negligence supports this interpretation. What defines negligence under the Hand Rule is the total risk from untaken precaution. According to Hand's definition, the doctor is negligent if the additional burden of a C-section is less than the resulting reduction in foreground and background risk: $B < P_f L_f + P_b L_b$. The foreground risk associated with the baby's large size and the background risk from an umbilical knot both count in the definition of negligence, so they both count as compensable types of harm.

Assigning numbers to the example, assume that vaginal delivery causes a foreground risk of 60 that a C-section avoids, including risk from the baby's large size. In addition, vaginal delivery causes a background risk of 30 that a C-section avoids, including risk from a knot in the umbilical cord. Finally, the costs of delivering by a C-section are 80. Given the combined reduction of the two types of risks, a C-section is cost-justified (30 + 60 > 80). Nevertheless, a medical provider who bears the costs of a C-section and liability for its foreground risks, but not the background risks, would find it more profitable to deliver vaginally (because 60 < 80) in these circumstances.[13]

This numerical example often reflects reality. One could imagine how a reasonable care provider would issue guidelines for delivering babies. A reasonable care provider would compare the cost of alternative deliveries and all risks—not only foreground risks—and issue guidelines accordingly.

D. Causal Link Distinguished

Liability for damages caused by negligence should include background risks. Background risks should not be excluded by liability limitations under negligence per se or by the wrongful risk limitation in common law negligence.

---

[13] One possible counterargument is that doctors tend to prefer C-sections to vaginal deliveries for other reasons, reasons that more than offset the incentives described in the text in favor of vaginal delivery. See *infra* chapter 10. Another complication arises from the fact that much of the cost of C-sections is borne by the mothers, not the doctors or medical care providers. This in itself could be a reason for reducing physician liability for negligently choosing a vaginal delivery to a C-section. See Ariel Porat, *Offsetting Risks*, 106 Mich. L. Rev. 243 (2007).

Despite this inclusive view of liability, we support a different kind of limitation on liability that decreases liability for harm under a negligence rule. Liability should be restricted to wrongdoing that increased the probability of the injury occurring.[14] In negligence cases, the plaintiff should prove that the defendant's negligence increased the risk of the harm that actually materialized.[15] Guido Calabresi called this condition for establishing liability the "causal link."[16] The causal link is explicit in the mathematical Hand Rule, where the probability of harm is a decreasing function of the defendant's care.

To illustrate, modify example 3 (Delivering a Baby), so vaginal delivery and C-section are equally likely to result in the baby's death from an umbilical knot. In mathematical terms, the probability of death by umbilical knot does not vary over choice of delivery method, although the specific way in which the risk materializes is different for the two methods of delivery. The doctor chooses vaginal delivery, which is negligent because avoiding other risks to the baby required a C-section. The baby dies during delivery due to a knot of the umbilical cord. A C-section would have avoided the specific way in which the risk materialized. Under these circumstances, the doctor should not be found liable because her negligence did not increase the risk from a knot in the umbilical cord.[17]

Here are three cases in which the lack of a causal link between the negligence and the harm that materialized should be the grounds for dismissing the suit. Instead, the courts dismissed each case on grounds of what we have called the "liability limitation." The courts reached the right conclusion for the wrong reasons.

In *Rauh v. Jensen*,[18] the plaintiff, while riding his motorcycle, swerved to the right to avoid colliding with a moving car, but in the process collided with another car parked in front of a fire hydrant and too close to the intersection. The plaintiff sued the driver of the parked car for two acts of negligence per se. First, the defendant breached an ordinance prohibiting parking next to a fire hydrant. The court reasoned that the purpose of this ordinance was to permit access to the fire hydrant in the event of fire. Second, the defendant breached an ordinance prohibiting parking so close to an intersection. The court reasoned that the purpose of this ordinance was to prevent obstruction of view for motorists and pedestrians. The court dismissed the suit because neither breach was

---

[14] *Berry v. Sugar Notch Borough* 43 A. 240 (Pa. 1899); DOBBS, *supra* note 1, § 187; RICHARD A. EPSTEIN, TORTS § 10.7 (1999); H.L.A. HART & TONY HONORÉ, CAUSATION IN THE LAW 121–22 (2d ed. 1985).

[15] RESTATEMENT (THIRD) OF TORTS: LIABILITY FOR PHYSICAL AND EMOTIONAL HARM § 30 (2010).

[16] GUIDO CALABRESI, *Concerning Cause and the Law of Torts: An Essay for Harry Kalven, Jr.*, 43 U. CHI. L. REV. 69, 71 (1975).

[17] It is possible, of course, to concretize the risk and argue that the specific risk we should consider is not the baby's risk emanating from a knot of the umbilical cord but its risk emanating from a knot in the umbilical cord *that is typical to vaginal delivery*.

[18] *Rauh v. Jensen* 507 P. 2d 520 (Mont. 1973).

a proximate cause of the injury. In referring to "proximate cause," the court was apparently using different terminology to refer to the limitations on liability under negligence per se.

The court could have reached this conclusion without considering the purpose of each statute. Parking a car next to a fire hydrant or near an intersection presumably does not increase the risk that the driver of another vehicle will collide with that parked car while swerving to avoid a collision with a third vehicle. There is no causal link between the unlawful parking and the resulting injury. The court was certainly right to dismiss the suit, but it should have done so without referring to the liability limitations.

In *Storke v. St. Johnsbury Trucking Co.*[19] the plaintiff was a passenger in her husband's car who suffered injury from a head-on collision when the car swerved into the opposite lane of traffic, colliding with an oncoming tractor-trailer driven by the defendant's employee. The plaintiff argued that the truck driver had violated a "slow-speed" statute, which obliges slow-speed vehicles to drive along the right-hand side of the highway, and should therefore be held liable under negligence per se. The plaintiff claimed that had the statute been complied with, the collision would not have occurred. The court rejected the claim, interpreting the statute as aimed at preventing the impeding of traffic going in the same direction, not head-on collisions. In the court's words, the statute "is helpful in the passing situation, since slow moving traffic in that context presents special problems, but not in the oncoming situation."[20]

As in the first case, the absence of a causal link between negligence and injury probably provides a better basis for dismissing the plaintiff's claim. It is at the very least unclear whether the risk of head-on collisions is decreased if slow-speed vehicles drive on the right-hand side of the road. Although, on the one hand, the risk of the vehicle coming into contact with oncoming traffic may be reduced, on the other hand an oncoming vehicle may have greater difficulty "escaping" the slow-moving vehicle's path once it has entered its lane. The court should probably dismiss the case on grounds of no causal link. Or, if the court thinks that there is such a link, it should reach a decision for the plaintiff.[21]

In a third case, *Coughlin v. Peters*, the court also decided the claim based on the argument that the liability limitations apply, rather than on the lack of a

---

[19] *Storke v. St. Johnsbury Trucking Co.* 443 F. 2d 89 (2d Cir. 1971).

[20] *Id.* at 91.

[21] If the risk of collision is reduced when slow-speed vehicles drive on the right-hand side of the road, then the accident would be causally linked to the violation of the statute. In this event, we see no reason to assume that the legislature did not intend to reduce such a risk: perhaps it is the aggregation of both the risks related to the obstruction of traffic and the risks of head-on collisions that justifies the enactment of the "slow-speed" statute. Regardless, there is no sense in dismissing the plaintiff's claim because of the liability limitations. It should either have been dismissed due to a lack of causal link or accepted because of the existence of such a link.

causal link between the breach of statutory duty and the injury.[22] In this case a car hit and killed a child. One of the defendants was the owner of another car parked in violation of a statute that prohibited parking in the same place for longer than ten hours during the day. The plaintiff argued that the parked car had obstructed the view of the driver and the child, and that had the statute not been violated, the car would not have been parked there and the accident would have been avoided. The court dismissed the claim on the grounds that the liability limitations apply. In particular, the court reasoned that the statute was not intended for the benefit of the plaintiff and that it was entirely different from a statute completely prohibiting parking in a given location.

The court could have easily dismissed the case for the lack of a causal link between the injury and the negligence. Had the driver of the parked car obeyed the statute, he would have parked in a different spot, and the risk resulting from obstructing the view of drivers and pedestrians would have been of the same magnitude. Furthermore, had he not parked his car for longer than ten hours, perhaps another car would have parked in the same spot at the time of the accident and created a risk similar to the risk created by the defendant's violation of the statute.

E. Where the Problem Is and What the Limits of the Argument Are

As we have seen, under both negligence per se and common law negligence, only risks that define the injurer's negligence should trigger liability. In negligence per se, these are the risks whose prevention (or reduction) was the purpose of the statute. The argument made here, rather, is that while the theory is right, its implementation by courts is sometimes wrong. Courts, in tending to focus on the foreground risks and ignoring the background risks, fail to grasp that the aggregation of both types of risks often motivated the enactment of the statute (in negligence per se cases) or underlies the definition of negligence (in common law negligence).

Why do courts disregard the background risks and consider only the foreground risks? This may be the result of a cognitive bias that some people—judges and jurors included—share, that makes them see unusual events as causes. Or perhaps they think that precautions almost never affect background risks.[23]

---

[22] *Coughlin v. Peters* 214 A. 2d 127, 129 (Conn. 1965).

[23] A different answer (which, we believe, contradicts the practice of American tort law) could be that many judges oppose the aggregation of risks across persons in applying tort law—an aggregation that is at the center of the argument made in this chapter. *Cf.* Kenneth W. Simons, *Tort Negligence, Cost-Benefit Analysis, and Tradeoffs: A Closer Look at the Controversy*, 41 Loy. L.A. L. Rev. 1171 (2008) (discussing the question of whether, and under what circumstances, deontologists would allow aggregation of risks across persons).

Courts should consider background risks more often than they do, but we do not assert that *all* harms that the injurer could have prevented or reduced by reasonable behavior should trigger liability. We do not suggest abandoning foreseeability as a precondition for liability, a requirement with valid justifications.[24] Moreover, in common law negligence, policy considerations occasionally dictate that negligent injurers not be held liable for harms caused by their negligence. Policy considerations include the desire to restrain excessive litigation and to avoid the chilling effect of liability on desirable activities.[25] In the absence of policy considerations that exclude liability, liability should be imposed for all foreseeable harms that materialize from risks increased by the injurer's negligence.

Negligence per se raises a special concern with statutes that impose affirmative duties on defendants, which common law negligence usually does not impose.[26] The legislature could limit injurer liability by allowing only a subset of victims to sue or making only some harms recoverable. A breach of a statutory duty would thus create a *prima facie* case for liability and nothing more. In example 1 (The Stairway Railing), the legislature might have imposed a duty on the employer to install railings where common law negligence would not impose such a duty. The legislature might have wanted to ease the employer's burden by limiting his liability to employees and excluding visitors. Exempting visitors from the right to damages would reduce employers' incentives to install railings, which would lead to less protection for everyone, employees and visitors alike. Perhaps the legislature thinks that breaching the statutory duty is not reprehensible enough to justify extending the liability of employers to everyone, or perhaps the legislature fears the chilling effect of comprehensive liability on employment.

This reasoning, however, has far less force—if any at all—when the victim is an employee, even an able-bodied one, as in example 1. In such circumstances, courts should be alert to the possibility that the aggregate risk to able-bodied and disabled employees motivated the enactment of the statute. The same sensitivity to legislative intent is pertinent with respect to example 2 (The School-Zone Speed Limit).

---

[24] See EPSTEIN, *supra* note 14, § 10.12, at 270 (arguing that in cases of "freakish events," the bizarre consequences could never have influenced a defendant's primary conduct and, hence, should not generate liability for the defendant, whose negligence is defined with reference to some standard, nonfreakish set of consequences).

[25] RESTATEMENT (THIRD) OF TORTS: LIABILITY FOR PHYSICAL AND EMOTIONAL HARM § 7 cmt. a (2010); KEETON ET AL., *supra* note 10, § 53, at 358; ARIEL PORAT, *The Many Faces of Negligence*, 4 THEORETICAL INQUIRIES L. 105, 109 (2003); STEPHEN D. SUGARMAN, *A New Approach to Tort Doctrine: Taking the Best from the Civil Law and Common Law of Canada*, 17 SUP. CT. L. REV. 2D 375, 387–89 (2002) (Can.).

[26] RESTATEMENT (THIRD) OF TORTS: LIABILITY FOR PHYSICAL AND EMOTIONAL HARM § 37 cmt. b (2010); RESTATEMENT (SECOND) OF TORTS § 314 (1965); EPSTEIN, *supra* note 14, § 11.1; ERNEST J. WEINRIB, *The Case for a Duty to Rescue*, 90 YALE L.J. 247, 247 (1980).

Why should courts presume that the legislature was more likely to have wanted to exempt visitors rather than able-bodied employees from employer liability? Suppose that a statute obliges employers to provide safety clothing to people at the workplace. One possible reading of the statute is that employees are entitled to this protection, but not visitors. The justification could be that employees are exposed to higher risks than nonemployees, or that the employer is expected to protect her employees more than others. Unlike stairway railings, safety clothing can be supplied to employees without supplying it to visitors. The employer's incentive to provide employees with protective clothing is apparently the same whether or not visitors can recover damages for injuries that protective clothing would have prevented. In contrast, the employer's incentive to provide disabled employees with a railing is higher when able-bodied employees can also sue for injuries that a railing would have prevented.

Thus, a typical case for exempting the injurer's liability toward a particular class of victims under negligence per se occurs when the precautions required under the statute are taken separately toward the potential victims.[27] In such cases, even a *prima facie* case for recognizing liability is not warranted. If employees are intended as the only beneficiaries from a statute requiring employers to supply safety clothing, then failing to supply safety clothing to visitors does not breach the statutory duty. All other cases of negligence per se discussed in this chapter involve joint precautions (the same act protects all potential victims) rather than separate precautions (individual acts protect different victims). In the examples of joint precaution, the statute was unquestionably violated, so the only remaining issue is whether the victim should be entitled to recover.

F. Conclusion

The principle is right that liability should be imposed only for risks that a statute was intended to prevent, but its implementation by the courts is often wrong. The most plausible interpretation of a safety statute is that everyone who will benefit from its protection should recover from any injury caused by its breach. An exception is the case when the precautions required under the statute could be taken separately toward the potential victims. The doctrine of negligence per se should not contradict this principle and limit recovery, unless explicit statutory language provides the limitation. The doctrine of negligence

---

[27] *Cf. Teal v. E.I. DuPont de Nemours & Co.* 728 F.2d 799 (6th Cir. 1984). In this case, the appellant was injured from falling off a ladder while working at the appellee's plant on behalf of his employer. The appellant claimed that the appellee had failed to provide a safe place to work, safe equipment, or proper safety devices. The trial court found the defendant liable but did not discuss the question of whether the failure to provide safety equipment constituted negligence per se, leading the appellate court to reverse and remand.

per se often leads courts to the wrong outcome when a background risk materializes. Courts should appreciate that background risks often combine with foreground risks to justify the enactment of a safety statute, so the materialization of either risk attributable to breach of the statute should trigger liability. In contrast, the doctrine of negligence per se often leads to the right outcome for the wrong reason when breach of a statutory duty did not increase the plaintiff's risk. Courts often find no liability because the statute excluded this type of victim or injury by its definition of the statutory duty. Instead of this frail argument, courts should reach the same outcome by the robust argument that breach of duty had no causal link to the accident. These arguments, in much the same way, also apply to common law negligence.

Lapses and Substitution

he making and execution of decisions can go wrong and result in harm in various ways. The harm caused can be attributed to misjudged distances, underestimated probabilities, unforeseen consequences, quavering hands, clumsy feet, slips of the tongue, or an eye's blink—among endless other possibilities. Given the chance that such lapses will occur, actors cannot simply choose a specific level of precaution. Instead, they draw their precaution from a probability distribution. Here is an example.

Example 1: Driver's Lapse. A motorist sets out on the long, straight drive from San Francisco to Los Angeles on Interstate 5. The speed limit is 70 mph, which is also the reasonable speed. The car lacks a mechanical device to maintain constant speed ("cruise control"). The driver aims for 65 mph. Not being a machine, the driver cannot possibly stay at a constant speed of 65 mph with no fluctuation. The driver makes reasonable effort to maintain constant speed, but occasional lapses in attention cause the driver to exceed or fall short of 65. Near the end of the trip, the driver has an accident while traveling at 72 mph. He would have avoided the accident if he had been driving 70 mph or less.

The driver in this example draws his speed from a probability distribution encompassing a range of possibilities, 65 being likely and 72 unlikely. When the driver lapses, his speed increases to an uncharacteristically high rate, given the probability distribution. A reasonable driver takes precaution against lapses, but their optimal level is not zero. With imperfect realization of intentions, a reasonable person can unintentionally breach a legal standard. Even a reasonable driver has lapses from time to time, which can cause an accident. When a lapse causes an accident, the driver has "bad luck" because fault occurred when none was intended.[1] Under an objective legal standard in tort law, the lapse is negligent and the driver is liable for the resulting harm.

---

[1] Liability for lapses is closely related to the moral luck literature, and to the question of whether outcome liability is morally justified. See, e.g., JEREMY WALDRON, *Moments of Carelessness and Massive Loss*, PHILOSOPHICAL FOUNDATIONS OF TORT LAW 387 (1995, David G. Owen ed.); TONY HONORE, *Responsibility and Luck: The Moral Basis of Strict Liability,* 104 L. Q. REV. 53 (1988);

Liability for lapses distorts incentives, as in this example.

Example 2: Cruise Control. The same facts obtain as in example 1, except the car has a mechanical device to maintain constant speed ("cruise control"). The motorist intends to drive 65 mph. The law allows her to rely on either cruise control or human skill. The danger from cruise control is inflexibility, and the danger from human skill is lapses. By relying on cruise control instead of human skill, she can expect to have more accidents and less liability. By relying on human skill instead of cruise control, she can expect to have fewer accidents and more liability. She decides to use cruise control, and while traveling at a speed of 65 mph she has an accident that she would have avoided if she had not been using cruise control.

A negligence rule makes an actor liable for accidents caused by a lapse, but not for "unavoidable accidents." The accident in example 2 was apparently "unavoidable" when the car had its cruise control mechanism engaged, which the law allows. The driver in example 2 replaced human skill that lapses with a machine that has unavoidable accidents. A negligence rule gives injurers an incentive to substitute activities with unavoidable accidents for activities with lapses.

In example 2, substitution reduced liability and increased the overall risk of accidents. To dampen the substitution effect, courts could modify the negligence rule to allow a "lapse defense." A "lapse defense" would require the injurer to prove that he took reasonable precaution against the lapse that caused the accident. In example 1, the driver might show that he almost always drove 65 mph on the long trip to Los Angeles, and he strayed above 65 mph no more often than a reasonable driver. Advances in technology such as the GPS (global positioning system) simplify record keeping. Anticipating the value of this defense, the careful driver might retain records to prove that he took reasonable precaution against lapses.

Lapses are under-theorized in the economic analysis of law, although the idea itself is not new.[2] We will survey the openness of liability law to the lapse defense, describe some activities that substitute unavoidable harm for lapses,

---

CHRISTOPHER H. SCHROEDER, *Corrective Justice & Liability for Increasing Risks*, 37 UCLA L. REV. 439 (1990); ARTHUR RIPSTEIN, *Closing the Gap*, 9 THEORETICAL INQ. L. 61, 62-80 (2008); BENJAMIN C. ZIPURSKY, *Two Dimensions of Responsibility in Crime, Tort and Moral Luck*, 9 THEORETICAL INQ. L. 97, 98-106 (2008); JOHN GOLDBERG & BENJAMIN ZIPURSKY, *Tort Law and Moral Luck*, 92 CORNELL L. REV. 1123, 1127, 1153-4 (2007).

[2] Steven Shavell observed that an injurer subject to a negligence rule would have a motive to choose optimal levels "only to those dimensions of care that are incorporated in the due care standard.... Some dimensions of care will usually be omitted from the due care standard because of difficulties that courts would face in ascertaining them ... or in determining proper behavior in respect to them." STEVEN SHAVELL, FOUNDATIONS OF ECONOMIC ANALYSIS OF LAW 181-2 (2004). The substitution effect analyzed in this chapter results from the failure of negligence rules to incorporate precaution against lapses.

and show how the lapse defense dampens inefficient substitution and increases collection of supporting information. Our analysis of substitution and information is apparently novel, as is our advocacy of a lapse defense.

A. Lapse Defenses in Prevailing Law

In some circumstances, courts are open to a defense based on the reasonableness of the behavior affecting the probability of a lapse, although tort law has no general lapse defense. First, consider road accidents. Lapses appear to be a common cause of road accidents, possibly the most common cause.[3] In road accidents, courts are reluctant to admit a lapse defense.[4] A driver's lapse from a legal standard of care usually triggers liability for any resulting harm. In three categories of cases, however, drivers' lapses are *in*sufficient for imposition of liability.

The first category concerns *guest statutes* that govern the liability of a driver toward a guest in his car. Under these statutes, a lapse in precaution is not enough to satisfy the requirements of driver's liability to a guest. Liability to a guest in the car requires the driver's gross negligence or willful and wanton misconduct.[5] Gross negligence and willful and wanton misconduct imply a knowing or deliberate choice of unreasonable precaution, not a lapse.

The second category concerns *sudden emergencies*.[6] If the actor took reasonable care before the sudden emergency, then the sudden emergency doctrine lowers the standard of care applicable to the emergency. According to one court's formulation, this doctrine lowers the standard of care for a motorist during an emergency and does not lower the standard of care before the emergency occurs.[7] The sudden emergency doctrine cannot be invoked by someone who has not used due care to avoid the emergency or by someone who has brought the emergency on himself by his own wrong.

In the third category, courts refuse to consider a momentary lapse of attention as negligence per se in some exceptional cases.[8]

---

[3] Examples are speeding, not stopping at a stop sign, reacting too slowly in dangerous situations, taking eyes off the road, not maintaining a proper lookout, failing to slow down when necessary, and not keeping adequate distance from other cars.

[4] For driving cases that discuss and reject the lapse defense, see *Porter v. State* 88 So. 2d 924 (Fla. 1956); *Bobstein v. Splinter* 168 So. 2d 560 (Fla. 1964); *Pedersen v. Kinsley* 25 Ill. App. 3d 567 (Ill. 1975); *Rosbottom v. Hensley* 209 N.E. 2d 655 (Ill. 1965); *Security Timber & Land Co. v. Reed* 398 So. 2d 174 (La. 1981).

[5] See *Hoffman v. Slocum* 219 Cal. App. 2d 100 (Cal. 1963); *Porter v. State, supra* note 4; *Bobstein v. Splinter, supra* note 4.

[6] *Hickman v. Southern Pacific Transport Company* 262 So. 2d 385 (La. 1972).

[7] *Dick v. Phillips* 218 So. 2d 299, 302 (La. 1969).

[8] See *Plowman v. Digatono* 1995 Minn. App. LEXIS 1291.

Turning from road accidents to medical malpractice, many medical accidents result from errors caused by lapses in making decisions and executing them.[9] Lapses in decisions include failing to diagnose, choosing the wrong drug to administer, choosing the wrong technique to perform, using the wrong medical equipment, omitting tests needed to diagnose the patient's illness, or deciding to operate too early or too late. Lapses in execution include administering a different drug from the one intended, incorrectly performing a medical technique, using medical equipment improperly, misreading results of diagnostic tests, operating on the wrong patient or the wrong body part, leaving a sponge inside a patient's body, failing to sterilize medical equipment, and failing to monitor the patient's condition.[10]

The case law suggests that doctors are more likely to be found liable for lapses in execution than for lapses in making decisions.[11] Courts sometimes exempt physicians from liability for an error of judgment if they acted in good faith.[12] Similarly, when doctors prepared reasonably, courts often exempt them from liability for the wrong decision. Doctors who act in good faith and prepare for a decision appear to have a lapse defense for faulty decisions. When a doctor decides to deliver a baby by Caesarean, courts will ordinarily not check the reasonableness of his decision so long as they are convinced that he prepared

[9] For a profound analysis, both positive and normative, of errors, lapses, and related occurrences in the field of medicine, see ALAM MERRY & SMITH MCCALL SMITH, ERRORS, MEDICINE AND THE LAW 72-97, 127-151 (2006). For data on medical errors and their huge contribution to patients' injury, see ROBERT JAMES CIMASI, *Medical Malpractice and Tort Reform Risks*, INSURANCE AND RISK MANAGEMENT STRATEGIES FOR PHYSICIANS AND ADVISORS 186-8 (2004, David Marcinko ed.). For the argument that systemic errors are major causes for most medical accidents even if typically combined with individual errors, and for a comprehensive account of all types of medical errors based on extensive empirical evidence, see MICHELLE M. MELLO & DAVID M. STUDDERT, *Deconstructing Negligence: The Role of Individual and System Factors in Causing Medical Injuries*, 96 GEO. L. J. 599 (2008).

[10] For a comprehensive list of causes for patients' injury which include those mentioned in the text and many others, see JAMES E. ORLIKOFF & AUDRONE M. VANAGUNAS, MALPRACTICE PREVENTION AND LIABILITY CONTROL FOR HOSPITALS 65-7 (2nd ed., 1988); MELLO & STUDDERT, *supra* note 9.

[11] Reluctance to second-guess doctors' judgments is reflected in Section 6.03 of the California Civil Jury Instructions, which states as follows:

Where there is more than one recognized method of diagnosis or treatment, and no one of them is used exclusively and uniformly by all practitioners of good standing, under the same or similar circumstances, a physician is not negligent if, in exercising [his] [or] [her] best judgment, [he] [or] [she] selects one of the approved methods, which later turns out to be a wrong selection, or one not favored by certain other practitioners.

Juries following these instructions will find no liability for many lapses in judgment. Thus a doctor's bad decision to deliver a baby by Caesarean, when vaginal birth would have been better, will seldom trigger liability.

[12] See *Dotson v. Hammerman* 932 S.W. 2d 880 (Mo. App. 1996); DAN D. DOBBS, THE LAW OF TORTS, §243, at 634 (2000).

properly to make it. In contrast, once the delivery method is decided, courts are reluctant to excuse faulty execution on grounds of reasonable preparation. (Note that lapses in execution are often easier to prove than lapses in professional judgment.[13])

Do statistics support the conclusion from doctrine that courts impose liability for faulty execution more readily than for faulty judgment? Some available data suggest a positive answer. The National Practitioner Data Bank (2005)[14] includes 191,082 medical malpractice claims, both tried and settled, brought by patients in 1991-2005. The claims are arranged by category. Upon examination, these categories suggest that roughly 80 percent of the claims were brought for faulty execution and 20 percent were brought for misjudgments.[15]

Turning to product liability, history reveals the creation and subsequent abolition of a lapse defense. Manufacturing inevitably results in some defective items, and quality control reduces the frequency with which defective items harm consumers. Thus a manufacturer of a soft drink must fill bottles, and he also must monitor the bottles for cracks or overcharging with gas. The more carefully the manufacturer monitors, the less often a cracked or overcharged bottle reaches consumers. A manufacturer monitoring for quality resembles a motorist self-monitoring for speed. Production of a defective item resembles a lapse of attention that caused a motorist to exceed reasonable speed.

At the beginning of the twentieth century, the common law imposed a negligence rule on manufacturers for defective products that harmed consumers. To recover damages, the consumer had to prove that a defective product caused the injury and the manufacturer's negligence caused the defect. The second part of the proof usually involved showing that the manufacturer's quality control was unreasonable.[16] Consumers usually lacked sufficient evidence about manufacturers' quality control processes to meet this burden of proof. To allow more recoveries by injured consumers, American courts in the early twentieth century applied the doctrine of *res ipsa loquitur*. According to this doctrine, the

[13] *Powell v. Kleinman* 151 Cal. App. 4th 112 (2007).

[14] Public Use Data File (computer file). Available at: http://www.npdb-hipdb.com/publicdata.html

[15] 37,805 claims were brought for failed diagnosis—probably more judgment than execution claims. Most of the rest were brought for various types of faulty execution. Thus 16,356 claims were brought for delay in treatment, 3,286 for failed monitoring, 3,943 for failed performance of a procedure, 12,275 for improper management, 28,931 for improper performance, 857 for improper use of equipment, 2,054 for administering treatment on a wrong body part, 1,562 for administering wrong dosage of medication and 1,913 for administering wrong medication.

[16] Imperfect quality control causes a few items in a manufacturing process to fall short of the design that the others satisfy. In contrast, a defect in design affects all items manufactured according to that design. Manufacturing (quality control) defects and design defects require a separate analysis in the law of torts. This chapter discusses the former and not the latter. For a discussion of the distinction, see RICHARD A. EPSTEIN, TORTS 406-8 (1999).

court should *infer* the defendant's negligence from facts that the plaintiff could usually prove.[17] Under these conditions, the manufacturer was liable when the consumer showed that he was injured by a defective product, unless the manufacturer could prove that its quality control satisfied the legal standard.[18] Thus the doctrine resembles a negligence rule with a lapse defense.

The change from the original liability rule to the rule of *res ipsa loquitur* reversed the burden of proof concerning whether precaution against lapses was reasonable or not. In the course of the twentieth century, most jurisdictions changed the rule again, this time to strict liability. If a product is unreasonably dangerous, the manufacturer is strictly liable for the harm the defect causes to consumers, and no amount of quality control excuses the manufacturer.[19] A defense resembling the lapse defense was abolished.

We explained that the prevailing rules of tort law sometimes allow a lapse defense, especially in emergencies or for faulty judgments by doctors. In addition, there are other areas of liability law with such a defense: violation of a statue,[20] defamation,[21] and business judgments by corporate officers.[22]

---

[17] For *res ipsa loquitur* to apply, the specific accident must belong to a type that regularly results from negligence, furthermore, the agency or instrumentality that caused the event was within the exclusive control of the defendant, and was not due to any voluntary action or contribution on the part of the plaintiff. See Epstein, *supra* note 16, at 172; Ariel Porat & Alex Stein, Tort Liability Under Uncertainty 84-92 (2001).

[18] *Richenbacher v. California Packing Corp.* 145 N.E. 281 (Mass. 1924); *Escola v. Coca Cola Bottling Co.* 150 P. 2d 436 (Cal. 1944).

[19] Epstein, *supra* note 16, at 389-94.

[20] Many courts excuse the violation of a statute when the violator shows that "he did what might reasonably be expected of a person of ordinary prudence, acting under similar circumstances, who desired to comply with the law." *Alarid v. Vanier* 327 P. 2d 897 (Cal. 1958); *Witham v. Norfolk & Western Ry. Co.* 561 N.E. 2d 484 (Ind. 1990); *Leikin v. Wilson* 445 A. 2d 993, 1002 (D.C. App. 1982). See also Dobbs *supra* note 12, §140, at 330; *Waugh v. Traxler* 412 S.E. 2d 756 (W.Va. 1991).

[21] To succeed in a defamation suit, a plaintiff who is a private individual must establish that the defendant was negligent. Dobbs *supra* note 12, § 419, at 1182. Even partial erroneous facts are often not enough for liability. It is sufficient for the defendant to show that the charge or imputation is "substantially true, or as it is often put, to justify the 'gist,' the 'sting' or the 'substantial truth' of the defamation." William Lloyd Prosser & Page Keeton, Prosser and Keeton on the Law of Torts 842 (5th ed., 1984). A different rule applies to public officials or public figures under the Supreme Court decision of *New York Times v. Sullivan* 376 U.S. 254 (1964), according to which liability for defamation is conditioned upon the defendant being guilty of publishing a knowing or reckless falsehood. Efforts to reduce the probability of an error—that could exonerate the defendant—include checking information and verifying its truth. See Dobbs *supra* note 12, § 419, at 1182. Robert Cooter formulated the gathering of information to support an assertion as an optimal problem. In this framework, negligence consists in stopping too soon. Robert D. Cooter, The Strategic Constitution 324-31 (2000); see also Oren Bar-Gill & Assaf Hamdani, *Optimal Liability for Libel*, 2 Contributions to Economic Analysis & Policy, Article 6 (2003).

[22] Stockholders sometimes sue corporate directors when they make bad decisions and lower the value of the company's shares. As formulated in *Smith v. Van Gorkom* 488 A. 2d 858, 872 (Del. 1985), the business judgment rule prohibits courts in such cases from second-guessing directors'

B. Substitution

Liability for lapses creates an incentive to switch to activities that are less susceptible to them. Sometimes these activities are inherently more dangerous. Self-interest causes actors to avoid lapses even when doing so increases unavoidable harm, as illustrated in example 2. Here is a numerical example.

Example 3: Substitution. Performing an activity without any precaution causes accidental harm of 500. The actor can choose between two alternative precautions. Precaution A costs 100 and reduces accidental harm from 500 to 300. Accidental harm and precaution sum to total social costs of 400. Alternatively, Precaution B costs 120 and reduces accidental harm from 500 to 350. Accidental harm and precaution sum to total social costs of 470. So Precaution A has lower social costs than Precaution B.

Now consider the private costs of the injurer in example 3 under the standard negligence rule. After taking Precaution A at a cost of 100, the remaining harm from accidents is 300. Assume that this harm is due to lapses by the injurer, so the injurer is liable for 300 under the standard negligence rule. Consequently, the injurer's private costs under Precaution A equal the cost of precaution and the harm from accidents, which sum to 400. Alternatively, taking Precaution B at a cost of 120 leaves the remaining harm from accidents at 350. Assume that this harm is unavoidable, so the injurer is not liable under the standard negligence rule. Consequently, the injurer's private costs under Precaution B equal 120. Social costs are lower with Precaution A than Precaution B, but the injurer's private costs under the standard negligence rule are lower with Precaution B than Precaution A. The standard negligence rule creates incentives to choose the form of precaution with higher social costs.

Allowing a lapse defense would reverse the incentives. The actor who chooses Precaution A has a defense against liability for lapses.[23] Now the actor's private costs equal 100 under Precaution A, whereas the actor's private costs equal 120 under Precaution B, so the actor will choose the socially efficient

---

substantive decisions. Instead, courts may consider only the quality of the directors' decision-making *process*, especially the information that they gathered before deciding. For a discussion, see LYNN A. STOUT & MARGARET M. BLAIR, *Truth, Trustworthiness, and the Behavioral Foundations of Corporate Law*, 149 U. PA. L. REV. 1735 (2001). The business judgment rule is considered to be the main reason for the rarity of court decisions imposing liability on directors: see BERNARD S. BLACK & BRIAN R. CHEFFINS, *Outside Director Liability across Countries*, 84 TEX. L. REV. 1385 (2006). The rule was adopted by most states including Delaware: NANCY E. BARTON, DENNIS J. BLOCK, & STEPHEN A. RADIN, THE BUSINESS JUDGMENT RULE: FIDUCIARY DUTIES OF CORPORATE DIRECTORS (5th ed., 1998).

[23] Alternatively, a court could hold Precaution A is reasonable because it is socially efficient, and Precaution B is unreasonable because it is socially inefficient. Equating "reasonable" with "efficient" requires that courts have substantial information on untaken precautions. For the general problem of evaluating untaken precautions, see MARK F. GRADY, *Untaken Precaution*, 18 J. LEGAL STUD. 139 (1989); EHUD GUTTEL, *The (Hidden) Risk of Opportunistic Precautions*, 93 VA. L. REV. 1389 (2007).

precaution.[24] The law should encourage forms of precaution that are inherently less dangerous, which sometimes requires a lapse defense.[25]

Here are some concrete examples of substitution favoring inherently more risky activities under the standard negligence rule without a lapse defense.

> *Example 4: Traffic Light and Policeman.* The municipality must decide whether to post a policeman in the intersection to direct traffic or to install a traffic light. A policeman is more flexible than the traffic light, so traffic flows more quickly. However, a policeman is more susceptible to lapses than traffic lights are susceptible to failures.

In example 4 the municipality chooses between a machine and a person. If the social benefits of flexibility exceed the cost of lapses, the policeman may be more efficient. However, the standard negligence rule creates an incentive for the municipality to replace a policeman with a traffic light, because the machine does not lapse. Even if traffic lights occasionally fail to operate properly, the municipality can argue in court that it used the best available technology, so it was not negligent.

The choice between labor and capital, or manpower and machines, often occurs in settings involving accidents. Employers must decide whether to reduce risks to employees in the workplace by using safer machines or by imposing safer work rules on employees. Hospitals and other providers of medical services must decide whether to monitor their patients' condition by sophisticated equipment or by their medical staff. Airport authorities and airlines must decide whether to promote passengers' safety by new technologies or by posting guards. Drivers must decide whether to rely on devices like cruise controls or on their human skills.

Technology is sometimes more effective than manpower in avoiding accidents, and sometimes the opposite is true. In either case, courts are more likely to find fault when humans lapse than when machines that are reasonably maintained fail. This fact biases the liability law in favor of machines and against humans.[26]

---

[24] The other way to restore efficient incentives, which we do not discuss here, is to impose strict liability for any harm resulting from the activity.

[25] A lapse defense would not always solve the problem of actors choosing the less efficient activity or precaution: it could be the case that one activity or one precaution entails more private costs for the actor *even with a lapse defense*, while the other activity or precaution entails more unavoidable harm. The actor would inefficiently choose the latter activity, which is less costly to him than the former. Thus, the substitution effect exists even with a lapse defense, but a lapse defense mitigates it.

[26] Interestingly, Grady argued that new technologies result in higher standards of liability, so tort liability obstructs innovation and development. Our argument points to an opposite influence. MARK F. GRADY, *Why Are People Negligent? Technology, Nondurable Precautions, and the Medical Malpractice Explosion*, 82 Nw. U. L. REV. 293 (1988).

A second form of substitution concerns human precautions with different susceptibility to lapses.

Example 5: Deliveries of Babies. Doctors must decide between vaginal and Caesarian delivery of a baby. Assume courts cannot verify *ex post* whether the doctor's decision was right or wrong, so no liability attaches to the doctor's *decision* to deliver by Caesarian, even when the decision was bad. Courts, however, can verify whether the doctor lapsed in executing the delivery, and also whether that lapse caused the injury.[27] Assume that doctors are more likely to lapse in executing a vaginal delivery than in executing a Caesarian delivery. Also assume that the average harm from vaginal and Caesarean deliveries is approximately the same.

In example 5, the prevailing negligence rule gives doctors an incentive to perform too many Caesarian deliveries.[28]

To illustrate numerically, assume that vaginal delivery harms the mother 1 percent of the time, and a lapse by the doctor is the cause in 50 percent of these cases. In the rest of the cases the harm is unavoidable. Thus vaginal delivery results in doctor's liability to the injured mother in 0.5 percent of cases. In contrast, assume that Caesarian delivery harms the mother 2 percent of the time and a lapse by the doctor is the cause in 12.5 percent of these cases. Thus Caesarian birth results in doctor's liability to the injured mother in 0.25 percent of cases. In the rest of the cases the harm is unavoidable. According to these numbers, the accident risk for mothers is twice as great from Caesarian birth as from vaginal birth and the liability risk for doctors is half as great from Caesarian birth as from vaginal birth.[29]

Similarly, substituting bureaucratic rules for human discretion can reduce an organization's liability under the standard negligence rule.

Example 6: Regulation by Rules vs. Discretion. The police department considers how to regulate policemen in various circumstances. One alternative is to regulate policemen's behavior by a comprehensive set of specific rules. The police can apply these rules mechanically with few lapses. However,

---

[27] For a discussion of the distortions caused by tort law with respect to Caesarian and vaginal birth, see *infra* chapter 10.

[28] We assume that doctors cannot adjust their prices to account perfectly for the different liability risks posed by each procedure.

[29] In general, doctors are advised by risk management experts to choose procedures that reduce their liability potential, when the enhanced risk is not captured by prices. See Charles F. Fenton III & David Edward Marcinko, *Risk Management in Modern Medical Practice*, Insurance and Risk Management Strategies for Physicians and Advisors 107, 133 (2004, David Marcinko ed.): "[Physicians] should evaluate their own practice and identify those procedures and those patient types that carry a high risk of malpractice for which the physician is not adequately reimbursed. Physicians then should tailor their practice so that they no longer provide those services. The revenue lost will be worth the risk of the malpractice suit and the collateral consequences."

comprehensive rules make the police inflexible and ineffective. Second, the police department can provide policemen with general principles. The application of general principles often results in lapses in judgment. However, general principles make the police more flexible and effective.

What will the police department do under the prevailing rule of negligence? It may wish to decrease its liability risks at the cost of decreasing its effectiveness by imposing specific rules that eliminate discretionary judgment. In general, an organization that imposes strict rules on employees who engage in risky activities may reduce its liability by reducing the frequency of lapses, even though the elimination of employee's discretion increases the total risk to the public.

Earlier we touched on the distinction between deciding what to do and executing the decision that you made. We noted examples of courts allowing actors to escape liability for bad decisions but not for faulty executions. When courts impose liability for faulty executions but not for faulty decisions, actors have an incentive to choose the precautions least susceptible to lapses in execution and more susceptible to lapses in judgment, even when the latter are less efficient than the former. Example 7 illustrates such a case.

Example 7: Treating Cancer. Hospital X must adopt Treatment A or Treatment B for a patient's cancer. Treatment A involves a particular procedure that is difficult to execute. Treatment B involves difficult choices among procedures that are easy to execute.

If courts are quick to find fault in the execution of a procedure, then Treatment A causes relatively high liability risk for the hospital. If courts are reluctant to "second-guess" the hospital's decisions, then Treatment B causes relatively low liability risk. Under the standard negligence rule, the hospital may save money by using Treatment B, even if it is inherently more dangerous than Treatment A. (We assume that the hospital cannot perfectly adjust prices for each treatment to reflect liability risks.)

C. Implementing a Lapse Defense

Implementing a lapse defense often requires the injurer to generate costly information. A doctor can record preparations for the operation and subsequently prove that he took adequate precautions against a lapse. A driver can record his speed and subsequently prove that his lapses in speed were reasonable. Generating information makes precaution against lapses observable. Under a negligence rule without a lapse defense, the injurer gains nothing by making sure the precautions he takes against lapses are observable. Indeed, if his precaution against lapses is below the reasonableness standard, recording this fact may help the plaintiff to get higher damages. Under a negligence rule with a lapse defense, the rational injurer generates the information for a lapse defense if it costs less than his reduction in expected liability.

An increase in precaution against lapses usually decreases the probability of an accident without reducing it to 0. This fact would create a dilemma for courts that are willing to allow a lapse defense. In standard tort doctrine, unreasonable behavior is the cause of an accident if it is more likely than not that reasonable behavior in the circumstances would have prevented the accident. If courts apply this doctrine literally with respect to lapses, negligent defendants will seldom be found liable because the plaintiff will rarely satisfy the standard of proof necessary to establish causation.

To see why, assume that the plaintiff can convince the court that reasonable precaution by the defendant would have reduced the probability of a lapse causing an accident. Even so, it might be difficult to convince the court that reasonable precaution against lapses would have prevented *this* accident. Assume that a driver's reasonable precaution would have decreased the probability of a lapse causing an accident from 4 percent to 3 percent. The actor fails to take reasonable precaution, a lapse occurs, and an accident results. The injurer would argue that it is more likely than not that the same accident would have been occurred in this specific case even if he had taken reasonable precaution against lapses.[30]

We offer no general solution to this problem, but we mention the consequences of some alternatives. A court might feel compelled by the prevailing causation doctrine to find "no liability" whenever the probability is 50 percent or less that reasonable precaution against lapses would have prevented the accident. In that case, the court gives injurers deficient incentive to take precautions against lapses in the usual circumstances. At the opposite pole, the court might presume that the defendant negligently caused an accident whenever his failure to take reasonable precautions against lapses increased their probability. This solution is a practical one, relatively easy to implement and certainly constitutes an improvement over the current rule under which a lapse defense is not allowed.

Intermediate rules locate between these polar types. First, a principle of probabilistic recovery can apply to lapses. Under this solution, a driver whose failure to take reasonable precautions against lapses increased the probability of a lapse that could cause an accident from 3 percent to 4 percent, would be liable

[30] See JENNIFER ARLEN & W. BENTLEY MACLEOD, *Malpractice Liability for Physicians and Managed Care Organizations*, 78 N.Y.U. L. REV. 1929 (2003); JENNIFER ARLEN & W. BENTLEY MACLEOD, *Torts, Expertise and Authority: Liability of Physicians and Managed Care Organizations*, 36 RAND J. ECON. 494 (2005). Arlen & MacLeod do not favor what we called "lapse defense." Such a defense is unnecessary in their model because courts do not need to use it to force injurers to reveal information about precaution against lapses. So the Arlen & MacLeod model applies to a world where precautions against lapses are observable, and our model applies to a world where they are revealable.

toward the victim for 25 percent of her harm.[31] However, probabilistic recovery raises many issues that we cannot discuss here.[32]

Alternatively, a rule of liability for excessive harm can be applied for repeat harms caused by lapses. Assume that an actor caused n units of harm by lapses over a certain period of time, while only m units of harm would have been produced by lapses if the actor had taken reasonable precautions against lapses. Thus "n" might refer to the actual annual harm in a hospital, and a lower rate "m" might refer to the annual harm that would have unavoidably occurred despite reasonable precaution against lapses. By the rule of *liability for excessive harm*, the hospital is liable for the excessive harm, which is $n - m$. (In chapter 5 we analyze the rule of liability for excessive harm, which economizes on information needed by courts to create efficient incentive.[33])

D. Conclusion

Under the prevailing tort rule, an actor is usually liable for the harm caused by a lapse, regardless of how much precaution he takes to avoid lapsing. The prevailing tort rule makes sense most of the time because courts can seldom verify the reasonableness of precautions against lapses. It is difficult to prove that a driver's self-monitoring was reasonable, or that a doctor made reasonable preparation for an operation, or that a policeman who lapsed in directing traffic did not succumb to these lapses more often than a reasonable policeman.

A negligence rule without a lapse defense, however, prompts actors to substitute in favor of activities that are less susceptible to lapses, even if they are inherently more dangerous. Actors sometimes substitute worse forms of precaution for better ones when machines substitute for people, bureaucratic rules substitute for human discretion, or risky judgments substitute for risky execution. A lapse defense dampens these perverse incentives. Prevailing law sometimes permits a lapse defense, and we advocate making it available more generally. The defendant should bear the burden of proving that his precaution against lapses was reasonable, rather than making the plaintiff prove the opposite. The burden of proof should fall on the defendant because he is better

---

[31] In one out of four cases, the lapse which caused the accident was caused by the failure of the injurer to take reasonable precautions against lapses. The probability that the lapse in question is the one caused by the failure to take reasonable precautions against lapses is therefore 25 percent.

[32] PORAT & STEIN, *supra* note 17, at 101-29.

[33] Applying this rule requires information on aggregate harm, both actual n and ideal m. However, applying this rule does not require information on individual harms. Avoiding proof on a case-by-case basis greatly reduces the information requirements for liability law. Notice that the optimal units of harm m are the annual number that still occur given a reasonable level of precautions against lapses.

situated than the plaintiff to produce evidence. A lapse defense provides incentives for potential injurers to take reasonable precautions against lapses and to make this fact observable to courts.[34]

[34] Here are two doctrinal issues that future research should explore. The first issue relates to the alternatives of reducing the level of lapses: should a defendant who failed to take reasonable precautions against lapses be allowed to show that at an earlier stage he took precautions against lapses beyond the ones required by reasonableness, and in general reduced lapses significantly? To illustrate, should a driver who lapsed and caused an accident be allowed to raise the argument that he installed in his car expensive safety devices which he was not obliged to install, thereby reducing risks dramatically, although given the existence of the devices his precautions against lapses were unreasonable?

The second issue relates to third parties' precautions against lapses: Should a doctor who lapsed due to fatigue and caused injury be allowed to show that the hospital required him to work too many extra hours? If such a defense is allowed for the doctor, it will be essential to impose liability on the hospital, conditioned upon establishing its negligence. *Cf.* MELLO & STUDDERT, *supra* note 10, who argue that instead of focusing on individual doctors' negligence, tort law should focus on institutions, and impose enterprise liability; and that systemic errors are major causes for most medical accidents even if typically combined with individual errors.

Total Liability for Excessive Harm

When several factories pollute a lake, officials may be able to measure the total pollution but not the individual pollution emitted by each factory. In these circumstances, total pollution is verifiable and individual pollution is unverifiable. Implementing a rule of strict liability or negligence in tort law requires verifying the emissions of each factory and the resulting harm. Similarly, a fine for excessive emissions, a pollution tax ("Pigouvian tax"), or transferable pollution rights also require verifying emissions of each factory. Traditional approaches to liability do not work when individual behavior is unverifiable, because officials cannot prove how much harm any injurer caused.

If officials can verify the total harm caused by all injurers but not the harm caused by each injurer, how can liability law control pollution? A novel liability rule provides the solution. Each individual injurer should be liable for the total harm that everyone causes in excess of the optimal harm. We call this rule *total liability for excessive harm*. The remarkable consequence of this rule is that injurers respond to it by causing optimal harm, so their liability is nil. Thus the environmental agency can set a target for clean air or water and announce that each factory in the area is liable for pollution by all factories in excess of the target. Since the liability rule induces the factories to hit the target, they pay no damages. The environmental agency gains control over emissions without having to monitor individual polluters, and the polluters do not have to pay damages or conform to bureaucratic regulations.

Here's why it works. Assume that five factories pollute a lake, causing aggregate harm of 750, whereas the socially efficient pollution level equals 500. Total excessive pollution thus equals 250. To clean up the lake, officials impose a rule of strict liability for excessive harm. Each factory is responsible for *all* of the *excessive* harm caused by the five factories, so each of them will be liable for 250. Each of them will respond by reducing its pollution until the cost of additional abatement equals the resulting reduction in liability. When each factory responds in this way, pollution will fall to the social optimum of 500 and the liability of each factory will fall to 0.

To appreciate our rule, contrast it to the usual negligence rule. With a negligence rule the expected liability of any one of several injurers is the difference between the actual expected harm and the optimal expected harm caused by *his* behavior.[1] With a rule of total liability for excessive harm the expected liability of any injurer equals the difference between the actual expected harm and the optimal expected harm caused by all injurers. Thus, a rule of total liability for excessive harm is analogical to a negligence rule that would be applied if all injurers merged into one entity.

The rule of total liability for excessive harm creates efficient incentives because each injurer internalizes the marginal social benefit from reducing his excessive pollution. This rule aligns *marginal* liability and the legal standard as required for efficiency. If any individual's care falls below the legal standard, the increase in harm equals the resulting increase in that individual's liability, holding constant the care of other injurers. In contrast, under the conventional negligence rule (and other legal rules), a decrease in the injurer's care so that it falls below the legal standard causes no change in his or her liability. Liability is unchanged because the court cannot verify the cause of the increase in harm. Assuming verifiable total harm and unverifiable causation by individuals, the rule of total liability aligns marginal liability and the harm from deficient care, whereas the conventional negligence rule misaligns them.

The rule of total liability for excessive harm has practical advantages that enable it to succeed where other alternative rules fail. We commend its use under three conditions: (i) total harm is verifiable, (ii) optimal total harm is calculable, and (iii) the number of injurers is not too large.[2] This chapter begins with

---

[1] See *supra* chapter 1.

[2] Our proposal builds on existing literature. Holmstrom's classic paper, "Moral Hazard in Teams," explains that a principal can provide efficient incentives to two agents with unverifiable outputs by paying bonuses that correlate with total output by both agents. BENGT HOLMSTROM, *Moral Hazard in Teams,* 13 BELL J. ECON. 324-40 (1982). Kaplow and Shavell suggest that when firms create indistinguishable externalities, the state can tax each firm at the rate of the marginal harm, which depends on the total level of the externality. LOUIS KAPLOW & STEVEN SHAVELL, *On the Superiority of Corrective Taxes to Quantity Regulation,* 4 AM. L. & ECON. REV. 1, 10-1 (2002). In the paper closest to our position, Segerson analyzes the consequences of taxing each polluter for total pollution that exceeds the social optimum. KATHLEEN SEGERSON, *Uncertainty and Incentives for Nonpoint Pollution Control,* 15 JOURNAL OF ENVIROMENTAL ECONOMICS AND MANAGEMENT 87 (1988). Also see THOMAS J. MICELI & KATHLEEN SEGERSON, *Joint Liability in Torts: Marginal and Infra-Marginal Efficiency,* 11 INT. REV. L. & ECON. 235 (1991). Miceli & Segerson proposed a form of total liability for ambient pollution, according to which underachievement of a group's abatement goal results in a tax and overachievement results in a subsidy. For underachievement, Miceli & Segerson's tax has the same consequences as our rule of total liability for excessive harm. For overachievement, however, Miceli & Segerson's subsidy creates a potentially fatal incentive problem. A group that reduces total pollution below the target receives a subsidy equal to a multiple of the total benefit created by their overachievement. Consequently, by overachieving they realize a private gain and cause a social loss. Overachieving is privately profitable and socially costly. The rule of total liability for excessive harm avoids this problem by not paying subsidies for overachieving relative to the target. A recent paper that responded to our proposal for total liability for excessive harm is ALAN C. MARCO, ADON S. VAN WOERDEN & ROBERT M. WOODWARD, *The Problem of Shared Social Cost,* 5 REV. L. ECON. 137 (2009). In their paper the authors propose an alternative mechanism to the one offered by us, which they call "Shared Social Costs." According to that mechanism, actors

alternative liability rules, shows their problems, and then explains our novel solution, concluding with a list of examples.

A. Individual Liability for Excessive Harm

We begin with an example contrasting strict liability and liability for excessive harm for an individual.

> *Example 1: Individual Harm Is Verifiable.* A factory emits smoke and causes harm h to the neighbors. Without abatement, harm h, which is verifiable, equals 150. Abatement to reduce pollution below 150 has two forms. First, by taking precautions costing 15, the factory reduces the actual harm by 30. Second, by reducing production at a cost of 10 in forgone profits, the factory reduces the actual harm by 20. Efficiency requires both forms of abatement—more precaution and less activity—so the socially optimal harm h^* equals 100.[3]

In example 1, a rule of strict liability causes the factory to choose between not abating and paying damages of 150, or abating at a cost of 25 and paying damages of 100. Since the latter is cheaper, the factory will abate at the socially optimal level for both precaution and activity level. Similarly, a rule of liability for excessive harm holds the injurer liable for the difference between the harm actually caused and the optimal harm. The factory chooses between not abating and paying damages of 50, or abating at a cost of 25 and paying damages of 0. Since the latter is cheaper, the factory will abate at the socially optimal level for both precaution and activity level.

In general, injurer i's liability for actual harm h_i, or injurer i's liability for excessive harm $(h_i - h_i^*)$, gives the injurer socially optimal incentives with respect to precaution and activity level. A rule of strict liability creates efficient incentives by making the injurer internalize the *total* social benefits and costs of precaution and activity level, which includes marginal and infra-marginal benefits and costs. In contrast, a rule of liability for excessive harm makes the injurer internalize the *marginal* social benefits and costs of precaution and activity level when harm is excessive. The difference between them is the allocation of infra-marginal costs h_i^*, which does not influence the rational individual's behavior.

To participate in an activity, an actor often has to make an initial investment. To illustrate, a motorist buys a car before driving, and a manufacturer builds

---

causing the harm share the total harm and abatement costs. In cases where the abatement costs for each firm are verifiable, the Shared Social Costs mechanism may provide efficient incentives to the firms to abate efficiently.

[3] Example 1 implicitly assumes that the neighbors can do nothing to reduce harm, and transaction costs prevent the factory and the neighbors from solving the problem by private bargaining.

a factory before manufacturing. After buying a car or building a factory, the actor must choose precaution against social harm (how safely to drive, how much to filter effluent) and level of activity (how far to drive, how much to manufacture). Infra-marginal costs $h_i^{'}$ affect the profitability of participating in the activity, but not the most profitable precaution or activity level. A rule of strict liability for actual harm causes each potential participant to internalize the social cost of participating, thus creating efficient incentives for participation. Does a rule of individual liability for excessive harm create efficient incentives for participation? Ideally, the answer is "Yes," because the ideal rule applies to excessive participation. When the rate of participation is excessive, a rule of individual liability for excessive harm ideally makes each potential participant internalize the social cost of participating. Conversely, when the rate of participation is socially optimal, a rule of liability for individual excessive harm ideally makes participants pay nothing for participation.

B. Strict Total Liability and Proportionate Liability

Now we modify example 1 to fit strict total liability—the principle that each injurer is liable for the harm caused by all injurers.[4]

> *Example 2: Only Total Harm Is Verifiable.* Each of m factories has the same costs as in example 1. Without abating, each factory causes harm of 150, so total harm caused by all factories equals $150m$. Socially optimal abatement by the socially optimal number of factories m^{*} results in total social harm equal to $100m^{*}$. While total harm and optimal total harm are verifiable, individual harms are unverifiable.

In example 2, a rule of strict total liability causes each factory to choose between not abating, or abating at a cost of 25 and reducing damages by 50 for everyone. Since the latter is cheaper, each factory will abate. Thus if there are five factories ($m=5$) and each causes harm of 150, the total social harm is 750. Each factory knows that if it abates at a cost of 25 its liability will be reduced by 50, regardless of what the other factories do. As a result, all five factories abate, and the total harm is reduced from 750 to 500, which is the optimal total harm.

The rule of strict total liability, however, has two decisive disadvantages. First, since each participant is liable for all of the harm that everyone causes, any injurer who reduces harm by $1 saves all injurers m. This fact gives injurers an incentive to collude and reduce social harm below the social optimum H^{*}. In general, a rule of strict total liability causes collusion, which results in

[4] For a discussion of the consequences of a rule of strict total liability, see DEVRA L. GOLBE & LAWRENCE J. WHITE, *Market Share Liability and Its Alternatives.* CENTER FOR LAW AND BUSINESS PAPER NO. 99-014 (1999). Available at SSRN: http://ssrn.com/abstract=209809.

too much precaution and too little activity. In example 2, the five factories know that for harm of 1 that anyone prevents, the liability of all of them falls by 5. As a result, they might agree among themselves to invest up to 5 in abatement for reducing harm by 1. Collusion will reduce total harm below 500 and in the extreme case it might fall from 750 to 0, at a total cost of more than 2500.[5]

Second, since participants are liable for more harm than the harm that they cause, too few will participate. In general, a rule of strict total liability causes too little participation in the activity that triggers liability.[6] Thus, in our example, even if all factories abate efficiently, each would be liable for 500, which is 5 times higher than the harm it actually caused. As a result, some of the factories that expect to gain more than their actual harm of 100, but less than the total harm of 500, would stop operating, even though the benefit of their operation is higher than its costs. Under the rule of strict total liability, participation is suboptimal, although the precaution and activity level of firms that participate are optimal.

An alternative rule that could be applied to example 2 is proportionate liability. Each factory would thereby bear liability in proportion to the risk it creates. Since the behavior of each factory in example 2 is nonverifiable, the agency or court applying proportionate liability would allocate total harm H equally among the m factories, resulting in each factory bearing liability of H/m. Proportionate liability would not provide efficient incentives to abate, because any \$1 reduction in harm by a factory reduces its liability by \$1$/m$. Factories would underinvest in abatement. In example 2, a factory that invests 25 in abatement reduces pollution by 50, which is socially efficient. However, the factory that invests 25 in abatement reduces its liability by 50/5. Self-interested factory owners will not spend 25 on abatement to save 10 in liability.

C. The Basic Model of Total Liability for Excessive Harm

Under a rule of total liability for excessive harm, each injurer is liable for the difference between the total harm and the optimal total harm. Now we apply this rule to example 2 and show that the social optimum is an equilibrium. Assume that each of m^* factories is abating optimally. Any factory that decreases expenditures on abatement from 25 to 0 will increase each factory's liability from 0 to 50, so no factory will reduce its abatement. Socially optimal abatement

[5] For reducing the first 250 of harm they would invest 125 in abatement. In the most extreme case they would invest an additional 2499 for reducing the remaining 500 to zero, because their total benefit from that reduction would amount to 2500; realistically, they would invest less, but still much more than 500.

[6] Inducing optimal participation under a rule of strict total liability requires a participation subsidy equal to $H^* - h'_i$, which can be a very large number.

is an equilibrium because each injurer internalizes the marginal social cost of decreasing his precaution or increasing his activity level.[7]

By the same reasoning, it is easy to see that if the pollution from the factories exceeds the social optimum, the rule of total liability for excessive harm will cause the factories to abate until pollution falls to the optimum.[8]

The rule of total liability for excessive harm does not suffer from the two decisive disadvantages of the rule of strict total liability. First, under this rule, collusion helps to achieve the social optimum. If anyone abates suboptimally, the others gain by helping him to correct his mistake and reduce everyone's liability. If everyone abates optimally, liability is zero, so the group cannot gain by colluding and abating further. Collusion helps the parties to find the social optimum and remain there.

Second, whereas the rule of strict total liability for actual harm results in too little participation, the rule of total liability for excessive harm ideally induces the socially optimal level of participation. Beginning at the social optimum for participation m^*, an additional participant would cause additional social harm denoted h_{m^*+1}. Relative to the social optimum, total harm is then excessive by h_{m^*+1}, so everyone's liability would increase by this amount. If the social optimum were a competitive equilibrium with zero profits, then each participant would suffer a loss of h_{m^*+1}. A potential entrant foreseeing this eventuality, when m^* already participate, can calculate that the contemplated activity would not pay, so m^* is an equilibrium.[9]

D. Comparing Liability Rules

Table 5.1 compares the verifiability requirements and efficiency of different liability rules. The first row indicates the familiar result that when the harm caused by individuals is verifiable, a rule of individual strict liability gives the injurer efficient incentives for precaution, activity level, and participation. The second row indicates that when the harm caused by an individual is verifiable

---

[7] In general, when total harm H is a convex function of individual abatement effort, socially optimal abatement h_i^* by all m^* individuals is an equilibrium.

[8] Assume again that there are five factories, which is the optimal number, and that the optimal total harm is 500. However, pollution from the factories equals 750 so that the excessive harm is 250. Under the rule of total liability for excessive harm, each of the factories will bear liability of 250. Each factory knows, however, that if it abates at a cost of 25, its liability will fall by 50, regardless of what other factories do. As a result each factory abates efficiently, and the total harm is reduced from 750 to 500.

[9] Fixed initial costs of an activity constitute nonconvexities. Relatively small nonconvexities do not threaten the usual efficiency analysis in microeconomics. KENNETH J. ARROW & FRANK H. HAHN, *Markets with Non-Convex Preferences and Production*, GENERAL COMPETITIVE ANALYSIS 169 (1971).

and comparable to the social optimum, a rule of individual liability for excessive harm gives the injurer efficient incentives for precaution, activity level, and participation. The third row indicates that when individual precaution can be verified and compared to the optimum, a negligence rule gives the injurer incentives for efficient precaution, excessive activity level, and excessive participation.

The fourth row indicates that when actual total harm is verifiable, a rule of strict total liability can be implemented. Under this rule, each injurer internalizes the marginal social cost of changing his precaution or activity level, so the rule provides efficient incentives for precaution and activity level. The rule of strict total liability, however, overburdens participating in the activity. Furthermore, by colluding, participants can reduce social harm below the social optimum H^* and save themselves liability costs.

The fifth row indicates that when actual total harm and ideal total harm are verifiable, a rule of total liability for excessive harm provides incentives for optimal precaution, activity level, and participation. In the usual case, collusion is benign because it helps the actors to reach the social optimum H^*.

Proportionate liability is another rule that can be used when individual harm is unverifiable. Applying a rule of proportionate liability requires verifying the actual total harm and then allocating it to individuals by using a verifiable measure of proportionality. The measure of proportionality indicated in the sixth row is the activity of each individual divided by the total activity of all individuals. The measure of activity might be market share in the sale of a good, miles driven, or fuel consumed. As indicated in table 5.1, liability in proportion to activity level creates incentives for too little precaution, and the incentives for activity level and participation are not generally optimal.[10]

E. Refining the Model

Next we discuss problems and possibilities for the rule of total liability for excessive harm.

1. ERRORS AND IRRATIONALITY

When applying the rule of total liability for excessive harm, the authorities may overestimate or underestimate the actual harm H or the ideal social harm H^*. Overestimating actual harm H and attributing more harm to injurers than they actually cause is mathematically equivalent to underestimating the socially optimal harm H^*. In either case, instead of observing excessive harm $H - H^*$, the authorities observe $H - H^* + \varepsilon$, where ε is an error term.

---

[10] Unless liability under the proportionate rule is imposed in proportion to the exact risks created. In that case liability equals the harm actually caused by the individual, so the rule of individual liability can be applied, and there is no need to apply a rule of proportionate liability.

Table 5.1.
Verification and efficiency of liability rules

Liability rule	Total harm H	Ideal harm H*	Actual individual harm h	Ideal individual harm h*	Actual individual precaution x	Ideal individual precaution x*	Actual individual activity	Precaution	Activity level	Participation	Collusion problem
Individual strict liability			Verifiable					Efficient	Efficient	Efficient	
Individual excessive harm			Verifiable	Verifiable				Efficient	Efficient	Efficient	
Negligence			Verifiable		Verifiable	Verifiable		Efficient	Too high	Too high	
Strict total liability	Verifiable							Efficient	Efficient	Far too low	Collusion
Total liability for excessive harm	Verifiable	Verifiable						Efficient	Efficient	Efficient	
Proportionate liability	Verifiable						Verifiable	Too low	Inefficient	Inefficient	

Consider the consequences when liability is too low because $H - H^* + \varepsilon < H - H^*$. By satisfying the observed legal standard $H - H^* + \varepsilon$, each injurer's liability is nil, so participants respond with too little precaution and too much activity relative to the social optimum. Now consider the consequences when liability is too high because $H - H^* + \varepsilon > H - H^*$. To escape liability, the injurers must reduce harm below the social optimum. At the social optimum, however, the cost to each injurer of reducing social harm exceeds the resulting reduction in actor's liability. Injurers, consequently, respond with the socially optimal precaution and activity. As in the case of strict total liability discussed above, this behavior is susceptible to collusion and the participation level is too low.

We apply these conclusions to the case where error ε is a random variable. With random errors, each injurer faces the possibility that liability is too low, in which case it would pay to respond with too little precaution and too much activity. Each injurer also faces the possibility that liability is too high, in which case it would pay to respond with optimal precaution and optimal activity level. If the random error is biased toward liability that is too low ($E(\varepsilon) < 0$) or unbiased ($E(\varepsilon) = 0$), then each injurer will respond with too little precaution and too much activity. If the random error is biased toward liability that is too high ($E(\varepsilon) > 0$), then, as the bias increases, each injurer will respond by increasing precaution and reducing activity level until these values approach the social optimum.

Having discussed errors by authorities, we extend our analysis to errors by injurers. Assume that some injurers fail to act in their rational self-interest. In notation, let H denote the total harm that is individually rational, and let ε denote the error caused by some actors failing to act in their rational self-interest. The actual harm equals $H + \varepsilon$, and everyone is liable for $H - H^* + \varepsilon$. As the notation makes clear, this form of error by some actors is mathematically identical to errors by the authorities in applying the liability rule. We have already explained the incentive effects on rational actors when ε is negative, positive, or a random variable.

The preceding discussion assumes that errors by authorities or injurers add to, or subtract from, the actual harm H or the optimal harm H^*. Additive error is relatively simple to analyze because it often does not affect marginal values. We will not explicitly analyze any other forms of error, but we mention briefly how they can change our conclusions. Our conclusions would be different if the error multiplied the actual harm H or optimal harm H^*. To illustrate multiplicative error, the authorities may underestimate actual harm by 10 percent, or the authorities may overestimate the socially optimal harm by 15 percent, or an injurer may underestimate his individually rational precaution by 20 percent. Multiplicative errors change the preceding conclusions because they affect marginal values.

If there are many injurers, the possibility is high that at least one of them will make an error and cause excessive harm. Furthermore, when there are many injurers, excessive harm caused by a few of them imposes liability costs on many others. For these reasons, the rule of total liability for excessive harm ceases to be practical when the number of injurers becomes very large. For example, the rule is impractical for assessing damages against drivers in Los Angeles for excessive pollution.

2. SEARCH

When actors make errors, they can also learn from their mistakes and correct them. Thus when the authorities have difficulty estimating the optimal social harm H^*, they might search for the optimum and converge toward it by iteration. To begin the search, they might set the legal standard, denoted H_t, above the social optimum H^* in the first year, and thus allow more harm than the social optimum. When H_t is higher than the social optimum H^*, all the firms will meet the target and pay no damages. In the next year, the authorities might decrease the legal standard H_t. The authorities can repeat this process over several years. As H_t decreases, eventually a point will be reached at which further increases in abatement cost firms more than their reduction in liability, so the firms will fall short of the target and begin to pay damages $H - H_t$. When this happens, the authorities know that H_t is marginally lower than H^*, so they should increase H_t slightly and stop making changes. In brief, the authorities can proceed iteratively until the firms reveal that their marginal cost of abatement equals the marginal social cost of the social harm. This is essentially the same process proposed in theoretical models of search for the Hand Rule standard of negligence or the optimal Pigouvian tax.[11]

After searching and finding the social optimum H^*, the authorities should be alert to the possible emergence of new technologies that lower abatement costs and cause the optimal harm H^* to decrease. In response to technical improvement, the authorities must decrease the target H_t in order to keep it equal to the social optimum H^*. If they do not, actors will have deficient incentives to adopt new technologies.

3. VICTIMS' INCENTIVES

We have been assuming that injurers can reduce social harm and victims cannot reduce it. Now we assume that victims can reduce social harm and we discuss very briefly the incentives that alternative liability rules give them. Our discussion is very brief because its conclusions are familiar in the existing economic analysis of accidents. In general, when victims do not receive compensation, they internalize the benefits as well as the costs of their actions, so victims' incentives are socially efficient.[12] Consequently, if injurers are liable to the state

---

[11] Robert Cooter, Lewis Kornhauser & David Lane, *Liability Rules, Limited Information, and the Role of Precedent*, 10 Bell J. Econ. 366 (1979).

[12] See *infra* chapter 6, section B.

and not liable to the victims, as with a pollution tax, then victim's incentives are efficient.

Instead of being liable to the state, tort law makes injurers liable to the victims. To simplify the analysis of total liability for excessive harm, assume that there is only one victim who receives all damage payments from m injurers. Under the rule of total liability for excessive harm the victim will try to increase his harm beyond the optimal total harm (H^*) as much as he can, since for every harm of 1\$ he receives compensation of m\$.

This problem arises as long as the authorities set compensation equal to the difference between actual harm and socially optimal harm, $H - H^*$. To avoid the problem, the authorities could replace actual harm H in this formula with the hypothetical harm $H\sim$ that would result from the actual behavior of injurers and socially optimal behavior of victims. When liability follows this formula, victims cannot increase the compensation that they receive by deviating from the socially optimal precaution and activity level. [13]

4. BANKRUPTCY

Externalizing risk through the possibility of bankruptcy is a familiar problem for any liability rule. The problem, however, affects the rule of total liability for excessive harm differently from how it affects a rule of individual liability. Under the former rule, each injurer pays for the total excessive harm regardless of the ability of other injurers to pay. If an insolvent actor takes large risks of harming others and the harm materializes, all of the solvent injurers will suffer an increase in their liability costs. Each injurer, consequently, has an incentive to prevent others from behaving irresponsibly. This incentive does not exist under a rule of individual liability for separate harms, where the irresponsible behavior of one injurer does not affect the liability of another injurer. [14]

5. STRATEGY

The circumstances for adopting the rule of total liability for excessive harm include the inability of the authorities to verify the harm caused by individuals. Under these circumstances, individuals may be unable to observe the harm that each of them causes. One person cannot react strategically to another's unobservable behavior. Consequently, the assumption of nonstrategic behavior is the natural way to begin to analyze the rule of total liability for excessive harm. For nonstrategic actors, we have shown that the social optimum is an equilibrium under the rule of total liability for excessive harm.

---

[13] *Cf. infra* chapter 6, section D, where we explain that when damages in contract law are liquidated, the promisee will not over-rely since reliance will not affect the level of damages.

[14] When several injurers create one inseparable harm for which they are all jointly and severally liable, however, the injurers have contribution claims against each other. In these circumstances, the insolvent injurer's proportion of liability will be borne by the solvent injurers, so each one has an incentive to constrain the others, as under the rule of total liability for excessive harm.

The polar opposite of nonstrategic behavior is perfect collusion. Perfect collusion implies that all actors cooperate with each other to maximize their joint payoffs. In our model, the aim of collusion is to minimize the total cost of liability and abatement for the parties. Under the rule of total liability for excessive harm, the parties minimize their total cost of liability and abatement by meeting the target H^* and avoiding liability. Thus, when the parties collude perfectly, the rule of total liability for excessive harm induces socially optimal results. Indeed, collusion has the advantage of enabling actors to help correct each others' mistakes.

These facts suggest that the rule of total liability for excessive harm will prove robust and practical. There is a danger, however, that collusion over liability and abatement might prompt other harmful forms of collusion, such as collusion over prices. The tools of antitrust law are available to deal with this problem. Another fear is that collusion over liability will lead to political lobbying to set the target level of harm H_t above the social optimum. The problem of setting standards and escaping political distortions is common to all liability rules.

Another topic to explore is forms of strategic behavior that do not involve cooperation. Assume that each actor can observe the individual harm caused by each of the other actors. A sinister possibility is that an actor threatens to impose liability on himself and everyone else unless they take steps to eliminate liability for everyone. This is a form of the game of "chicken." To play chicken under the rule of total liability for excessive harm, an injurer refuses to abate efficiently in order to force other injurers to abate excessively. Acting on this threat, however, lowers the actor's payoff, so it is not credible. For the threat to be effective, people must believe that the party making it is irrational. Playing chicken requires making others believe that you are irrational. This possibility is too unlikely to present a general objection to the rule of total liability for excessive harm.[15]

Another sinister possibility is that an injurer increases the harm that he causes in order to increase the costs of his competitors. A firm might engage in the pollution equivalent of predatory pricing. Predatory pricing refers to a situation in which a firm temporarily prices below cost in order to drive a competitor out of the market, and then raises the price exorbitantly in the absence of competition. With a rule of total liability for excessive harm, a firm might temporarily create excessive harm in order to drive a competitor out of the market. After the competitor withdraws from the market, the remaining firm returns to optimal harm and no liability. Or a firm might pursue entry-limiting

---

[15] Notice that without collusion among the other actors the first actor would never play "chicken." To illustrate, suppose that the first actor does not abate and each of the other actors believes that his refusal to abate is credible. Nevertheless, after the other actors reduced their excessive harm to zero, none of them will abate, because by definition, each actor's costs of additional abatement are higher than the harm that additional abatement could reduce. This proposition is valid with respect to each and every actor, regardless of how the other actors behave.

pollution. Under a rule of total liability for excessive harm, the incumbent firm increases pollution until the liability for a new firm entering the market makes such entry unprofitable.

These problems should not occur often or prove unmanageable. When firms do not compete in the same product markets, they have no reason to practice predatory polluting or limit polluting.[16] If firms that compete with each other engage in these behaviors, the authorities can extend exiting legal remedies for limit pricing and predatory pricing to these new behaviors.

F. EXAMPLES

To show that the rule of total liability for excessive harm is practical, consider some real and hypothetical situations in which the rule could be applied to great advantage.

Industrial Pollution of the Kishon River: Two petrochemical plants and five fertilizer plants discharge a variety of pollutants, especially metals, into the final 7 kilometers of the Kishon River where it flows into the Mediterranean Sea at Haifa.[17] Measuring the extent of these metals in the river is feasible, but not the individual contributions of polluters. In 1994, the "Kishon River Authority" assumed responsibility for full ecological rehabilitation of the river by 2010.[18] The Kishon River Authority could pursue its goals by applying the principle of total liability for excessive harm. For each metal, the small number of firms that discharge it would be totally liable for concentrations in the river that exceed the Kishon River Authority's targets.

Everglades and NPS: Phosphorus runs off of farms into the Florida Everglades. Beginning in 1995-1996, phosphorus loadings are compared to a baseline derived from loadings recorded from 1979-1988.[19] If basin-wide reductions in nutrient load into the Everglades do not meet statutory targets over time, the "Agricultural Privilege Tax" imposes a property tax increase on all farmers,

---

[16] However, even if the firms do not compete in the products market, the firms could still compete over the "right" to pollute. Thus, if the environmental protection agency allows a certain amount of pollution in a specific area, some polluters could find it beneficial to increase pollution in order to drive other polluters out of the area. If the former polluters succeed in their efforts, fewer polluters will later share the "right" to pollute. This concern disappears, however, if the environmental protection agency adapts H^* to encompass the number of polluters acting in the area.

[17] KISHON RIVER AUTHORITY, *Information on the Kishon River and Quality of Its Waters* (2001), Available at: http://www.kishon.org.il/pages/publications/information.php (in Hebrew). Pollution in the river especially caught the attention of the Israeli public because of the fate of an elite army squad that trained in the polluted water and now has at least 88 documented cases of malignant tumors in its men. The incidence of cancer in this army unit far exceeds base rates.

[18] KISHON RIVER AUTHORITY, *Master Plan for the Kishon River* (2001), Available at: http://www.kishon.org.il/pages/publications/tochen.php (in Hebrew)

[19] See U.S. Environmental Protection Agency, *A Tax Incentive for Installing Ag BMPs in the Everglades,* 46 NON-POINT SOURCE NEWS-NOTES 17 (1996). Available at: http://water.epa.gov/polwaste/nps/outreach/upload/2007_11_02_info_NewsNotes_pdf_46issue.pdf

beginning at $24.89 per acre in 1996 and increasing every four years to a maximum of $35 per acre from 2006 through 2014. However, the farmers in the designated area can escape the tax increase by exceeding an overall 25 percent basin-wide phosphorus reduction goal.

Such a tax, whose form corresponds to a rule of total liability for excessive harm, can apply more generally to nonpoint source pollution (NPS). Section 303(d) of the U.S. Clean Water Act provides the Environmental Protection Agency with the power to set the Total Maximum Daily Load (TMDL) for a type of pollutant and a body of water. Section 319 of the 1987 Clean Water Act requires states to identify water bodies in which control of nonpoint source polluters is necessary, and to establish management programs. Sometimes a small number of major sources account for almost all NPS pollution. In these circumstances, each polluter could be held liable for total harm caused by pollution that exceeds the TMDL.

Fish Cages at Eilat: As of 2004, 70 percent of the coral reef in the Gulf of Eilat in the Red Sea was dead or seriously damaged, primarily because of fish farms operated by two companies, which the authorities are threatening to close.[20] To avoid closure, the two companies could contract into a rule of total liability for excessive harm, which is practical because the total harm caused by the two companies is verifiable and the individual contributions are unverifiable. Such a contract could halt further damage and remove the public pressure to close the fish farms.

To conclude, we briefly mention some hypothetical examples that show more possibilities. If Coke bottles explode either because Company A supplies defective bottles or Company B overcharges the bottles when filling them, the consumer protection agency could collect a fine from both companies for injuries that exceed the expected rate of injury for companies following the best practices. Similarly, if Hospital A diagnoses melanoma and refers its patient to Hospital B for treatment, the hospital authority could hold each of the hospitals liable for deaths exceeding the expected rate from optimal care by both hospitals.[21] If a city suffers from pollution by buses operated by three companies, and if city officials can determine with reasonable accuracy the amount of total pollution caused by all buses, the city could fine the three companies for excessive pollution. Finally, if three municipalities around a lake want to prevent

---

[20] THE ISRAELI MINISTRY OF ENVIRONMENT & THE AUTHORITY FOR NATURE AND GARDENS (Opinion Paper), *The Effects of the Fish Farms on the Gulf of Eilat and the Coral Reef* (2004). Available at: http://www.sviva.gov.il/Enviroment/Static/Binaries/News/eilat_madanim_1.pdf

[21] The two hospitals might respond by refusing to take patients whose survival prospects are below average. For example, Hospital A might not admit patients who delay too long and come to the hospital with an advanced stage of melanoma. This is the same problem of adverse selection that afflicts private medical insurance markets. This problem diminishes or disappears in so far as hospitals must accept all patients in need of care.

overfishing, they could agree to collection of a tax from each of them whenever the stock of fish falls below an accepted target.

G. CONCLUSION

In the last century, the rule of strict liability for consumer product injuries displaced the rule of negligence. Problems of proof compelled the change. For certain kinds of harm, we believe the same consideration will eventually compel replacing individual liability with the rule of total liability for excessive harm. The rule is practical under three conditions: (i) total harm is verifiable, (ii) optimal total harm is calculable, and (iii) the number of injurers is not too large. When these conditions are met and the harm caused by individuals is difficult to verify, we recommend adopting the rule of total liability for excessive harm and avoiding the administrative burden of individualized liability, taxes, fines, or transferable rights.

Moralists might reject this recommendation because it imposes "collective punishment." On the path to equilibrium, actors could find themselves paying for harms caused by others, and errors or strategic behavior might continue this result in equilibrium. However, the *excessive* harm caused by everyone is usually less than the *actual* harm caused by each individual actor. "Collective punishment" under the rule of total liability for excessive harm is typically less than the actual harm that the individual caused. The complaint that total liability for excessive harm is unfair seems hollow when liability is clearly below the harm that the injurer caused. Indeed, liability will usually be nil.[22]

The fact that the rule of total liability for excessive harm creates socially optimal incentives should make it attractive to people who want to promote the public interest. The fact that injurers escape bureaucratic regulation and each injurer's liability equals zero in equilibrium should make the rule more attractive to injurers than most alternatives. In order for people to be attracted to the rule, however, they must understand its consequences. As this discussion shows, some consequences are counterintuitive.

---

[22] The argument for the rule's fairness resembles the utilitarian justification of an effective deterrent: An "effective" deterrent is fair because it does not have to be used. Utilitarian and deontological traditions disagree about whether a very harsh penalty that perfectly deters and never requires use should be praised for its good consequences or condemned for its excessive threat. For a contribution to this debate that favors the utilitarian tradition, see Louis Kaplow & Steven Shavell, *Fairness versus Welfare*, 114 Harv. L. Rev. 961 (2001). For environmental law application, see Shi-Ling Hsu, *Fairness versus Efficiency in Environmental Law*, 31 Ecology L. Q. 303 (2004), which argues for more economics and more efficiency-thinking in environmental law.

Contracts and Victims' Incentives

A contract changes the incentives of the promisor who makes a promise and the promisee who receives it. You might expect that theories of contract law would analyze the incentives of both parties. Surprisingly, however, contract theories focus mostly on the promisor's incentives. The promisee's incentives are commonly ignored as if she were passive and unable to advance the contract's purposes. In fact, the promisee can often affect the probability and value of performance and breach in at least three ways.[1] First, the promisee's *reliance* on the promise increases the gain from performance and the loss from breach. Second, promisee's *assistance* to the promisor lowers the latter's cost of performance and decreases his probability of breach. Third, promisee's *mitigation* of the harm caused by a promisor's breach lowers its costs. Analysis is underdeveloped for all three—reliance, assistance, and mitigation.[2] *The second claim of this book is that contract law and theory should respond more to the promisee's incentives, especially to the problems of over-reliance and under-assistance.*

Neglect of victim's incentives afflicts legal theory more in contracts than torts. Economic models of tort law have analyzed the incentives of both parties from the beginning with Ronald Coase in 1960, through Guido Calabresi and Richard Posner in the early seventies, and Steven Shavell, Robert Cooter and Thomas Ulen in the eighties. By comparison, the promisee's incentives were underdeveloped in contract law during these years. What explains this difference? Perhaps the victim's behavior is analyzed more thoroughly in tort theory than in contract theory because of a difference in legal doctrine. For tortious accidents, courts throughout the United States recognize the victim's comparative fault as a defense against liability. The comparative fault defense forces the victim's behavior out of the background and into the foreground of

---

[1] But see ROBERT COOTER, *Unity in Tort, Contracts and Property: The Model of Precaution*, 73 CAL. L. REV. 1 (1985).

[2] In early economic models of contracts, the most thorough analysis of promisee's incentives concerns mitigation. See CHARLES GOETZ & ROBERT SCOTT, *The Mitigation Principle: Toward a General Theory of Contractual Obligation*, 69 VA. L. REV. 967 (1983).

legal disputes and theory. For breach of contract, the comparative fault defense is weak or nonexistent, except in a few countries other than the United States.[3] Absent a comparative fault defense, contract doctrine allows the promisee's behavior to remain in the background of disputes and theories.

Underdeveloped analysis of the victim's behavior causes confusion in contract theory. To illustrate, consider three arguments against a comparative fault defense in contract law. First, with such a defense, the promisee could no longer be certain of full compensation for nonperformance, so she might rely too little on the promise. Under-reliance would interfere with planning and coordination.[4] Second, instead of "sitting and waiting" for the promisor to perform, the promisee might feel compelled by a comparative fault defense to provide uncompensated help that the promisor never bargained to receive. Third, fear of incomplete compensation from breach might cause the promisee to mitigate damages excessively.

According to these arguments, a comparative fault defense causes the promisee to rely less, assist more, and mitigate more. Will these changes in the promisee's behavior increase or decrease the contract's value? Answering this question requires an explicit standard of optimal reliance, assistance, and mitigation. The preceding arguments cannot withstand scrutiny in light of an explicit standard of optimal behavior, as we will show.

Part II of this book analyzes problems and solutions concerning the incentives of the promisor and promisee. Chapter 6 (Unity in the Law of Tort and Contracts) explains that if we analyze the incentives of the promisor and promisee simultaneously, the analysis of contracts is much the same as the analysis of torts. The economic analysis of tort law usually begins with the goal of minimizing social costs. The injurer and the victim obviously affect the social cost of accidents by their precautions and activities. Similarly, the economic analysis of contract law usually begins with the goal of maximizing the value of contracts. The promisor can affect the contract's value by performing, and the promisee can affect the contract's value by relying, assisting, and mitigating.

Some form of negligence rule, such as comparative negligence, decides liability for many accidents. Unlike tort law, however, contract law makes the

---

[3] ARIEL PORAT, *A Comparative Fault Defense in Contract Law*, 107 MICH. L. REV. 1397 (2009). The comparative fault defense has spread into contract law of some countries such as Canada and the United Kingdom, mainly in cases of concurrent tort and contract liability, or where a party breached a contractual duty of reasonable care. See, e.g., *Law Comm'n, Contributory Negligence as a Defence in Contract* para. 1.4 (1993). For *refusal* to apply the comparative fault defense to contracts, see *Fortier v. Dona Anna Plaza Partners* 747 F. 2d 1324 (10th Cir. 1984). For willingness to apply the defense to contracts, see *American Mortgage Inv. Co. v. Hardin-Stockton Corp.* 671 S.W. 2d 283 (Mo. Ct. App. 1984). There is an increasing willingness to apply the comparative fault defense to implied-warranty cases. See JAMES J. WHITE & ROBERT S. SUMMERS, UNIFORM COMMERCIAL CODE § 11-8, at 758–60 (5th ed. 2006).

[4] See *Law Comm'n, id.*, paras. 4.5-4.7.

promisor's liability contingent on breach, not negligence. Reasonable effort by the promisor to perform, or the lack of reasonable effort by the promisee to assist, are not defenses against liability for breach of contract.

A negligence rule can provide efficient incentives for injurers and victims to take precaution against accidents. With a negligence rule, one party takes reasonable care to avoid liability, and then the other party takes reasonable care because she bears the cost of accidental harm. Tort law solves the problem of incentives for both parties by some type of negligence rule such as comparative negligence. Contract law does not make liability turn on negligence. However, the parties could write terms into the contract that mimic tort law. The contract could say that the promisor is not liable unless his negligence caused the breach, and the extent of his liability will be reduced according to the promisee's comparative negligence.

Contract terms that require reasonable behavior, however, are vague and their enforcement requires a large amount of information. The courts cannot ordinarily verify whether or not a party to the contract satisfied such a vague obligation. The two chapters that conclude this part of the book offer two novel mechanisms to circumvent the problem of verification and to solve the promisee's incentives problem: Anti-Insurance (chapter 7), and Decreasing Liability Contracts (chapter 8). The first mechanism is a theoretically perfect solution. We believe that in the future, once its potential is fully captured, it may even be a practical solution. The second mechanism is less perfect, but more practical, even nowadays. We indicate some limited use of decreasing liability contracts in current markets, even if under different names. Understanding the concept of decreasing liability contracts, their pros and cons, may contribute to their wider spread and efficient use.

Unity in the Law
of Torts and Contracts

Variables in an economic model can be redefined and the model repurposed, in a process similar to recycling aluminum. The hard work of analysis transfers from one topic to another, revealing unity in complexity. This chapter repurposes the model of torts. In the basic torts model, the injurer and the victim can reduce the probability and severity of accidents by taking precaution. "Precaution" against accidents can be reinterpreted to fit contracts and other bodies of law.[1] For contracts, precaution is reinterpreted as effort to fulfill a promise and avoid breaching a contract. By allocating the cost of harm from accidents and broken contracts, liability law creates incentives for precaution. The simplest, most basic model of precaution reduces social costs to the cost of harm and precautions against it. At this basic level of analysis, the model of precaution unifies the law of torts and contracts. After building the basic model of precaution, other social costs can be inserted such as the cost of information, risk aversion and dispute resolution.

A. Forms of Precaution

The parties affected by an accident or breach of contract can usually take steps to reduce the probability or magnitude of the harm. The potential victim and injurer in an accident can reduce its probability or destructiveness. When contracting, the promisor can avoid breach or reduce its probability, and the promisee can help the promisor to perform. The promisee can also reduce the destructiveness of breach by reducing his reliance on the promise. Extending the ordinary meaning of "precaution" makes it a term of art referring to any such action that reduces harm.

---

[1] The original essay on which this chapter is based repurposes the torts model to contract and also property. Specifically, the model of precaution applies to the risk that the state will take property and the risk that one property owner will create a nuisance for another. See ROBERT COOTER, *Unity in Tort, Contract, and Property: The Model of Precaution*, 73 CAL. L. REV. 1 (1985).

B. The Paradox of Compensation

When each individual bears the full benefits and costs of his precaution, economists say that social value is internalized. The individual sweeps all social values affected by his actions into his calculus of self-interest. The incentives of private individuals are socially efficient when costs and benefits are fully internalized. Conversely, when an individual bears part of the benefits or part of the costs of his precaution, economists say that some social value is externalized. The individual's calculus of self-interest excludes some values affected by his actions, so his incentives are socially inefficient.

In situations when both the injurer and the victim can take precaution, internalization requires both parties to bear the full cost of the harm. Suppose that smoke from a factory soils the wash at a commercial laundry, and the parties fail to solve the problem by private negotiation. A pollution tax equal to the harm caused by the smoke can solve the incentive problem. The factory will bear the tax and the laundry will bear the smoke, so pollution costs will be internalized by both of them, as required for social efficiency.[2] In general, when precaution is bilateral, the efficiency principle requires both parties to be fully responsible for the harm. Efficient incentives require *double responsibility at the margin.*[3]

Compensating victims is usually inconsistent with double responsibility at the margin. Instead of paying a tax to the government, the factory in the preceding example may pay compensation to the laundry. With compensation the laundry externalizes the harm from smoke, which undermines its incentives for precaution against it. Here is the paradox: If the factory can pollute with impunity, then the factory externalizes the resulting harm. Conversely, if the factory must pay full compensation,[4] the laundry externalizes the harm. In the intermediate case where the factory must pay partial compensation, the factory and the laundry each externalize part of the harm. No level of compensation can achieve double responsibility at the margin. When efficiency requires

---

[2] For a full discussion of the tax remedy, See ROBERT COOTER, *The Cost of Coase*, 11 J. LEGAL STUD. 1 (1982). Like other remedies, the tax remedy assumes that there is no bargaining between the injurer and the victim. If bargaining is possible, however, it will pay the injurer to bribe the victim to take more than the socially efficient amount of precaution, thus reducing the injurer's tax liability.

[3] "The margin" refers to the change in harm brought about by a small change in precaution by either party. The economic concept of the margin corresponds to the mathematical concept of the first derivative.

[4] Perfect compensation, by definition, is the level of compensation at which the laundry becomes indifferent to the level of pollution. Costs are internalized, by definition, when a decision-maker's self-interest perfectly coincides with an economic conception of the public interest. In other words, costs are internalized when minimized private costs correspond to minimized social costs. Costs are externalized when they are not minimized.

bilateral precaution, strict liability for any fraction of the harm from zero percent to 100 percent is inefficient.[5]

How does liability law combine compensation with double responsibility at the margin? It has evolved three distinct mechanisms for solving this paradox, each of which is found in the law of torts, contracts, and elsewhere.

C. Accidents

Assume that Xavier and Yvonne are engaged in activities that sometimes result in accidents. If an accident occurs, Yvonne's property is damaged and Xavier's is not. For this reason we will call Xavier the injurer and Yvonne the victim, regardless of who is at fault. The probability that an accident will occur depends on the precautions taken by both of them, which are costly. The relationship between harm and precaution is easy to visualize in concrete cases. Drawing on a famous example,[6] suppose that Xavier operates a railroad train that emits sparks that sometimes set fire to Yvonne's cornfield. Xavier can reduce the harm to the corn by installing spark arresters, running the trains more slowly, or running fewer trains. Similarly, Yvonne can reduce the harm by planting her corn farther from the tracks, planting cabbage instead of corn, or leaving the fields fallow.

There are two rules that assign liability without regard to fault. The first is the rule of no liability, which means that the injurer need not compensate the victim. Under this rule, the victim bears the full cost of accidents. The second rule is strict liability, which means that the injurer must compensate the victim. As noted by Ronald Coase, the rule of law makes no difference from the viewpoint of social efficiency if Xavier and Yvonne can bargain with each other and agree on the reallocation of social costs.[7] In order for the rule of law to make a difference, obstacles must prevent potential injurers and victims from bargaining together.

With bargaining obstructed, the legal rule for allocating accident costs determines Xavier's and Yvonne's incentives for precaution. If the rule is no liability, the injurer has no economic incentive to take precaution and so will minimize expenditure on precaution by taking none. If the rule is strict liability

---

[5] An implicit assumption of the paradox of compensation is that this inefficiency cannot be overcome by private bargaining, e.g., that transaction costs block an efficient solution by private agreement. See, generally, RONALD H. COASE, *The Problem of Social Cost*, 3 J. L. & ECON. 1 (1960).

[6] This example was presented in Coase, *supra* note 5, at 29-34, and extended in Cooter, *supra* note 2, at 2-4.

[7] See, generally, Coase, *supra* note 5. Thus, if the legal rule is no compensation, Yvonne will be willing to pay Xavier to take efficient precautions to reduce Yvonne's exposure to harm. This will reduce her total costs. Conversely, if Xavier is required by law to compensate Yvonne, he will be willing to pay Yvonne to take efficient precautions so that her harm will be minimized.

with perfect compensation, the victim is indifferent whether or not an accident occurs. Since she has no economic incentive to take precaution, she will minimize her expenditure on precaution by not taking any. Thus, no liability and strict liability with perfect compensation are symmetrical opposites.[8]

The desirability of no liability or strict liability can be evaluated from the viewpoint of economic efficiency. Efficient levels of precaution minimize the social costs of accidents.[9] In the simple model of precaution, social costs equal the sum of the parties' precaution and the expected harm. For most accidents, precaution is bilateral in the sense that social efficiency requires both injurer and victim to take at least some precaution.[10] The rule of no liability and the rule of strict liability with perfect compensation both lack incentives for one of the parties to take precaution, so these rules cannot be efficient for bilateral accidents.

A similar consideration applies when compensation is imperfect rather than perfect. Compensation is less than perfect if the victim would prefer no accident to an accident with (imperfect) compensation. Under a rule of strict liability with less than perfect compensation, the injurer externalizes the uncompensated portion of the harm and the victim externalizes the compensated portion of the harm. Since neither of them internalizes the full cost of harm, both have inadequate incentives for precaution.[11] When efficiency requires bilateral precaution, rules of no liability or strict liability provide inadequate incentives for precaution, regardless of the level of compensation.

Instead of no liability or strict liability, law can assign responsibility for harm according to the fault of the parties. A simple negligence rule requires the injurer to compensate the victim if, and only if, the injurer is at fault. Under a simple negligence rule, the injurer will satisfy the legal standard in order to avoid liability. If the legal standard corresponds to the efficient level

---

[8] This is the standard conclusion first proved by JOHN P. BROWN, *Toward an Economic Theory of Liability,* 2 J. LEGAL STUD. 323, 328 (1973).

[9] For any given technology of care, some potential precautionary steps will be efficient, i.e., will return a reduction in harm greater than the cost of implementation. Liability rules have the effect of assigning to one party or the other the incentive to take particular precautionary steps, but the socially efficient level of precaution is a function of the technology of care (the costs of particular precautions and the resulting reduction in harm). The socially efficient level of precaution is independent, at least in the simple model, of the assignment of incentives to the parties.

[10] Some efficient precautions may cost less when taken by one party or the other. Precaution is bilateral when at least one such precaution for each party exists. Workplace injuries, consumer product injuries, automobile collisions, and pedestrian accidents are all examples of accidents that are bilateral with respect to precaution.

[11] Assume for example that if either party took a particular precaution costing $100 annually, the annual cost of accidents would be reduced by $150. This is an efficient precaution since total social costs would be reduced by $50 annually if the precautionary step were taken. Yet under a rule of strict liability with imperfect compensation, say, one that requires the injurer to compensate the victim for half the cost of accidents, each party will externalize half the accident cost, and neither will be willing to spend $100 to avoid a cost of $75.

of precaution, the injurer's precaution will be efficient. Since the injurer avoids liability, the victim knows that she bears the cost of the harm. She internalizes the costs and benefits of precaution, so her incentives are efficient. In sum, if the legal standard of fault corresponds to the efficient level of care, both parties will take efficient precaution.[12]

Consider the marginal costs of the parties under a simple negligence rule. To avoid liability, the injurer exactly fulfills the legal standard of care. A small reduction in his care will cause his precaution to fall below the legal standard and make him liable.[13] Absent that reduction in care by the injurer, however, the victim bears the cost of the harm. Thus, each party bears the full cost of the increase in harm caused by the decrease in precaution. This is double responsibility at the margin.

Besides simple negligence, other fault rules include negligence with contributory negligence, strict liability with contributory negligence, and comparative negligence.[14] Under any fault rule, one of the parties can escape responsibility by satisfying the legal standard, so an efficient legal standard will cause his behavior to be efficient. The other party bears the cost of harm and thus internalizes the costs and benefits of precaution. So long as the legal standards correspond to efficient precaution, all such rules create double responsibility at the margin. Since all forms of the fault rule are efficient, a justice-minded lawmaker can choose the form that best accords with his sense of fairness.

D. Contracts

Yvonne and Xavier enter into a contract in which Yvonne pays for Xavier's promise to deliver a product in the future. Obstacles might arise that will prevent Xavier from performing as promised. The probability of timely performance depends on Xavier's costly efforts to avoid the obstacles that prevent performance.

One purpose of contracting is to give Yvonne confidence that Xavier's promise will be performed, so that she can rely upon his promise. Reliance on the

---

[12] In the simple model we assume that the statistical cost of harm is perfectly known by the parties.

[13] In reality, legal standards tend to be vague. The negligence theory does not change qualitatively, however, when a model with vague legal standards is adopted. A theory of negligence with fuzzy standards is discussed in ROBERT COOTER & THOMAS ULEN, LAW AND ECONOMICS 220-222 (7th ed. 2011). See also RICHARD CRASWELL & JOHN E. CALFEE, *Deterrence and Uncertain Legal Standards*, 2 J. L. ECON. & ORG. 279 (1986); LOUIS KAPLOW & STEVEN SHAVELL, *Accuracy in the Determination of Liability*, 37 J. L. & ECON. 1 (1994).

[14] For a critical account of comparative negligence given uncertainty and asymmetric information between the parties, see OMRI BEN-SHAHAR & OREN BAR-GILL, *The Uneasy Case for Comparative Negligence*, 5 AM. L. ECON. REV. 433 (2003).

contract increases the value to Yvonne of Xavier's performance. However, reliance also increases the loss suffered in the event of breach. The more the promisee relies, therefore, the greater the benefit from performance and the greater the harm caused by breach.

To make this description concrete, suppose that Xavier is a builder who signs a contract to construct a store for Yvonne by the first of September. Many events could jeopardize timely completion of the building; for example, the plumbers' union may strike, the city's inspectors may be recalcitrant, or the weather may be inclement. Xavier can increase the probability of timely completion by taking costly measures, such as having the plumbers work overtime before their union contract expires, badgering the inspectors to finish on time, or rescheduling work to complete the roof before the rainy season arrives. Yvonne, on the other hand, must order merchandise for her new store in advance if she is to open with a full line on the first of September. If she orders many items for September delivery and the store is not ready for occupancy, she will have to place the goods in storage, which is costly. The more merchandise she orders, the larger her profit will be in the event of performance, and the larger her loss in the event of nonperformance.

The injurer in torts and the promisor in contracts resemble each other. Precaution against accidents by the potential tortfeasor parallels precaution against breach by the promisor. The parallel between the tort victim and the promisee in contracts is more subtle. *More* precaution by the tort victim is like *less* reliance by the promisee, because each action reduces the harm caused by an accident or a breach. The victim's precaution against accidents and the promisee's reliance upon the contract are inversely symmetrical.

If Xavier does not perform as promised, then a court must decide whether Xavier is liable or excused. The excuses that law recognizes include deficient quality of assent to the contract due to mistake, incapacity, duress, or fraud; unconscionable contract terms; or impossible or impractical performance. If the court narrowly construes excuses, usually finding nonperformance to be a breach, then Xavier will usually be liable. If the court construes excuses broadly, usually finding nonperformance to be justified, then Xavier will seldom be liable.

The incentive effects of a broader or narrower construction of excuses are similar to the effects of strict liability and no-liability rules in tort. If defenses are narrowly construed and perfect expectation damages are awarded for breach,[15] the promisee will rely as if performance were certain. Specifically, Yvonne will order a full line of merchandise as if the store were certain to open

---

[15] In many occasions, however, compensation is not perfect. See, e.g., MELVIN A. EISENBERG & BRETT H. McDONNELL, *Expectation Damages and the Theory of Overreliance*, 54 HASTINGS L.J. 1335, 1357 (2003); JASON SCOTT JOHNSTON, *Investment, Information and Promissory Liability*, 152 U. PA. L. REV. 1923, 1930 (2004). When compensation is below actual harm the promisee will have incentives to restrain reliance (but less than at the efficient level), and the promisor will have incentives to take precautions (also less than at the efficient level).

on the first of September. A promisee's over-reliance parallels a tort victim's under-precaution.

A broad construction of excuses has the symmetrically opposite effect: the promisor expects to escape liability for harm caused by his breach, so he will not undertake costly precautions to avoid nonperformance. Specifically, if Xavier is unconcerned about his reputation or the possibility of future business with Yvonne, and if nonperformance due to a plumbers' strike, recalcitrant inspectors, or inclement weather will be excused, say, on grounds of impossibility, then Xavier will not take costly precautions against these events. The promisor's lack of precaution against possible obstacles to performance corresponds to the injurer's lack of precaution against tortious accidents.[16]

Social efficiency requires Xavier to hire the plumbers to work overtime if the additional cost is less than the increase in Yvonne's expected profits from timely completion. Suppose, however, that inclement weather excuses tardiness regardless of whether or not Xavier hired the plumbers to work overtime. Anticipating this possibility, Xavier may not hire the plumbers to work overtime, even though social efficiency may require him to do so. In general, excuses externalize some expected cost of breach, so that the promisor takes too little precaution and the probability of breach is too high.

Social efficiency also requires Yvonne to restrain her reliance in light of the objective probability of breach. Specifically, the marginal benefit of ordering additional merchandise equals the resulting increase in profit from anticipated sales in the new store multiplied by the probability that Xavier will finish the store on time. The marginal cost equals the cost of storing the goods multiplied by the probability that Xavier will finish the new store late. Social efficiency requires Yvonne to order additional merchandise until the marginal benefit equals the marginal cost. Suppose, however, that Xavier must compensate Yvonne for her storage costs if he finishes late. Self-interest motivates Yvonne to multiply storage costs by the probability of breach without compensation, which is smaller than the probability of breach. Yvonne's marginal cost is too low and her reliance is excessive and inefficient. In general, compensation externalizes some of the costs of reliance, so the promisee relies too heavily and breach results in excessive harm.

Like tort law, contract law has a solution to the paradox of compensation, but the contract solution is different from the tort solution. If the contract

---

[16] Since the purpose of many contracts is to facilitate planning and coordinate behavior, the possibility of excessive reliance may be difficult to grasp at first. Upon reflection, however, it is apparent that efficient reliance in many contractual contexts is less than the level that would maximize profits if performance were certain, and not merely likely. In the construction contract example, it is probably inefficient for Yvonne to order bulky merchandise with high storage costs, even though this would maximize her profits if timely construction were certain. For such contracts, efficiency requires the promisee to restrain her reliance.

stipulates damages for breach—say it requires Xavier to pay $200 per day for late completion—then the promisor has an incentive to prevent breach. Xavier may find that paying the plumbers to work overtime is cheaper than running the risk of late completion. If the promisee receives the stipulated damages as compensation, then the level of her compensation is independent of her level of reliance. Since she receives the same compensation for high or low reliance, she bears the extra risk from high reliance. Specifically, if Yvonne receives $200 per day in damages for late completion whether or not she orders the bulky merchandise, she may avoid the risk and not order it. In general, stipulated damages create an incentive for the promisee to restrain reliance.

Like a negligence rule in torts, stipulated damages in a contract create double responsibility at the margin: the promisor is responsible for the stipulated damages and the victim is responsible for the actual harm. By adjusting the level of stipulated damages, efficient incentives to take precautions can be achieved for both parties.[17] Stipulated damages are efficient when they equal the loss that the victim would suffer from breach if her reliance were efficient. Assume that efficient reliance requires Yvonne to order compact merchandise, not bulky merchandise. Furthermore, assume that if Yvonne orders the compact merchandise she will lose $200 in profits for each day that Xavier is late in completing the new store, whereas she will lose $300 if she orders bulky merchandise. Under these assumptions, liquidating damages at $200 per day for late completion provides efficient incentives for both Xavier and Yvonne.

Under the stated assumptions, stipulating damages at $200 per day will cause Yvonne to order the compact merchandise and not the bulky merchandise. Consequently, the actual harm that Yvonne will suffer in the event of breach is $200 per day. Thus the stipulation of damages at the efficient level is a self-fulfilling prophecy: the stipulation of *efficient* damages causes the actual damages to equal the stipulation. Since Xavier internalizes the actual harm caused by breach, and Yvonne bears the risk of reliance, there is double responsibility at the margin as required for efficiency.

Since stipulating damages prevents over-reliance, clauses stipulating damages, which are also called liquidated damages clauses, should be found in contracts where efficiency requires restraining reliance. Rather than liquidating damages, however, many contracts leave the computation of damages until

---

[17] For the argument that liquidation of damages could create inefficient incentives at the stage when the promisor decides whether to breach or perform (as opposed to the time when he takes precautions in an earlier stage) because the actual damages could be either below or above the stipulated ones, see ROBERT E. SCOTT & GEORGE G. TRIANTIS, *Embedded Options in the Case against Compensation in Contract Law*, 104 COLUM. L. REV. 1428, 1449 (2004). For the argument that with the assumption of renegotiation, liquidation of damages could create inefficiencies, see GERHARD WAGNER, *In Defense of the Impossibility Defense*, 27 LOY. U. CHI. L.J. 55, 70 (1995); RICHARD CRASWELL, *Offer, Acceptance, and Efficient Reliance*, 48 STAN. L. REV. 481, 492 (1996).

after the breach has occurred. When damages are not stipulated, various legal doctrines can restrain reliance. Liquidated damages restrain reliance by making damages invariant with respect to reliance. Courts restrain reliance by applying other legal doctrines that make damages similarly invariant.

The goods supplied by different firms in a perfectly competitive market are substitutes. When the promisor fails to perform in a competitive market, damages are ordinarily equal to the cost of replacing the promised performance with a close substitute (the replacement-price formula[18]). Specifically, if the seller breaches his promise to supply a good at a specified price, the damages paid to the buyer may include the additional cost of purchasing the good from someone else. In technical terms, damages equal the difference between the good's contract price and its spot price. In a competitive market, no single buyer or seller can influence these prices. Consequently, damages computed by the replacement-price formula are invariant with respect to the level of the promisee's reliance. Thus, replacement price damages in a competitive market have the same efficiency characteristics as liquidated damages.

For noncompetitive markets, other legal doctrines can dampen or prevent variance in damages due to reliance.[19] Thus recovery may be limited to damages that were foreseeable at the time the promise was made, and excessive reliance may be unforeseeable for purposes of law. Thus, the foreseeability doctrine can prevent compensation for excessive reliance. (The mitigation of damages defense could also be extended to cover over-reliance.[20])

Other doctrinal approaches to damages have similar effects. For example, suppose that Xavier fails to complete the building on time and Yvonne has to rent elsewhere temporarily. The court might award damages based on the additional rent, not on speculations about Yvonne's lost profits.[21] If the additional rent is less than Yvonne's lost profits, then she has less incentive to over-rely. As another example, failure to perform on a franchise agreement may result in an award of damages equal to the profit of similar franchise establishments, but not the "speculative profits" lost by the particular plaintiff. In general, if compensation is restricted to nonspeculative damages that vary less with respect to

---

[18] See U.C.C. §2-713. The concept of replacement damages is developed at much greater length in ROBERT COOTER & MELVIN A. EISENBERG, *Damages for Breach of Contract*, 73 CAL. L. REV. 1432 (1985).

[19] See, e.g., U.C.C. § 2-715(2).

[20] Reliance occurs after a promise is given and before performance is complete, whereas the duty to mitigate ordinarily applies after a breach has occurred. Courts could extend the mitigation of damages defense and apply it to behavior anticipating breach. Under such an extension, a promisee who over-relied would not be entitled to compensation for his excessive reliance because he failed to anticipate the possibility of breach and to mitigate his damages accordingly.

[21] The problem of speculative profits is discussed in CHARLES J. GOETZ & ROBERT E. SCOTT, *Liquidated Damages, Penalties and the Just Compensation Principle: Some Notes on an Enforcement Model and a Theory of Efficient Breach*, 77 COLUM. L. REV. 554 (1977).

reliance than the actual harm, then restricting compensation to nonspeculative damages reduces the incentive to over-rely.[22]

Restraining reliance is the main form of promisee's precaution against breach. Besides reliance, another form of precaution involves the promisee co-operating with the promisor to make performance more likely. Thus Yvonne could help Xavier to complete the building on time by influencing the city inspectors who issue building permits. Perfect compensation for breach gives the promisee no incentive to cooperate with the promisor in order to make performance more likely. In this respect, the effect of perfect compensation for breach on the promisee's cooperation is like the effect of perfect compensation for an accident on the victim's precaution.

Moreover, stipulated damages do not solve this incentive problem. A perfectly compensatory liquidated damages clause leaves Yvonne indifferent between performance and breach, so she has no incentive to take costly measures to reduce Xavier's probability of breaching. As compensation for breach diminishes, however, Yvonne's incentives to cooperate with Xavier increase. Reducing damages by under-liquidation, or reducing expected damages by the contract doctrines discussed above, thus ameliorate the problem of under-cooperation by the promisee. (Chapters 7 and 8 discuss two innovative contracts to solve the compensation paradox: Anti-Insurance and Decreasing-Liability Contracts.[23])

E. Nuisance

In discussing tortious accidents, our example was a railroad train emitting sparks that sometimes burned a farmer's fields. Instead of describing such fires as tortious accidents, however, the farmer might have described the sparks as a nuisance. The choice of description has no effect on the nonlegal aspects of the situation, such as the need for bilateral precaution, but there is a difference in the legal remedy. The traditional remedy for tortious accidents is compensatory damages, while the traditional remedy for nuisance in property law is injunctive relief.

When the remedy is injunctive, the paradox of compensation cannot arise. Nonetheless, injunctions have efficiency problems. An injunction is a coercive order issued by a court. Assuming a failure in private negotiations by the disputants, if a coercive order is to be efficient, it must demand efficient

---

[22] For the argument that various fault-based rules in contract law mitigate the promisee's over-reliance problem, see GEORGE M. COHEN, *The Fault Lines in Contract Damages*, 80 VA. L. REV. 1225, 1245-1316 (1994).

[23] In various jurisdictions, mostly outside the U.S., a comparative fault defense applies in contract law. One of the justifications for this defense is that it provides incentives to the promisee to cooperate and restrain reliance, even if this is at the expense of the promisor's efficient incentives. See ARIEL PORAT, *A Comparative Fault Defense in Contract Law*, 107 MICH. L. REV. 1397 (2009).

behavior. However, the authorities who issue the order may be too remote from the facts to know what behavior is efficient, or they may not be motivated to demand it.

The preceding argument recapitulates a critique of regulation frequently made by economists. A regulation is a coercive order issued by a government agency. People subject to a regulation are likely to possess information that the regulator needs to identify the correct command, but it may be difficult for the regulator to obtain this information. The cost of gathering such information is especially high because the people who possess it gain from not divulging the truth. "Command and control" regulation requires too much information, as well as disinterestedness, on the part of regulators.

Economists often urge regulators to enable the parties with information and motivation to work out the best course of action among themselves. Nuisances should be remedied by private bargaining, a view that has been developed at length in the continuing commentary on the Coase Theorem.[24] The central conclusion of this literature is that private bargaining among a small number of people with well-defined rights usually has an efficient outcome. Experimental evidence also suggests that breakdowns are rare in two-person bargaining games with clear stakes but are more common when several people must agree.[25]

These conditions—small numbers of bargainers and well-defined rights— are often satisfied in nuisance disputes. The harmful externality is often limited

---

[24] See COASE, *supra* note 5; GUIDO CALABRESI & A. DOUGLAS MELAMED, *Property Rules, Liability Rules, and Inalienability: One View of the Cathedral*, 85 HARV. L. REV. 1089 (1972); COOTER, *supra* note 2; LOUIS KAPLOW & STEVEN SHAVELL, *Property Rules Versus Liability Rules: An Economic Analysis*, 109 HARV. L. REV. 713 (1996). The Coase Theorem proposes that "the structure of the law which assigns property rights and liability does not matter so long as transaction costs are nil; bargaining will result in an efficient outcome no matter who bears the burden of liability." COOTER, *supra* note 2, at 14.

[25] See ELIZABETH HOFFMAN & MATTHEW L. SPITZER, *The Coase Theorem: Some Experimental Tests*, 25 J. L. & ECON. 73 (1982). The number of affected people should influence the willingness of courts to give injunctive relief. Courts have sometimes relaxed the traditional right to injunctive relief in nuisance cases affecting many people and awarded damages instead. See, e.g., *Spur Indus. v. Del E. Webb Dev. Co.* 494 P. 2d 700 (1972) (injunction granted, but conditioned on plaintiffs' indemnification of defendant's reasonable costs); *Boomer v. Atlantic Cement Co.* 257 N.E. 2d 870 (1970) (injunction granted to enjoin nuisance, but conditioned on defendant's payment of damages). However, bargaining can break down for strategic reasons, even when only a few people are involved.

The proposition that people cannot cooperate even in simple bargaining situations, which is the antithesis of the Coase Theorem, has been called the "Hobbes Theorem." See COOTER, *supra* note 2. Hobbes apparently thought that a sovereign, having power sufficient to coerce everyone and to resist attempts to coerce him, was required to preserve peace among his squabbling subjects. The implication is that people cannot spontaneously cooperate for mutual advantage because they always fall to quarreling over the division of the cooperative surplus.

to contiguous pieces of real estate, and thus a small number of affected property owners. Noise, foul odors, and pollution diminish rapidly with distance from the source. The owners of property contiguous to the nuisance, who are the ones substantially harmed by it, often number only a few.

For some kinds of nuisance the rights are well-defined, and contiguity keeps the number of affected parties small, suggesting that private bargaining will solve the problem. The central claim of the Coase Theorem is that private bargaining will achieve efficiency regardless of who is assigned the well-defined rights, because the rights will be bought and sold until the final owner values them more than anyone else. It does not matter from an efficiency perspective whether the injurer has the right to make a nuisance or the victim has right to enjoin it. To illustrate, if the law gives the injurer the right to create a nuisance, and the victim values freedom from the nuisance more than the injurer values his right to create the nuisance, then the victim can always buy the right from the injurer. Conversely, if the law gives the victim the right to enjoin a nuisance, and the injurer values the ability to make a nuisance more than the victim values being free from it, then the injurer can always buy the right from the victim.[26]

One purpose of the remedy of injunctive relief in nuisance cases is to strengthen the bargaining position of victims. The right to an injunction enables victims to bargain from a position of strength. If victims have the right to enjoin a nuisance, they will not accept an injurer's settlement offer unless it involves a combination of abatement and compensation that the victims prefer to an injunction. In economic jargon, the right to injunctive relief establishes the victims' threat point in bargaining; the injurer cannot induce the victims to settle unless the terms of the cooperative solution benefit the victims more than the advantage they derive from exercising their threat.

Because of private bargaining, the right to injunctive relief against nuisances offers the potential for combining compensation with efficiency. However, these two goals are usually not achieved unless the parties settle. Exercising the right to an injunction usually indicates a breakdown in the bargaining process. When bargaining breaks down, an injunction cannot cause efficient behavior unless the coercive order prescribes it, which is unlikely given the court's limited information. Consequently, from an efficiency perspective, injunction is an appropriate remedy for classes of cases in which settlement is usual and trials are rare. From this perspective, therefore, injunctive rights are socially desirable creations in inverse proportion to the frequency with which they are exercised.

---

[26] Of course, giving the legal right in the first instance to the party who values it most saves the cost of a transaction.

F. Summary and Conclusion

For many types of harm, efficiency requires precaution by both injurer and victim. Incentives for precaution are efficient when both parties bear the harm caused by their marginal reductions in precaution (double responsibility at the margin). A rule of strict liability erodes the victim's incentives for precaution, whereas a rule of no liability erodes the injurer's incentives for precaution. Liability uses three mechanisms to combine compensation and incentives for efficient precaution. The first mechanism is the fault rule. Under the ideal negligence rule, the injurer takes efficient precaution to avoid legal responsibility and the victim takes efficient precaution because she bears residual responsibility.

The second mechanism is invariant damages. A liquidation clause in a contract stipulates a dollar amount to be paid as compensation in the event of breach.[27] When damages are liquidated, the breaching party is responsible for the stipulated damages and the victim of the breach is responsible for actual damages. Thus, invariant damages encourage double responsibility at the margin—the promisor balances the cost of precaution against the stipulated damages and the victim balances the benefits of reliance against the potential loss. But liquidation of damages does not give the promisee an incentive to help the promisor to perform.

The third mechanism is a coercive order from a court, such as an injunction against a nuisance. Economists are unenthusiastic about coercive orders for reasons developed at length in the critique of regulation. However, the right to an injunction may have desirable economic effects if it is used as a bargaining chip rather than actually exercised.[28] The right to obtain an injunction may enable nuisance victims to achieve adequate compensation by private agreement with the injurer, and the parties to the bargain can both benefit by making its terms efficient.

Fault rules are prominent in tort law, invariant damages are frequently found in contracts, and injunctions are a common remedy in nuisance law. However, each of the three mechanisms can be found in other branches of the law. For example, workers' compensation law stipulates damages for accidents, and specific performance provides an injunctive remedy for breaches of contract. These three legal mechanisms solve the paradox of compensation most of the time. The next chapter describes a contractual mechanism that could solve it perfectly, except that these contracts do not exist—not yet.

---

[27] This is an idealized liquidation clause. Often the contract will instead contain clauses that stipulate how damages are to be computed in the event of a breach, rather than stipulating an exact dollar amount.

[28] ROBERT COOTER, STEPHEN MARKS & ROBERT MNOOKIN, *Bargaining in the Shadow of the Law: A Testable Model of Strategic Behavior*, 11 J. LEGAL STUD. 225 (1982) develops the theory of dispute resolution through bargaining, while HOFFMAN & SPITZER, *supra* note 25, provide empirical evidence on bargaining experiments conducted in the laboratory setting.

Anti-Insurance

Distrust defeats many business deals like this one.

Example 1: Warranty for Transmission on Used Car. Buyer offers to buy a used car from Seller, provided that Seller repairs the transmission and provides a one-year warranty (a promise to pay for replacing the transmission if it fails within one year). Seller replies that Buyer might abuse a warranted transmission by racing the car. Buyer proposes that abuse of the transmission should void the warranty. Seller rejects this proposal as useless because he could not prove Buyer's abuse. Seller offers a three-month warranty, Buyer rejects the offer, and no sale occurs.

A short warranty erodes Seller's incentives to install a good transmission, and a long warranty erodes Buyer's incentive to use the transmission carefully. This is the paradox of compensation. A clause voiding the warranty for abuse cannot solve the problem unless it is easily verifiable in court.

When several actors affect a risk, efficient incentives require each of them to bear the full risk.[1] Specifically, when promisor and promisee affect the probability or magnitude of the contract's breach, efficient incentives require each of them to bear 100 percent of the resulting harm, so their total risk sums to 200 percent. Liability law cannot solve this problem because the parties' total risk sums to 100 percent. Conditional liability, such as voiding the warranty for abuse of the transmission, cannot solve the problem when some relevant acts are unobservable and unverifiable. Unobservable and unverifiable acts often block conventional solutions to the paradox of compensation.

A novel contract could solve the problem. Under the novel contract, which we call "Anti-Insurance," the promisor who fails to perform as promised owes

---

[1] One could imagine a legal regime under which damages for breach of contract are collected by the government. Such taxation of transactions will improve incentives to perform, to restrain reliance and assist performance, but at the same time it will reduce incentives to enter into contracts. *Cf.* Nuno Garoupa & Chris William Sanchirico, *Decoupling as Transactions Tax*, 39 J. Legal Stud. 469 (2010).

damages to a third party, not to the promisee.[2] In example 1, Third Party purchases Buyer's right to damages from Seller for transmission failure. Third Party pays for the liability right before anyone knows whether or not the transmission will fail. If the transmission fails, Buyer will not receive any compensation. This fact gives Seller confidence that Buyer will not abuse the transmission. If the transmission fails, Seller must pay damages to Third Party. This fact gives Buyer confidence that Seller will supply a good transmission.

Liability to the third party makes the promisor internalize the costs of breach, so the promisor has efficient incentives to perform. No damages for the promisee makes her internalize the costs of promisor's breach, so she has efficient incentives to restrain reliance and assist performance.[3] By improving incentives, anti-insurance increases the value of the underlying transaction. The increase in the transaction's value can be divided among the three participants so that each of them expects to gain. Later we provide a numerical example in which anti-insurance benefits all three parties.

Anti-insurance inverts insurance. In an insurance contract, the insurer reduces the insured's risk, thus weakening the insured's incentive to take precaution. Thus when an insurance company assumes the car owner's risk of theft, the owner has less incentive to prevent theft. In an anti-insurance contract, the anti-insurer increases the anti-insured's risk, thus strengthening the anti-insured's incentive to take precautions. Compared to a traditional warranty, on which the parties in example 1 were unable to come to terms, anti-insurance increases the risk of transmission failure borne by Buyer. Generalizing, anti-insurance is a third-party contract that increases the promisee's loss from nonperformance without reducing promisor's costs of nonperformance. Anti-insurance strengthens incentives for precaution by magnifying risk, whereas insurance erodes incentives by spreading risk.

When anti-insurance imposes the *full* value of a shared risk on everyone who can affect it, anti-insurance makes everyone internalize the risk as required for efficient incentives. In example 1, anti-insurance makes Seller pay the full

---

[2] For a contract allowing a third party to collect damages in case of a breach, see *The N. O. St. Joseph's Association v. Magnier* (1861) 1861 La. Lexis 206. In that case hatters agreed to close stores on Sunday, and stipulated that any hatter violating the agreement should pay a fine of $100 to the asylum of the St. Joseph's Orphans. The court refused to enforce that latter clause. In the diamond industry, arbitrators may sometimes impose sanctions on the party in breach involving not only compensation to the aggrieved party but also a donation to charity. See LISA BERNSTEIN, *Opting Out of the Legal System: Extralegal Contractual Relations in the Diamond Industry*, 21 J. LEGAL STUD. 115, 134-5 (1992). For a suggestion that under certain circumstances large liquidated damages would be paid to a third party instead of to the aggrieved party, see CHARLES R. KNOEBER, *An Alternative Mechanism to Assure Contractual Reliability*, 12 J. LEGAL STUD. 333 (1983).

[3] Sometimes nonlegal sanctions create the same incentives. See *infra* chapter 11 (Nonlegal Sanctions); ARIEL PORAT, *Enforcing Contracts in Dysfunctional Legal Systems: The Close Relationship Between Public and Private Orders*, 98 MICH. L. REV. 2459 (2000).

risk of transmission failure to Third Party, and Buyer also pays the full cost of replacing the transmission. Seller internalizes the full risk and so does Buyer.

Instead of internalization, an alternative approach directly controls the acts that affect a risk. To illustrate direct control in example 1, Buyer could promise to keep the gears lubricated, not to shift gears roughly, not to accelerate too fast, etc. Seller, however, cannot observe and verify Buyer's performance of these promises. That is why the transaction failed in example 1. In contrast, the anti-insurer can probably observe and verify transmission failure. Verifying the fact of loss is often easier than verifying its cause. Internalizing a joint risk by anti-insurance often carries lower transaction costs than contracting over the acts that significantly affect it.

A. Numerical Example

The following example will show how anti-insurance works. Assume the promisee pays the promisor 90 for a promise whose performance creates 100 in value for the promisee. In the event of nonperformance, the contract requires the promisor to return the purchase price of 90 to the promisee and to pay expectation damages of 10. With performance or breach, the promisee's net gain from the contract equals 10. However, the promisor's cost of performance can be small or large, depending on uncontrollable events. When the cost of performance is small, the promisor performs. Specifically, with probability .6, performance costs the promisor 80. Sometimes, however, performance is prohibitively expensive. When the cost of performance is large, the promisor breaches and pays damages. Specifically, with probability .4, performance costs more than 100, so the promisor breaches and pays damages. Promisor's expected net gain from the contract equals $.6(90 - 80) + .4(90 - 100) = 2$.

The promisee can assist or not assist the promisor's performance. Assistance increases the probability that the promisor's cost of performance will be small. Specifically, promisee's assistance increases the probability from .6 to .8 that performance costs the promisor 80. With promisee's assistance, promisor's expected net gain from the contract equals $.8(90 - 80) + .2(90 - 100) = 6$. Thus assistance increases the promisor's expected net gain from 2 to 6.

The contract, however, provides an incentive for the promisee *not* to assist the promisor. Assistance costs the promisee 1. The promisee receives 100 in value from performance of the contract and 100 in damages from nonperformance of the contract, so the promisee loses 1 from assisting. Gaining the surplus requires modifying the contract so the promisee has an incentive to assist the promisor.

To solve the problem directly, the promisee could promise to assist the promisor. At a cost of 1, the promisee's assistance increases the promisor's expected net value of the contract from 2 to 6. Thus the promisee's assistance creates a surplus of 3. To share the surplus, the promisor could pay 2 to the promisee in exchange for the promise of assistance. In practice, such a promise is often ineffective because it cannot be enforced. It is unenforceable because promisee's assistance is unobservable by the promisor and unverifiable in court.

A direct solution to the problem of promisee's assistance is impractical, but anti-insurance can solve the incentive problem indirectly. To supplement the primary contract, the promisor and the promisee need to contract with an anti-insurer. Recall that promisee's assistance creates a surplus of 3. Let's calculate the terms of the anti-insurance contract that would divide the surplus of 3 equally among the parties.[4] In the anti-insurance contract, the anti-insurer and promisor pay a price to the promisee and she assigns her right to damages in the event of the promisor's breach to the anti-insurer. To divide the surplus created by the anti-insurance contract equally among the promisor, promisee, and anti-insurer, each must gain 1. A straightforward calculation shows that each gains 1 when the promisee assigns her liability right to the anti-insurer in exchange for a payment of 1 by the anti-insurer and a payment of 3 by the promisee.[5] Figure 7.1 depicts this anti-insurance contract.

Our example assumes that the parties have equal bargaining power and they divide the surplus equally. If the anti-insurance market were perfectly competitive, however, the anti-insurer would lack bargaining power, because competition would drive the price of anti-insurance down to its cost. Assuming that perfect competition deprives the anti-insurer of bargaining power, promisor and promisee in the numerical example will divide the profits that otherwise go to the anti-insurer. To achieve this result, the anti-insurer pays the promisee 2 for the liability right, and the promisor pays the promisee 2.5 for agreeing to the anti-insurance contract, as depicted in figure 7.2.

B. Propositions—Anti-Insurance vs. Controls

What generalizations underlie this example? Several acts by different actors typically affect the probability and extent of a risk. Distinguish these acts into two types by their legal consequences. Acts with legal or contractual sanctions

---

[4] An equal division of the surplus is the Nash bargaining solution.

[5] With anti-insurance, the promisee receives no damages in the event of breach, so the promisee will assist the promisor in order to reduce the probability of breach. The anti-insurance contract will induce the promisee to assist the promisor and the probability of breach will equal .2. With breach, the promisor returns the price of 90 to the promisee, and pays 10 in additional damages. The expected value of a liability right to 10 with probability .2 is $.2 \times 10 = 2$. With anti-insurance, the promisee assigns a liability right to the anti-insurer that is worth 2. To net a gain of 1, the anti-insurer must pay 1 for the liability right. The promisor gains the promisee's assistance, which increases his value of the contract by 4. To net a gain of 1, he must pay 3 for assistance. Summing the payments of 1 by the anti-insurer and 3 by the promisor, a total of 4 is paid to the promisee. In exchange for 4, the promisee gives up a liability right that is worth 2 and she provides assistance that costs 1, for a net gain of 1.

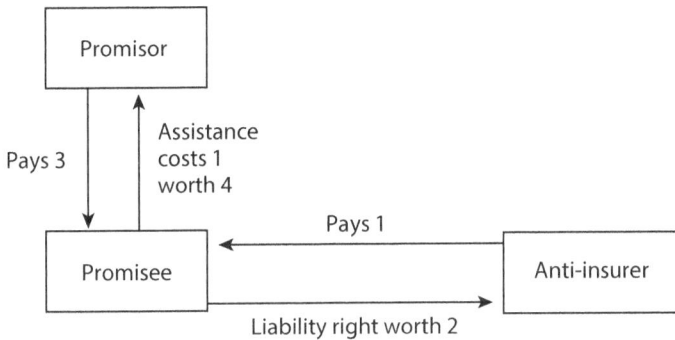

FIGURE 7.1. Contract with Anti-insurance

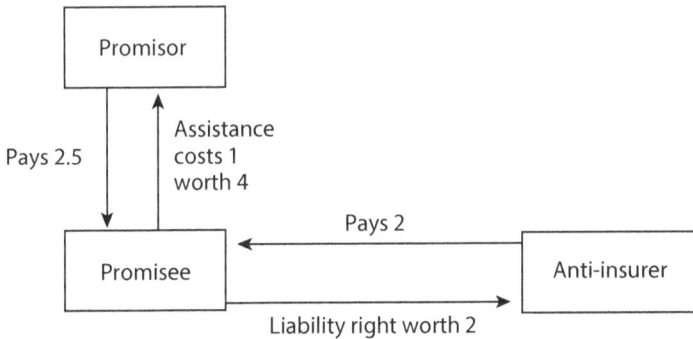

FIGURE 7.2. Perfectly Competitive Anti-insurance Contract

attached to them are legally *controlled*. Acts without legal or contractual sanctions attached to them are legally *uncontrolled*. In our numerical example, the promisor's performance is legally controlled, and the promisee's assistance is legally uncontrolled.

The distinction between controlled and uncontrolled acts relates to two ways that contracts can affect risk. The first alternative is to control the acts by a stipulation in the contract. In example 1, the risk of transmission failure increases as Buyer continues to drive the car. The number of miles driven is easily read off the speedometer. So Seller might warrant the transmission for 10,000 miles. This warranty helps to control how far Buyer drives. Seller, however, cannot easily observe and verify Buyer's hard driving, such as shifting gears quickly and accelerating rapidly, so these acts are not controllable by law or contract.

The second alternative is to make the actors who significantly affect a risk internalize its social cost. Internalization, which implies that each actor pays 100 percent of the social cost of the risk, creates efficient incentives for all the acts that affect a risk, regardless of whether they are controlled or uncontrolled.

Anti-insurance is the contractual device to make several actors internalize the social cost of a risk affected by each of them. Thus anti-insurance provides Buyer with efficient incentives for every act that affects the transmission, including less driving, shifting gears smoothly, accelerating moderately, and keeping the gears greased.

The first proposition expresses a familiar tautology about the meaning of "internalization."

> *Proposition 1*: Assume that an actor bears the cost of his own acts that affect a risk. Internalization of the risk of harm by the actor gives him efficient incentives to affect the risk.

Instead of internalizing risk, the actors who affect a risk often share its cost. Risks are shared by definition when they sum to 100 percent. Examples of sharing rules include liability of injurer to victim for the full harm, liability for part of the harm, and liability for none of the harm. In the presence of uncontrolled acts by the parties that affect the risk, all of these rules are inefficient.

> *Proposition 2*: Assume that actors bear the cost of their own acts that affect a risk. Any rule for sharing the risk of harm among the actors provides one or more of them with inefficient incentives to affect the risk.

Proposition 2 implies the inefficiency of the rules of no liability, strict liability, and shared liability. Proposition 2 also implies that any contract among the parties who create a risk cannot give all of them efficient incentives. A contract among the parties can only share losses, whereas efficiency requires magnifying losses. Magnifying losses requires introducing an outsider into the bargain—the anti-insurer.

This point can be expressed in terms of the budget constraint on a contract. Cooperation in a risky activity creates a potential surplus, which the parties can divide among themselves. Assume that cooperation by the promisor and promisee will yield a surplus of 200 with probability .5. If the surplus materializes, the parties can divide it among themselves. When dividing the surplus, the parties' payoffs must sum to 200, which is their "budget constraint." Internalizing the risk, however, requires their payoffs to sum to 400, which implies breaking their budget constraint. Breaking the budget constraint requires a third party, such as an anti-insurer, to inject more money for the parties to share. (This point about the budget constraint was made by Holmstrom in a model with a principal and several agents.[6])

---

[6] ". . . group incentives alone can remove the free-rider problem. Such incentives require penalties that waste output or bonuses that exceed output. In both cases the principal is needed, either to enforce the penalties or to finance the bonuses. Thus, the principal's primary role is to break the budget-balancing constraint." See B. HOLMSTROM, *Moral Hazard in Teams*, 13 THE BELL JOURNAL OF ECONOMICS 324, 325 (1982).

Anti-insurance provides efficient incentives by internalizing risk, not by legal controls on risk-taking. Instead of anti-insurance, a contract or law may try to achieve efficiency by legal controls on risk-taking. When an actor does not internalize a risk, efficient incentives require controlling *every* act that significantly affects the risk. When controls are used, however, *some* acts usually escape legal or contractual controls because they are unobservable by the potential plaintiff or unverifiable in court. Sharing rules, consequently, cannot control all forms of inefficient behavior. Given uncontrollable acts, proposition 2 implies the inefficiency of the rules of negligence, negligence with a defense of contributory or comparative negligence, and strict liability with a defense of contributory or comparative negligence.

Unlike controls, anti-insurance can overcome the inefficiencies of sharing rules. By definition, anti-insurance magnifies a risk so that every party to the contract internalizes it. When risk sharing distorts incentives, anti-insurance can correct the distortion by imposing the full cost of the risk on everyone who significantly affects it, as formulated in the following proposition.

Proposition 3: For any sharing rule, an anti-insurance contract can internalize the risk for the actors.

We can restate the relationship between controls and internalization in terms of transaction costs. To achieve efficiency, direct controls require all the people who significantly affect the risk to agree to contractual terms covering all the acts that affect it. All the acts of all the people must be observable and verifiable. To achieve efficiency, anti-insurance requires all the people who significantly affect a risk to contract with a third party. The realization of the risk must be observable and verifiable, not the acts that affect the risk. For many risks, a contract that covers all the acts that affect the risk is more costly than the alternative proposed here—namely, all the people who affect the risk contracting with an anti-insurer. The next proposition summarizes these facts.

Proposition 4: To choose between anti-insurance and direct controls, balance:

(a) the cost of observing and verifying the realization of the risk;
(b) the cost of observing and verifying the acts that influence the risk;
(c) the distortions created by direct controls due to uncontrollable acts.

With respect to the budget constraint, anti-insurance also has some structural similarity to an idea proposed by Barry Adler in an unpublished paper entitled *Avarice-Based Forfeiture* that was given at the American Law and Economics Association's annual meeting in 1998. Adler proposed a fund that would receive stochastic payments from parties to a contract based on outcome and transfer the expected amount of such payments to the parties regardless of outcome.

C. Scope for Anti-Insurance: Variables

How widely does anti-insurance apply? Here are some factors affecting its scope.

Observation and Verification Costs: Proposition 4 compares controls and anti-insurance as different approaches to managing risk. Enforcing a contract to control the acts that affect a risk requires observing and verifying these acts. Enforcing an anti-insurance contract requires observing and verifying the realization of the risk. Anti-insurance is especially attractive when the costs of observing and verifying the acts that affect the risk are high relative to the costs of observing and verifying the realized risk.

Attitudes toward risk: Most people are averse to risks involving a large proportion of their wealth, and they are not averse to risks involving a small proportion of their wealth. Insurance is attractive when people bear large risks relative to their wealth, and anti-insurance is attractive when people bear small risks relative to their wealth. Thus anti-insurance is attractive in example 1 because the cost of a transmission is small relative to the wealth of most car buyers.

Responsiveness to risk: The promisee can often decrease the expected loss from nonperformance of a contract by revealing information useful to the promisor, assisting the promisor's performance, avoiding over-reliance, and mitigating damages. The more promisees respond to risk, the larger the loss from spreading risk by insurance and the larger the gain from magnifying risk by anti-insurance. In example 1, the more car buyers harm transmissions in response to a warranty, the more a warranty costs and larger the gain from substituting anti-insurance for warranties. Conversely, the less the promisee or victim responds to risk or can influence it, the lower the gain from magnifying risk by anti-insurance.

Pricing costs: The anti-insurer has to figure out how much to pay for liability rights. Pricing a contingent commodity is a difficult actuarial problem whose costs usually fall with volume. Viable anti-insurance may require a large scale. In general, the need for a high volume of transactions to lower the costs per transaction presents an obstacle to the development of anti-insurance markets.

Adverse selection: Many people with a high probability of a claim seek insurance, which causes the premium to rise. Some people with a low probability of a claim respond to the rise in premiums by dropping their insurance, which causes another rise in premiums, and so forth. This process selects against quality in the market. Adverse selection occurs in insurance markets whenever the customers know more about their individual risks than the insurer knows.

The same problem occurs with anti-insurance. In an anti-insurance contract, the anti-insurer bargains with the promisor and promisee to acquire the promisee's liability right. The value of the promisee's liability right presumably differs from one case to another. One party to the bargain often knows less than others about its value. The relatively uninformed party, who lacks knowledge of the particular case, may rely on the average value of liability rights in similar cases. In these circumstances, the owners of liability rights with above-average value will tend to withhold them from sale, and the owners of liability rights with below-average value will tend to sell them. If the promisee and promisor know that the liability right is worth more than average, and if the anti-insurer does not know this, then the anti-insurer may offer the average price and the others may refuse to sell. The severity of the problem of adverse selection depends especially on the extent of the difference in information about liability rights among the parties. Thus the anti-insurance market suffers from the same selection against quality that occurs in markets for health insurance or used cars.

Victim's reporting problem: If the promisee transfers his liability right to the anti-insurer, then the anti-insurer must know when breach occurs in order to know when to assert a claim. If the anti-insurer cannot observe nonperformance, the anti-insurer may need to rely on promisee's report of harm to know when to assert a claim. The *victim's reporting problem* refers to the problem of inducing the promisee to report the promisor's nonperformance to the anti-insurer. In an illustration derived from the scenario in example 1, Anti-Insurer needs Buyer to report transmission failures so that Anti-Insurer can assert liability rights against Seller. Should Buyer's transmission fail, however, Buyer gains nothing from disclosing this information to Anti-Insurer.

To solve the victim's reporting problem, the promisee may promise to provide a report to the anti-insurer. In addition, the anti-insurer may pay the promisee a fixed fee or a percentage of damages for making a report. These payments correspond to deductibles or co-insurance in standard insurance contracts. To illustrate from the situation in example 1, Anti-Insurer might pay Buyer to provide evidence of transmission failure. Alternatively, instead of Anti-Insurer paying promisee to report nonperformance, the anti-insurance contract may require promisee to pay stipulated damages for failing to report nonperformance.

Changed circumstances and renegotiations: When circumstances change, the parties can sometimes benefit by renegotiating the contract. The renegotiated contract often allows the promisor to modify performance rather than performing as originally promised. Both parties can benefit from renegotiations in changed circumstances. When the anti-insurer acquires the promisee's liability right, however, a modification of the promise affects the anti-insurer as well as the promisor and promisee. Anti-insurance can cause a dispute over whether performance of the renegotiated contract equates to performance of the original contract, in which case damages are not owed, or nonperformance of the original contract, in which cases damages are owed. Since both the promisor and the promisee share the interest in depriving the anti-insurer of its right to damages, they have an incentive to make unproductive modifications that avoid breach of the original contract. Conversely, the promisor and promisee have an incentive not to make productive modifications that might count as breaching the original contract.

In principle, negotiations with the anti-insurer can overcome these distorted incentives, but a third party obviously complicates negotiations in practice. Consequently, if the need for contract modification is rare, anti-insurance works better than if the need for such modification is frequent. With stable circumstances the need for modification is rare, so stable circumstances favor anti-insurance. Automobiles are statistically predictable products, and the circumstances of their use seldom change in unforeseeable ways that vitiate anti-insurance.

Recontracting: The standard principal-agent model suffers from a particular recontracting problem identified by Grossman and Hart.[7] In the standard formulation, a risk-neutral principal puts an asset under the control of a risk-averse agent. The agent's effort, which is noncontractible, creates value.[8] Value materializes later. The efficient contract assigns the risk partly to the principal (because he is risk-neutral) and partly to the agent (so he exerts himself). Risk spreading and effort-incentives trade off. After the agent exerts himself, the effort-incentives have done their work and they are no longer needed. Consequently, the parties can gain by transferring all of the risk to the principal. Foreseeing the advantage of recontracting, however, undermines the effort-incentives in the original contract. When the agent decides how much to exert himself, he may foresee that he will subsequently rid himself of risk by recontracting, so he will exert himself less. To make the original contract work, the parties need to preclude future recontracting some way or another.

Anti-insurance has a similar problem. The anti-insurance contract magnifies risk to improve incentives. After the parties act, however, anti-insurance has done its work, so the parties may wish to purchase insurance in order to spread the risk. Foreseeing the purchase of insurance will undermine the incentives created by anti-insurance.

Fortunately, anti-insurance attenuates the recontracting problem for three reasons. First, unlike principal-agent models, anti-insurance does not have risk aversion at its core. Indeed, the simplest form of the anti-insurance model assumes risk-neutrality. With risk-neutrality, there is no reason to spread risk by recontracting. Second, no identified renegotiation moment exists in many anti-insurance contracts. To illustrate by example 1, there is no moment at which the driver stops putting the transmission at risk by stopping driving. Third, institutional barriers may prevent recontracting by raising its transaction costs.

Repeat transactions: Long-run relationships generally inhibit opportunistic behavior, which reduces the need for all contracts, including anti-insurance.

---

[7] See SANFORD J. GROSSMAN & OLIVER D. HART, *An Analysis of the Principal-Agent Problem*, 51 ECONOMETRICA 7 (1983).

[8] For example, see STEVEN SHAVELL, *Risk Sharing and Incentives in the Principal and Agent Relationship*, 10 BELL JOURNAL OF ECONOMICS 55 (1979).

Conversely, one-shot transactions increase the need for anti-insurance to improve promisees' incentives. To illustrate by example 1, high stakes and tentative relationships make used car sales notoriously opportunistic. Impersonal trade on a wide scale thus favors anti-insurance.

Collusion and Fraud: Like most three-party contracts, anti-insurance is susceptible to cheating when two parties collude against the third party. Three possibilities exist.

- First, collusion between promisor and promisee. The promisor has an incentive to breach the anti-insurance contract and to pay the promisee not to report the harm. In a modified version of example 1, for instance, Seller might offer to pay Buyer half the cost of repairing a broken transmission in exchange for not disclosing the transmission's failure to Anti-Insurer. Seller and Buyer then both benefit at the expense of Anti-Insurer. Collusion between promisor and promisee generally deprives the anti-insurer of the value of the liability right.[9]

- Second, collusion between promisee and anti-insurer. The anti-insurer may pay the promisee to reduce precautions and assistance, thus increasing the value of the liability right. In another version of example 1, Anti-Insurer might subsidize Buyer's participation in drag races. Or the anti-insurer and the promisee may secretly agree to divide between themselves the damages that the anti-insurer will collect from the promisor.[10] Collusion between promisee and anti-insurer generally deprives the promisor of the advantages of strong incentives for the promisee to reduce the probability and cost of nonperformance.

- Third, collusion between promisor and anti-insurer. The promisor might secretly pay the anti-insurer for a promise not to collect damages in case of harm to the promisee. In example 1, Anti-Insurer and Seller might secretly agree that in case of transmission failure Seller will pay little or nothing to Anti-Insurer. Consequently, Buyer would be purchasing the car under the mistaken belief that Seller has strong incentives to provide a good transmission. Collusion between promisor and anti-insurer generally deprives the promisee of the advantages of strong incentives for the promisor to reduce the risk of harm.

---

[9] Similarly, another way that the promisor might reduce the value of the liability right owned by the anti-insurer is by secretly paying the promisee to assist performance. To illustrate by example 1, Seller might offer to pay Buyer to drive fewer miles than planned.

[10] To illustrate by example 1, the anti-insurance contract signed by Buyer, Seller, and Anti-Insurer may stipulate that Anti-Insurer will give Buyer 10 percent of the value of any reported claim. Anti-Insurer gives Buyer 10 percent so Buyer has an incentive to report harm. In addition, a secret agreement between Buyer and Anti-Insurer may stipulate that Buyer by paying Anti-Insurer will acquire a right to more of the value of the reported claim, say 50 percent of that claim. After acquiring this right from Anti-Insurer, Buyer saves costs by reducing precaution and Seller's expected damages increase. If effective, the secret agreement decreases Buyer's incentives to care for the transmission, whereas Seller mistakenly supposes that Buyer has strong incentives for care.

The contract among the parties will contain terms to suppress collusion. At a minimum, collusion will breach the anti-insurance contract. In addition, collusion may involve torts or crimes that make the collusive agreement unenforceable and indeed punishable. Trust between the parties is a necessary condition for collusion. In example 1, assume that Seller pays Buyer for the promise not to report transmission failure to Anti-Insurer. This contract is illegal, so Buyer's promise is unenforceable. Seller runs the risk that Buyer might ask Seller for a second payment in exchange for another promise not to report the transmission failure. Seller also runs the risk that Buyer will take the money and then negotiate a reward from Anti-Insurer for reporting the transmission failure. Foreseeing all these risks, Seller will not collude with Buyer unless they trust each other.

Even if Seller trusts Buyer to keep his promise, other mechanisms may obstruct collusion. Unlike Buyer, Anti-Insurer probably does repeat business with Seller. Consequently, in colluding against Anti-Insurer Seller risks detection and destruction of a valuable business relationship. In addition, disclosure may ruin Seller's reputation and prevent contracts with other anti-insurers. Various disclosure mechanisms might serve to deter collusion, such as requiring Seller to disclose his account books to Anti-Insurer.

Parties can also reduce the risk of collusion by carefully choosing their business partners. Buyer might reduce the risk of collusion between Seller and Anti-Insurer by insisting that Anti-Insurer should be a large corporation with a valuable reputation among consumers or a corporation certified by a consumer organization.

D. Anti-Insurance for Losses: Examples

We have developed a general theory of anti-insurance, but much of its value resides in its applications. Example 2 is identical to example 1, except that the car is *new*, not used, which makes a big difference.

> *Example 2: Warranty for Transmission on New Car.* Manufacturer makes and sells new cars. As proof that transmission is well-designed and made, Manufacturer promises that the transmission will work for one year. Transmission failure within one year obligates Manufacturer to pay its replacement cost. Some buyers want Manufacturer to guarantee the transmission for three years, but Manufacturer knows that some buyers abuse a warranted transmission and abuse is not provable in court. To solve this problem, Manufacturer proposes a contract extending the liability right to three years and requiring Buyer to assign the liability right to Anti-Insurer, who offers to pay for the liability right.

The critical difference between used and new cars concerns individualized versus standardized quality. In example 1, Seller offers to repair the transmission of a used car for an individual buyer, whereas in example 2 Manufacturer supplies the same quality of transmission to all buyers. Manufacturer has a strong incentive to provide high quality transmissions when many buyers have anti-insurance, but any single buyer's anti-insurance has little influence on Manufacturer. Consequently, no individual buyer wants to pay for anti-insurance and all individual buyers want everyone else to pay for it. Since all buyers benefit from everyone having anti-insurance and no individual buyer wants to pay for it, the manufacturer may include anti-insurance in the bundle of non-negotiable terms of sale. In general, each buyer of a new, mass-produced product wants to "free-ride" on others' anti-insurance, and the seller can stop free-riding by a non-negotiable sale's terms.

Here is another example from a different kind of contract with the same advantages for anti-insurance as in example 1.

Example 3: At-Will Employment Contract for Unverifiable Work. Employer offers Worker an employment contract for one year. The contract stipulates that Employer can fire Worker for any reason or no reason after giving one month's notice. Worker is reluctant to accept these terms, since if he quits his present job in reliance on the new employment contract he would run too high a risk of getting fired from the new job.[11] To avoid this problem, Worker proposes to replace the "at will" clause with a "for cause" clause, which stipulates that Employer can only fire Worker for one of the causes enumerated in the contract such as insufficient effort at work. Employer refuses because "cause" is too hard to prove in court. Instead, Worker proposes retaining the "at will" clause and adding a clause stating that if Employer fires worker then Employer must pay damages to Anti-Insurer.

The motivation for anti-insurance in example 3, as in example 1, is to induce good behavior by the promisee when bad behavior is not provable in court. An important difference in the examples, however, is transaction costs. Employment contracts are more individually tailored, so the anti-insurer will have more difficulty deciding how much to pay for the promisee's liability rights. If, however, Employer is a large company with many employees, the transaction costs may be low enough to make the anti-insurance contract benefit everyone.

Next, we modify example 3 to illustrate a problem with mitigation of damages after breach of contract.

Example 4: At-Will Employment Contract When Efforts to Mitigate Damages Are Unverifiable. Worker asks Employer for a one-year employment contract requiring Employer to pay damages for firing Worker without cause. Employer refuses on grounds that a fired worker may increase the damages

---

[11] *Cf. Grouse v. Group Health Plan, Inc.* 306 N.W. 2d 114 (Minn. 1981).

by delaying the search for another job. Worker makes a counterproposal for Employer to pay damages for firing Worker to Anti-Insurer, not to Worker.

In this example, Employer fears that Worker will not mitigate in spite of a legal burden to mitigate. Anti-insurance solves the problem by creating incentives for the Employer not to fire the worker as well as for the worker to mitigate damages from being fired.

Now we turn to an example in which the promisee should assist performance and restrain reliance.

> *Example 5: Construction Contract.* Restaurateur wants Builder to promise to construct a larger facility by September 1 and to compensate Restaurateur for losses if construction is delayed. Builder refuses to make this promise because it will undermine Restaurateur's incentives to help Builder in procuring the required permits from city building inspectors in a timely fashion. Also, the promise would give Restaurateur an incentive to order too much food in advance of the scheduled September 1 opening. Restaurateur overcomes these objections by offering to assign his liability rights for Builder's late completion of the project to Anti-Insurer, who pays in advance for the liability rights.

In example 5, imposing a legal duty on Promisee to assist performance and restrain reliance is ineffective because it is unverifiable. In contrast, anti-insurance only requires the verifiability of completion of the building, which is easily observed.

E. Anti-Insurance for Gains

When several actors affect a risk, efficient incentives require each of them to bear the *full risk*. So far we have applied this proposition to the risk of losses, and now we apply it to the risk of gains.

> *Example 6: Agency Contract.* Principal and Agent need each other's cooperation and effort to sell business computers. Agent must locate interested buyers, and Principal must negotiate and tailor the contract to the buyers' needs. Total sales depend upon effort and luck. The current contract requires Principal to give 50 percent of profits from sales to Agent.[12] To incentivize both parties fully, Agent must receive 100 percent of value created by a sale and Principal must also receive 100 percent. To achieve this goal, the parties buy anti-insurance. Principal and Agent pay Anti-Insurer a fixed sum in advance of sales, and the Anti-Insurer matches dollar for dollar the revenue from sales. By matching all profits with anti-insurance, the Principal and Agent each receive 100 percent of the value created by their joint efforts.

---

[12] *Cf. Wood v. Lucy, Lady Duff-Gordon* 118 N.E. 214 (N.Y. 1917).

In this example, anti-insurance causes the Principal and Agent to internalize the entire profits from sales, so they work harder. Because expected profits increase, they can pay the anti-insurer enough in advance for everyone to benefit.

Now we state the precise difference between anti-insurance for gains and anti-insurance for losses. Anti-insurance for gains means that promisor and promisee pay the anti-insurer a flat fee in advance for his promise to pay them an amount equal to any gain that they subsequently realize. Anti-insurance for losses means that the anti-insurer pays a flat fee in advance for the promise of the promisor and promisee to pay him an amount equal to any loss that they subsequently realize. Mixed cases also arise when realizations can be positive or negative.

Here is an example from legal practice.

Example 7: The Law Firms. Two law firms work together for the plaintiff on a bodily injury case for a contingent fee. Firm A is responsible for proving liability, Firm B is responsible for establishing damages. Their effort is unobservable and unverifiable. With optimal effort by each of them, the probability is .30 that they will win the case and receive a fee of 200. Initially they agree to split their winnings equally, but then they realize that they have suboptimal incentives. Each firm will externalize half of the benefit associated with its effort, so self-interest compels each firm to exert effort until its marginal cost equals half of the resulting marginal gain to both of them. The probability will be .15 that they will win the case and receive a fee of 100. To improve incentives, they buy anti-insurance for gains. If they win the case, the anti-insurer pays them an amount equal to the fee. Now both parties have optimal incentives, so the probability is .30 that the anti-insurer will pay them 200. In exchange for anti-insurance, the two firms pay the anti-insurer 60 in advance, which is the anti-insurer's expected cost. The anti-insurer expects to break even (his expected costs are .30 × 200), and the two law firms expect their payoff to increase by 45. (Their payoff is .15 × 100 without anti-insurance, and −60 + .30 × 400 with anti-insurance.)

In example 7, anti-insurance for gains solves an incentive problem involving teamwork. Anti-insurance for gains is especially attractive in cooperative ventures when the surplus depends on behavior by both parties that is unobservable and unverifiable. The two law firms in example 7 face essentially the same problem as the plaintiff and the plaintiff's lawyer in many liability cases. The next example illustrates how anti-insurance can completely solve the attorney-client problem that contingent fees partially solve.[13]

[13] Polinsky and Rubinfeld solve the motivation problem for the plaintiff's lawyer (but not the plaintiff) by an alternative mechanism. Whereas anti-insurance raises the lawyer's payoff to the same fraction as his costs, specifically 100 percent, the Polinsky-Rubinfeld mechanism reduces the lawyer's costs to the same fraction as the lawyer's contingency. To illustrate: given a 30 percent contingency, the plaintiff and attorney pay an upfront fee to an "administrator" who promises to

Example 8: Attorney-Client Relationship. Success in a suit for damages requires attorney and client to put effort into winning the case. Attorney takes plaintiff's case on a contingent fee of 30 percent. Attorney will balance her costs of working on the case against 30 percent of the judgment, and the plaintiff will balance his costs of working on the case against 70 percent of the judgment. To maximize their expected joint payoff, however, each of them should balance his own costs against 100 percent of the judgment. Recognizing this, they enter into an anti-insurance contract. The anti-insurer promises to match the judgment dollar for dollar, so the plaintiff receives 100 percent of the judgment and the plaintiff's attorney also receives 100 percent of the judgment. In exchange, they pay the anti-insurer a flat fee at the beginning of the case. (In perfect competition with zero transaction costs, the flat fee equals the expected judgment.)

Will anti-insurance for gains work in the real world? We have previously explained the variables that affect the feasibility of anti-insurance for losses. These same variables affect the feasibility of anti-insurance for gains. Without repetitively discussing all of them, we focus here on the most important. In analyzing anti-insurance for losses, the victim's reporting problem formed a major obstacle. Recall the problem is that the promisee may under-report his losses to the anti-insurer. An analogous problem arises with anti-insurance for gains. Here the problem is that the two cooperators may over-report their gains, so the anti-insurer will pay them more than they are owed. This is the *beneficiary's reporting problem.*

Anti-insurance for gains also motivates cooperators to make side payments to induce excessive exertion, which transfers wealth from the anti-insurer to themselves. In example 7, Firm A and Firm B expect to receive money from the trial judgment, which we call the "product," and money from the anti-insurer, which we call the "transfer." Being rationally self-interested, Firm A works until another $1 worth of its exertion causes an increase of $1 in its expected payoff. This exertion by A also causes an increase of $1 in Firm B's expected payoff. Half of the joint gain of $2 comes from production and half comes from transfer. Since Firm A's effort costs $1 and produces $1, Firm A's effort is efficient. However, Firm B has an incentive to make a side payment to A in order to induce even more effort from Firm A. By doing so, Firm B can cause the anti-insurer to transfer more money to Firms B and A.

---

reimburse 70 percent of the attorney's costs. Thus the attorney balances 30 percent of the judgment against 30 percent of his costs. Like anti-insurance, market competition makes the whole thing work. Note that Polinsky and Rubinfeld's administrator must observe the lawyer's costs in order to pay 70 percent of them, whereas our anti-insurer must observe the judgment in order to pay 100 percent of it. See A. MITCHELL POLINSKY & DANIEL L. RUBINFELD, *Aligning the Interests of Lawyers and Clients,* 5 AM. L. ECON. REV. 165 (2003).

Significant obstacles, however, may prevent side payments. First, the inability of each party to observe the other's effort will also inhibit side payments for effort. Second, side payments between Firms A and B are a form of collusion that will violate the anti-insurance contract and possibly violate the law of torts and crimes. Collusion will trigger sanctions if detected, so collusion often requires more trust than the parties have in each other.

Another problem concerns pricing. With anti-insurance for losses, the anti-insurer has to figure out how much to pay for the promisee's liability rights. With anti-insurance for gains, the anti-insurer has to figure out how much to charge the cooperators for giving them entitlements. For losses or gains, pricing anti-insurance is a difficult institutional and actuarial problem.

F. Choosing between Anti-Insurance for Gains and Losses

Public finance economists recognize that taxes and subsidies can achieve identical incentive effects in principle, although they differ sharply in fact. The same is true of anti-insurance for losses and gains. Recall that "anti-insurance for gains" means that promisor and promisee pay the anti-insurer a flat fee in advance for his promise to pay them an amount equal to any gain that they subsequently realize. In contrast, "anti-insurance for losses" means that the anti-insurer pays a flat fee in advance for the promise of the promisor and promisee to pay him an amount equal to any loss that they subsequently realize. The following proposition states the equivalence theorem:

> *Proposition 5: Equivalence of Anti-Insurance for Gains and Losses.* For each efficient anti-insurance contract for gains there corresponds an efficient anti-insurance contract for losses, and vice versa.

The explanation of proposition 5 is straightforward. A risk has relatively good and bad realizations. For example, the promisor can perform or not perform. Adding or subtracting a constant number to the good and bad realizations does not change the difference between them, which measures the risk. Since the risk does not change, the rational actor's behavior does not change. (We implicitly assume that the losses and gains are small enough for the actors to remain risk-neutral.[14]) Subtracting a constant can change anti-insurance for gains into anti-insurance for losses, and adding a constant can change

---

[14] Strictly speaking, the constant that is added or subtracted to the possible realizations should be measured in utils (a theoretical unit of utility), not dollars. We rely on the fact that a Von Neumann-Morgenstern utility function can be transformed linearly without changing the optimal values. In practice, dollars can be added or subtracted rather than utils, provided that the risk is small enough for the actor to be risk-neutral.

anti-insurance for losses into anti-insurance for gains, without changing the behavior of promisor and promisee.

To illustrate, assume that the promisor's performance creates 100 for the promisee, and nonperformance creates 0. First, consider anti-insurance for gains, which doubles the gain of 100 from performance. To implement this result, the promisor and promisee pay the anti-insurer a fixed sum in advance, and the anti-insurer pays 100 to promisor in event of performance. In the event of nonperformance, no one pays anything to anyone. Specifically, the nonperforming promisor does not pay damages to the promisee. Promisor and promisee thus internalize the difference of 100 that is at risk, as required for efficient incentives.

Now consider the equivalent anti-insurance contract for losses, which doubles the loss of 100 from nonperformance. To implement this result, the anti-insurer pays promisor and promisee a fixed sum in advance. In the event of performance, no one pays anything to anyone. In the event of nonperformance, the promisee gets paid nothing and the promisor pays 100 to the anti-insurer. Promisor and promisee thus internalize the difference of 100 that is at risk, as required for efficient incentives.

In the preceding example, anti-insurance for gains pays the promisor and promisee (100,100) for performance and (0,0) for nonperformance. Subtracting the latter from the former yields (100,100). Equivalently, anti-insurance for losses pays (0,100) for performance and (−100,0) for nonperformance. Subtracting the latter from the former yields (100,100). Since the difference in payoffs between performance and nonperformance remains the same, anti-insurance for gains and anti-insurance for losses have the same incentive effects on risk-neutral actors.

Although, in theory, anti-insurance for gains can create the same incentive effects as anti-insurance for losses, the practical consequences are different because enforcement requires different information. First consider anti-insurance for gains. If the promisor performs, then anti-insurance for gains requires the promisor to observe and verify how much the promisee actually gained from the contract in order to collect the payment owed to him by the anti-insurer. Second, consider anti-insurance for losses. If the promisor fails to perform, then anti-insurance for losses requires the anti-insurer to observe and verify how much the promisee actually lost from nonperformance in order to collect the payment owed to him by the promisor.

Now we can state the difference in information required by the two kinds of anti-insurance. Anti-insurance for gains requires the promisor to know how much the promisee actually gained from performance that did occur. Here the anti-insurer must observe the actual payoff from performance and subtract the hypothetical payoff from nonperformance. In contrast, anti-insurance for losses requires the anti-insurer to know how much more the promisee would have gained from performance than she actually gained from nonperformance.

Here the anti-insurer must observe the actual payoff from nonperformance and subtract it from the hypothetical payoff from performance.

The parties should typically choose the preferred form of anti-insurance (for gains or for losses) depending on the relative cost of proving in court the gains from performance or losses from nonperformance. To return once again to the situation in example 1, relatively few transmissions fail, so verifying that a few transmissions failed is cheaper than verifying that many transmissions did not fail. Thus, in this situation, anti-insurance for losses will have lower transaction costs than anti-insurance for gains.

G. Anti-Insurance vs. Other Legal Devices

In the absence of anti-insurance, the law has some mechanisms to give incentives to the promisee without eroding the promisor's incentives. We will discuss mitigation of damages, foreseeability of damages, comparative fault, and liquidated damages. We will also explain why all of these mechanisms are deficient.

According to the mitigation of damages rule, the breaching party is not liable for damages that could have been reasonably mitigated by the aggrieved party. The promisee thus bears the burden of mitigating. Mitigation of damages can only occur after the promisee knows that a breach occurred.[15] Before breach, more reliance by the promisee increases the damage that breach will cause. The burden of mitigation does not extend backward in time to encompass reliance. Consequently, the burden of mitigation cannot solve incentive problems concerned with reliance.

Contract law has not developed a burden of reasonable reliance. Rather, contract law has developed the doctrine that plaintiffs are entitled to the foreseeable losses caused by breach. The burden of unforeseeable losses falls on the promisee unless he can shift them by giving notice to the promisor. This doctrine, which offers some restraint on reliance, stops far short of providing optimal incentives for reliance.[16]

The comparative fault defense, which is generally not recognized in the realm of American contract law, works differently.[17] Under the comparative fault rule, over-reliance before breach, or unreasonable failure to assist the promisor in performance, may reduce damages from breach.[18] This defense suffers, however, from one main drawback that makes it inferior to anti-insurance. It is

---

[15] E. ALLAN FARNSWORTH, CONTRACTS 778-83 (4th ed., 2004). The mitigation of damages defense applies also to anticipatory breaches. See RESTATEMENT (SECOND) OF CONTRACTS§ 350 cmt. f. (1981).

[16] See *supra* chapter 6.

[17] *See* ARIEL PORAT, *A Comparative Fault Defense in Contract Law*, 107 MICH. L. REV. 1397 (2009).

[18] PORAT, *id.*

effective only when the behaviors of both parties are observable and verifiable. Otherwise the comparative fault rule cannot supply efficient incentives to the parties. Anti-insurance is especially attractive when behavior that affects value is neither observable nor verifiable.

Another solution available in contract law is liquidated damages, which stipulate damages that the promisor must pay the promisee for breach, regardless of the magnitude of the promisee's actual loss. If liquidated damages equal the expected damages of breach, the promisor has efficient incentives to perform. At the same time, since his right to damages is not contingent on the magnitude of his actual harm, the promisee has efficient incentives to restrain reliance and mitigate damages. A rule of liquidated damages, however, erodes the promisee's incentives to assist the promisor's performance. Liquidated damages cannot solve the problem of the promisee's incentives to assist.[19]

Like anti-insurance, nonlegal sanctions often extract a price from the promise-breaker without giving damages to the promisee. Another way to improve the promisee's incentives is for the court to deduct nonlegal sanctions from damages owed by the promisor. We examine this possibility in a separate chapter.[20]

The inadequacy of legal mechanisms to solve the incentive problems of promisor and promisee leave wide scope for the development of anti-insurance.

H. Extensions

Until now we discussed anti-insurance for nonperformance of contracts. Now we will discuss briefly anti-insurance for torts. Our aim is to show how anti-insurance might replace some mandatory legal rules in principle. The law typically imposes strict liability for bodily injuries caused by defective consumer products. Strict product liability improves manufacturers' incentives and erodes consumers' incentives to take care.[21] If consumers significantly reduce the care they exercise in particular situations, the law could allow manufacturers to substitute anti-insurance for strict product liability. Specifically, law would transfer the liability rights of consumers to anti-insurers, and in exchange the anti-insurers would pay a fixed fee to consumers. When a defective product harmed a consumer, the manufacturers would pay compensatory damages to the anti-insurer. Anti-insurance would restore incentives for care by consumers, without eroding incentives for care by manufacturers.

In addition, anti-insurance for consumer product injuries would solve an insurance problem. People need insurance against medical costs and lost wages

---

[19] *Supra* chapter 6.

[20] *Infra* chapter 11.

[21] Strict product liability also creates adverse selection problems: see GEORGE L. PRIEST, *The Current Insurance Crisis and Modern Tort Law*, 96 YALE L. J. 1521 (1987).

resulting from bodily injuries. However, people do not need insurance against pain and suffering. No one buys pain and suffering insurance in the private market. According to Viscusi's data, pain and suffering decreases the marginal utility of money, so insuring against pain and suffering is irrational.[22] By awarding damages for pain and suffering, the tort system over-insures potential victims.[23] Anti-insurance could eliminate the pain and suffering component of damages. Instead of receiving money that is not needed when a person suffers pain, uninjured people could receive a payment from the anti-insurer in exchange for the liability right. (This form of anti-insurance would, in a sense, set up a market for unmatured tort claims.[24])

Now we turn from consumer product injuries to implied warranties. Sometimes the law reads a warranty into a contract regardless of whether or not the parties agreed to it, as with the implied warranty of merchantability.[25] Often the law does not allow the parties to get rid of an implied warranty. The law should sometimes allow sellers to substitute anti-insurance for implied warranties. Specifically, the law should allow substitution in cases where the implied warranty significantly erodes the promisee's incentives to avoid triggering the warranty.[26]

I. Why Are There Currently No Anti-Insurance Markets?

When several actors affect a risk, contract or liability law often divides the risk and requires them to share it. Internalizing the risk, however, requires each actor to bear it fully. Anti-insurance is the perfect market solution for

---

[22] W. KIP VISCUSI & WILLIAM N. EVANS, *Utility Functions That Depend on Health Status: Estimates and Economic Implications*, 80 THE AMERICAN ECONOMIC REVIEW 353-374 (1990).

[23] *Cf.* SAMUEL A. REA, *Nonpecuniary Loss and Breach of Contract*, 11 J. LEGAL STUD. 35 (1982).

An exception, which can be explained, is uninsured motorist insurance, which typically gives the insured the right to recover damages, including pain and suffering, caused by an uninsured motorist.

[24] ROBERT D. COOTER, *Towards a Market in Unmatured Tort Claims*, 75 VA. L. REV. 383 (1989). *Cf.* ROBERT NOZICK, ANARCHY, STATE, AND UTOPIA, 77 (1974), who suggested a system that would allow individuals to sell their estates' potential future rights to compensation to a company that would purchase many such rights. For analyzing questions of risk customization, and the desirability of departing from society's default risk allocations, with or without third parties, see LEE ANNE FENNELL, *Unbundling Risk*, 60 DUKE L.J. 1285 (2011). For an argument in favor of using a third-party mechanism in order to make contract modifications harder, see KEVIN E. DAVIS, *The Demand for Immutable Contracts: Another Look at the Law and Economics of Contract Modifications,* 81 N.Y.U. L. REV. 487, 529 (2006).

[25] JAMES J. WHITE & ROBERT S. SUMMERS, UNIFORM COMMERCIAL CODE, 360-9 (5th ed., 2000).

[26] For an insightful proposal for using commitment bonds (much beyond contract law), according to which the buyer of the bond will be entitled to recover money payment from the seller of the bond if the latter breaches his commitment (either to third parties or even to himself), and for comparing this mechanism to anti-insurance, see MICHAEL ABRAMOWICZ & IAN AYRES, *Commitment Bonds*, 100 GEORGETOWN L. J. 605 (2012).

internalizing risk. Anti-insurance, however, is a novel concept, not an active market. Why are there no anti-insurance markets? We can think of two possible obstacles in legal doctrine. First, anti-insurance might be regarded as a penalty clause in a contract. In fact, anti-insurance does not involve penalties. With anti-insurance, the promisor pays exactly for the harm caused by nonperformance, no more and no less. The aggrieved party is not compensated, because he assigned his compensation rights to a third party, which contract law allows. Second, anti-insurance might be regarded as a gambling contract that is unenforceable on grounds of public policy. In fact, the anti-insurer is not a gambler but rather someone who increases the value of contracts by improving incentives.

If there are no legal obstacles, what are the nonlegal barriers? Three general factors reduce the scope for anti-insurance. First, when several actors affect a risk, but one actor affects it far more than the others, making one actor bear all the risk approximates efficient incentives. To illustrate, expectation damages creates efficient incentives for the promisor and inefficient incentives for the promisee, but the inefficiency is unimportant if the promisee cannot over-rely and cannot assist performance. Second, some nonmarket mechanisms reduce the need for anti-insurance by magnifying risk in business and law. Business examples include such simple devices as company prizes for employees[27] and replacing equity financing with debt financing.[28] Legal examples of risk magnification include processes whereby a losing defendant pays damages to a third party instead of paying the plaintiff.[29] Third, in a parallel with insurance markets, various forms of adverse selection and moral hazard impede anti-insur-

---

[27] To illustrate based on example 7, the law firm responsible for proving liability might merge with the law firm responsible for proving damages, and then the senior partners might offer large bonuses to the two teams in the event that they win the suit.

[28] More debt increases the risk that managers will lose the company through bankruptcy, hostile takeover, or special financing arrangement. Loss of the company magnifies the loss from lower stock values. To illustrate, assume that two people finance a new company themselves and the company is solvent. If each of them owns half of the stock, then each one bears half of the cost when one of them shirks. If, however, they borrow heavily, then shirking by either of them risks the loss of the company by both of them. So debt financing helps to discourage managerial shirking. For a novel financing proposal with some resemblance to anti-insurance, see GEORG NOLDEKE & KLAUS M. SCHMIDT, *Sequential Investments and Options to Own*, 29 RAND J. ECON. 633 (1998).

[29] Some organizations assess fines that must be paid to a charity. The National Basketball Association's Collective Bargaining Agreement contains such provisions. See Article VI, section 6 of the NATIONAL BASKETBALL ASSOCIATION'S COLLECTIVE BARGAINING AGREEMENT, at http://www.nbpa.org/cba/2005/article-vi-player-conduct. Class action settlements also sometimes involve payments to charities. *Cf. Howe v. Townsend (In re Pharm. Indus. Average Wholesale Price Litig.)* 588 F. 3d 24 (U.S. App. 2009); *McKinnie v. JP Morgan Chase Bank, N.A.* 678 F. Supp. 2d 806 (U.S. Dist. 2009); *Cohen v. Warner Chilcott Ltd. Co.,* 522 F. Supp. 2d 105 (U.S. Dist. 2007). For more examples, see ROBERT W. WOOD, *Resolving Litigation by Payments to Charity,* 109 TAX NOTES 633 (2005). Decoupling to improve plaintiff's incentives to sue is analyzed in A. MITCHELL POLINSKY & YEON-KOO CHE, *Decoupling Liability: Optimal Incentives for Care and Litigation,* 22 RAND J. ECON. 562 (1991).

ance markets. (We suggested above that the most serious form is the victim's reporting problem.)

While these three factors reduce the scope for anti-insurance, they do not explain its total absence. Perhaps the history of insurance provides the answer. Most forms of contemporary insurance were unknown in the nineteenth century. Lack of demand cannot explain this fact. People were presumably just as risk-averse then as now. There is little reason to think that people valued risk spreading more as they became richer. (Just the opposite is true.) Instead, the explanation must be that insurance markets are fragile because they are so susceptible to abuse. After decades (even centuries) of development and innovation, insurers eventually overcame these problems. Specifically, insurers developed better actuarial methods to price insurance, a wider market reduced transaction costs, and insurers developed better methods to limit the destructive scope of moral hazard and adverse selection.

Like insurance, anti-insurance is fragile and susceptible to abuse. Perhaps anti-insurance markets await better actuarial methods to price liability rights, a wide market to reduce transaction costs, and good methods to solve the victim's reporting problem. Working out the institutional forms will take time. We believe that promising market opportunities exist, notably for goods susceptible to consumer misuse (e.g., automobile transmissions), and goods or service contracts requiring the buyer's cooperation (e.g., building construction). We also believe that opportunities exist to improve the law, such as allowing sellers to substitute anti-insurance for implied warranties in some consumer transactions, and allowing manufacturers to substitute anti-insurance for strict product liability in some circumstances. Perhaps the necessary institutional innovations to sustain anti-insurance markets will appear in the twenty-first century. In any case, the prospects for anti-insurance markets will improve substantially after more people appreciate the concept.

8

Decreasing Liability Contracts
and the Assistant Interest

The anti-insurance contract discussed in the preceding chapter solves a basic incentive problem that we call the paradox of compensation, but, alas, anti-insurance is unavailable in the market. Existing contractual forms sometimes mitigate the compensation paradox, notably in contracts whose performance occurs in phases. In phased contracts, the promisor sinks more expenditure into performance as time passes and less expenditure remains. Consider this example:

> *Example1: Promisor's Sunk Costs.* Buyer and Developer make a contract in which Buyer immediately pays Developer 90 for the latter's promise to construct a building that Buyer values at 100. Developer spends 40 on architectural drawings and a concrete foundation, which cannot be recovered or reused. Developer then defaults. Buyer fails to find an alternative builder and abandons the project without receiving any benefit from it. Should Developer's liability to Buyer equal 100 or 60?

Under prevailing law, liability for breach of a phased contract equals promisee's expected value of performance minus benefit conferred by part performance.[1] In example 1, partial performance confers no benefits to Buyer, so Seller is liable for the entire loss of 100, regardless of when he breaches. Liability remains constant throughout the contract's phases.

Liability for breach, however, should ideally decrease throughout the phases of a contract, regardless of whether partial performance conferred benefits to the promisee. Compared to constant liability, a *decreasing liability contract* often improves incentives for two reasons. First, in many circumstances, the promisor will breach or perform depending on which is cheaper. When performance occurs in phases, less expenditure remains as time passes. Since the cost of

---

[1] RESTATEMENT (SECOND) OF CONTRACTS §347, Comment b (1981); E. ALLAN FARNSWORTH, CONTRACTS 775-6 (4th ed., 2004). Sometimes the promisee suffers other losses such as consequential losses, that we do not discuss here. Courts should award damages for those losses under either prevailing contract law or a decreasing liability legal regime.

completing performance falls with time, lower damages are typically sufficient to induce performance. This is true regardless of whether or not partial performance created any benefit. Second, promisee can often increase the probability of performance or lower its costs by assisting promisor. Buyer in example 1 may assist Developer in obtaining construction permits or reveal useful information after the contract was made. Reducing damages increases the promisee's incentives to assist performance by the promisor.

The two reasons given above imply that decreasing liability in the contract's later phases has a small negative effect on the promisor's incentives and a large positive effect on the promisee's incentive. When performance occurs in phases and promisor needs promisee's assistance, *a decreasing liability contract usually increases the contract's value relative to a constant liability contract.* Liability in example 1 equals 100 under existing law, unless the contract stipulates otherwise. The contract could stipulate that liability for breach will equal Buyer's loss minus Seller's investment in the event of partial performance. This stipulation, which allows the breaching Seller to deduct costs incurred rather than benefits conferred, creates a decreasing liability contract. With this stipulation, Seller in example 1 owes damages of 60, because Buyer's loss equals 100 and Seller incurred expenses of 40. If Seller needs Buyer's assistance to perform in example 1, then switching from constant liability of 100 to decreasing liability of 60 will induce Buyer to assist more and increase the contract's expected value.

The *assistance interest* refers to the promisor's interest in securing assistance from the promisee. To protect the assistance interest, explicit terms in contracts often require one party to assist the other. Thus, Buyer may have an obligation to assist Seller by preparing to receive a delivery of goods. Explicit contract terms, however, ineffectively protect the assistance interest when assistance is unobservable or unverifiable.[2] Reducing damages is often the most practical way to protect the assistance interest. Liability can decrease at many different rates in a phased contract. Scholars have neglected to find the optimal deduction from damages to protect the assistance interest. For practical reasons, we recommend setting liability for breach equal to promisee's value of performance minus breaching promisor's expenditures on performance. Deducting costs incurred from expectation damages provides an effective incentive for promisee to give unobservable assistance.

Scholars and lawyers do not currently use our phrases "assistance interest" or "decreasing liability contract." Yet many industries do use contracts requiring the buyer to make payments to the seller, termed progress payments, for costs incurred in completing each phase of a contract. Sometimes the buyer cannot recover past progress payments when the seller terminates before completing the project's final phases. Nonrecoverable progress payments closely

---

[2] Also, liquidating damages, although this mechanism effectively prevents promisee's over-reliance, are ineffective with respect to promisee's assistance. See *supra* chapter 6, section D.

resemble our recommended decreasing liability contract that deducts costs incurred from expectation damages.

A. Forms of Liability

Prevailing law encompasses three major damage measures—expectation, reliance, and restitution[3]—as illustrated in example 2 (which slightly modifies example 1).

> *Example 2: Alternative Damages.* Buyer and Developer make a contract in which Buyer immediately pays Developer 90 for the latter's promise to construct a building. In reliance on the contract, Buyer spends 5 in adapting his property for the new building. Buyer values performance at 100. Developer spends 40 on architectural drawings and a concrete foundation, which cannot be recovered or reused. Developer defaults. Buyer fails to find an alternative builder and abandons the project without receiving any benefit from it. What is Developer's liability?

Damages for loss of the contract's *expected* value, which is the usual legal remedy, require Developer to pay 100 to Buyer. Damages for *reliance* require Developer to return the payment of 90 and also pay 5 in compensation for Buyer's expenditures on adapting his property. *Restitution* only requires Developer to return the payment of 90. The axes in figure 8.1 represent the promisor's liability to pay damages and the promisee's entitlement to receive damages. Notice that this progression from expectation to reliance to restitution moves down the 45° line in figure 8.1 from (100,100) to (95,95) to (90,90).[4]

Figure 8.1 applies to all contracts. In a phased contract, decreasing liability implies that the contract moves down the 45° line as the promisor goes through the phases of performance. For practical reasons, we advocate moving down the 45° line at a particular rate. Specifically, we advocate taking expectation damages as the baseline and moving down the 45° line according to the extent of the breaching promisor's expenditures. Expectations are the baseline and the breaching promisor's actual expenditures are the deduction. To illustrate using example 2, Developer's breach *before* he makes any expenditures yields liability corresponding to point (100,100), whereas Developer's breach after he spends 40 yields liability corresponding to point (60,60). Thus we propose liability of 100 or 60 depending on whether or not the promisor has made expenditures of 40 by the time of breach.

---

[3] Lon L. Fuller & William R. Perdue, *The Reliance Interest in Contract Damages*, 46 Yale L. J. 52 (1936).

[4] Note that punitive damages and disgorgement damages can move up the 45° line past the point (100,100).

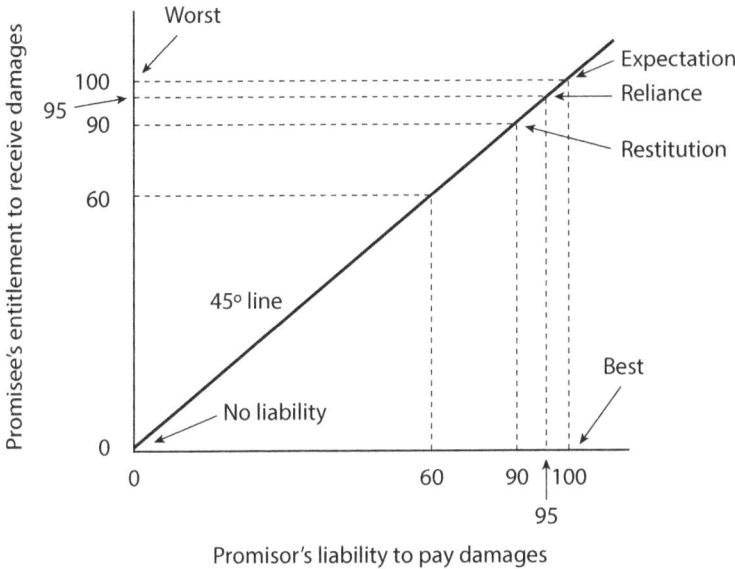

FIGURE. 8.1. Liability and Entitlement

B. Anti-Insurance Compared

How does moving down the 45° line affect the contract's value? Before answering this question, we will explain why the ideal point is *off* the 45° line. To have incentives to maximize the contract's value, each party should internalize the contract's costs and benefits for both of its parties. To supply both promisor and promisee with efficient incentives, each of them should bear the full loss that breach causes the other party, as well as his own loss.[5] In example 1, Developer internalizes the costs of breach when liability to pay damages equals 100. In the same example, Buyer internalizes the cost of breach when the entitlement to receive damages equals 0. Consequently, figure 8.1 describes the point (100,0) as "best" with respect to the incentives of the two parties.[6]

In private law, one party's liability to pay damages equals the other party's entitlement to receive damages. Thus the default rules of prevailing law can be represented as points on the 45° line. Like prevailing law, liquidation clauses stipulate that one party pays the other party for breach, so liquidated damages can also be represented as points on the 45° line. The best incentives for the two

[5] *Supra* chapter 6.
[6] Conversely, figure 8.1 describes the point (0,100) as "worst" with respect to the incentives of the two parties.

parties, however, require promisor's liability to exceed promisee's entitlement.[7] Specifically, the point (100,0) is best for the incentives of both parties.

To get off the 45° line, the parties must contract with a third party. In the preceding chapter we proposed a mechanism called "anti-insurance" to achieve this result. Anti-insurance is a contract that includes the two parties to the original contract and a third party called the "anti-insurer." In such a contract, the promisee assigns his potential right to damages to the third party before anyone knows whether a breach will occur, and the third party pays for this assignment. If a breach subsequently occurs, promisor pays expectation damages to the third party, and promisee receives no damages, which corresponds to the point (100,0) in figure 8.1. Consequently, both promisor and promisee internalize the full costs of the breach. By improving incentives, anti-insurance can significantly increase the value of a contract in principle and the three parties can share in the expected gain. We call such a contract "anti-insurance" because it improves incentives by increasing risk, whereas a standard insurance contract erodes incentives by spreading risk.

C. Best Constrained Point

Since anti-insurance is unavailable in markets, this chapter does not consider the best point in figure 8.1. Instead we confine consideration to alternatives on the 45° line where damages paid by the breaching promisor equal damages received by the promisee. We look for the point on the 45° line that creates incentives for the two parties to maximize the contract's value. Movement along the 45° line involves a tradeoff: Starting from any point on the 45° line, moving down the 45° line generally worsens promisor's incentives by externalizing more of the expected harm from breach. However, moving down the 45° line generally improves promisee's incentives to assist promisor's performance. Promisee's incentives improve because promisee internalizes more of the expected gain from assisting promisor's performance.

The 45° line represents different points of a tradeoff between the promisee's and the promisor's incentives. Expectation damages (100,100) are an unlikely candidate for the best constrained point. At this point the promisor has fully efficient incentives to perform, but the promisee has no incentive to assist the promisor. A small reduction in damages would decrease the promisor's incentive to perform and increase the promisee's incentive to assist. If the promisee's first dollar spent on assisting increases the contract's value by more than a dollar,

---

[7] Getting off the 45° line is called "decoupling" damages paid from damages received. See MITCHELL A. POLINSKY & YEON-KOO CHE, *Decoupling Liability: Optimal Incentives for Care and Litigation*, 22 RAND J. ECON. 562 (1991).

then moving *slightly* down the 45° line from the point (100,100) increases the contract's value.[8] The following proposition summarizes this argument.

> *Proposition 1*: Assume that promisor's liability for breach equals expectation damages. Assume that the promisor's expenditure on performance is positive. If a dollar spent on assistance by the promisee would increase the value of the contract by more than $1, then a small decease in liability will increase the contract's value.

In circumstances described by proposition 1, expectation damages do not maximize the contract's value. The best point on the 45° line, however, is usually much closer to expectation damages (100,100) than to no liability (0,0), because the promisor's incentives are usually more important to the contract's value than the promisee's incentives. Moving part of the way down the 45° line, but much less than halfway, will often improve incentives.

The point labeled "expectation" in figure 8.1 represents *perfect* expectation damages, which put the promisee in the same position as performance. In practice, expectation damages awarded by courts are imperfect. For example, courts tend to substitute objective measures for subjective measures that are difficult to prove. The usual error reduces compensation, which corresponds to movement down the 45° line in our figure. Therefore, imperfections in expectation damages tend to protect the assistance interest.

Replacing expectation damages with reliance or restitution damages also moves down the 45° line. Since reliance and restitution damages have this effect, the reader might expect us to advocate them. We accept that reliance or restitution damages often provide better incentives than perfect expectation damages. The gain from providing an incentive for promisee's assistance often exceeds the cost of reducing incentives for promisor's performance. However, the optimal distance to move down the 45° line bears no necessary relationship to reliance or restitution. Advocating reliance or restitution damages would disguise the fundamental reason for reducing damages below the perfect expectation level: protecting the assistance interest.

We have been discussing damages for breach generally. This chapter, however, focuses specifically on phased contracts. We will show that in contracts where promisor performs in phases and promisee's assistance matters, deducting breaching promisor's past expenditures from expectation damages typically provides better incentives than no deduction.

---

[8] When the promisor is liable for perfect expectation damages, the promisor is usually equating the marginal cost of more effort to perform against the marginal expected cost of breach. A small decrease in effort by the promisor reduces the cost of effort by the same amount as the resulting increase in the expected cost of breach. In contrast, the first dollar spent on assistance by the promisee usually reduces the expected cost of breach by more than a dollar. Shifting incentives from the promisor who is on the margin to the promisee who is not on the margin usually causes a net increase in the contract's value.

D. Basic Model of Phased Performance with Promisee's Assistance

As we further develop our model of phased contracts, in figure 8.2 we depict a promisor with numerous decisions. At time 0 promisor decides to accept price p in exchange for a promise whose performance creates value v for the promisee. To remain consistent with example 2, figure 8.2 sets p equal to 90 and v equal to 100. Expenditure on performance occurs in discrete phases enumerated $1, 2, \ldots T$. At any phase the promisor can choose to default or else make an expenditure that is necessary to proceed to the contract's next phase. The downward sloping curve in figure 8.2 indicates the promisor's costs that remain to complete performance, with the discrete points connected by a continuous curve. To illustrate concretely, at time 0 the promisor's expected remaining costs equal 80, so we have $C_0 = 80$. In figure 8.2, the present time is t. Expenditures before t are in the past, and expenditures after t are in the future. C_t denotes expected remaining costs at time t. At the particular time t in figure 8.2, promisor is half done: he has already spent 40, and he expects to spend an additional 40 to complete the job.

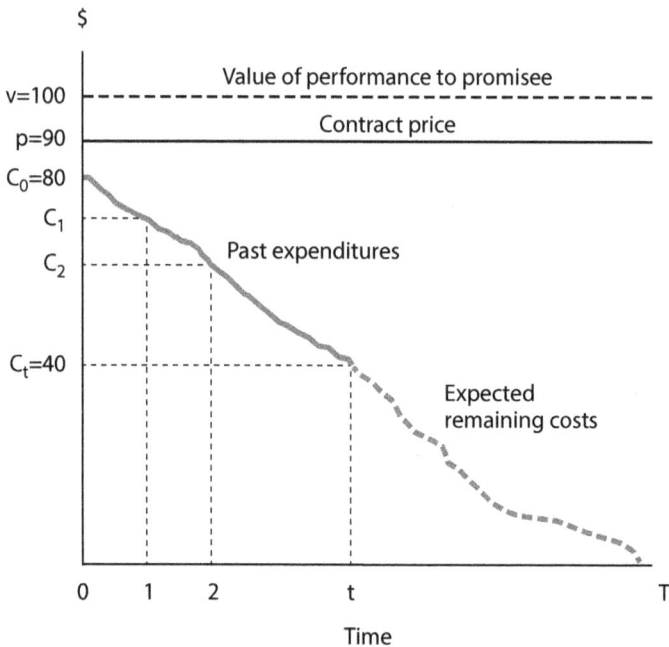

FIGURE 8.2. Decreasing Expected Costs in Phased Contract

Now we characterize how the promisor makes decisions. At each phase t, promisor defaults or continues performing according to whether the expected remaining expenditures C_t exceed liability L_t, which we write

$$C_t \leq L_t \qquad \rightarrow \qquad \text{continue performing.} \qquad (1)$$
$$C_t > L_t \qquad \rightarrow \qquad \text{default.}$$

Consider the promisor depicted in figure 8.2 who correctly anticipates future costs of performance. By decision rule (1), the promisor will perform provided that liability at each point in time exceeds expected future costs C_t. Consequently, we reach the following proposition:

Proposition 2: With each phase of the contract, the expected liability required to induce performance decreases.

Thus the minimal liability sufficient to induce performance at each phase corresponds to a decreasing liability contract.

Proposition 2 has several important implications. Compared to a constant liability contract, a decreasing liability contract can provide sufficient incentives for the promisor to perform, while also providing better incentives for the promisee to assist. Equivalently, a constant liability contract impairs the promisee's incentives unnecessarily, especially near the contract's final phase when very small damages are sufficient to induce performance by the promisor.

Now we consider a schedule in which liability equals expectation damages minus past expenditures. Figure 8.3 depicts this liability curve.[9] Note that the cost curve is below the liability curve everywhere in this figure, indicating that performance is cheaper than liability at each phase. This observation establishes the following proposition:

Proposition 3: If past expenditures are deducted from expectation damages, and if promisor correctly estimates future costs of performance, then promisor performs at every phase of the contract.

Proposition 3 has an important implication: Predictability favors deducting past expenditures from liability. When expenditures are predictable, deducting them provides sufficient incentives for promisor and better incentives for promisee.[10]

---

[9] The formula is $L_t = v - C_t$ at each point in time t. When promisor's expectations prove accurate, the liability curve always exceeds the expected future cost of performance by the difference between promisee's value of performance and promisor's initial expected cost of performance, or $v - C_0$.

[10] Note that if remaining future expenditure were observable, then liability could equal remaining future expenditure plus \$1. This rule would eliminate the problem of inefficient breach. Unfortunately, remaining future expenditures are usually unobservable, so this liability rule is impractical.

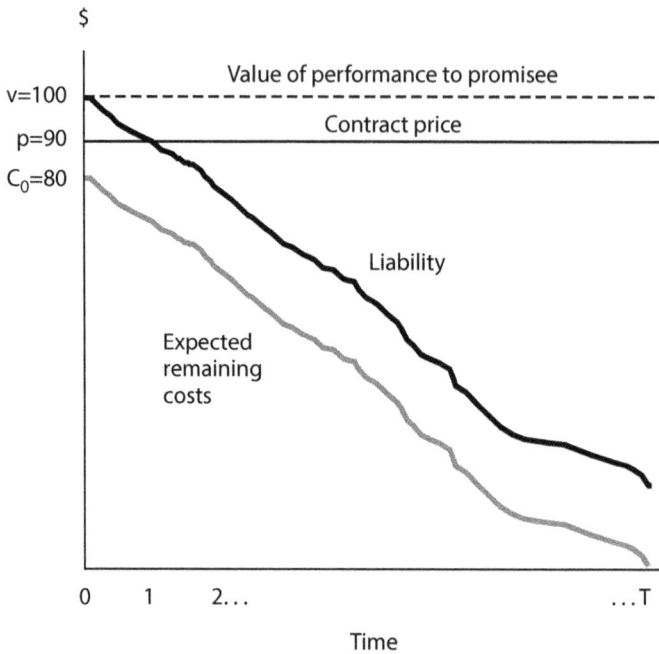

FIGURE 8.3. Decreasing Liability

In this contract, promisee's incentives to assist increase as promisor's performance progresses.[11] Thus, promisee has relatively weak incentives to assist at the contract's beginning and relatively strong incentives at its end. We do *not* recommend this arrangement because we think that promisee's incentives are typically more important at the contract's end than its beginning. Rather, we assume that promisor's incentives are more important than promisee's incentives, so promisee's incentive should be improved only when doing so does not undermine promisor's incentives. At an early stage of the performance, strong incentives for the promisee are too detrimental to the promisor's incentives, so the parties cannot afford them. At a later stage, after the promisor incurs past costs, the parties can afford to improve the promisee's incentives by reducing the incentives of the promisor.

---

[11] Sometimes the pattern is different. It may happen that breach occurs at a point in time when partial performance created value to the promisee that equals past costs. In these circumstances, a decreasing liability contract that deducts past costs from expectation damages fully compensates the promisee, because damages equal the value of full performance minus the benefit received from partial performance.

E. Surprises

When a promisor correctly anticipates future costs, a level of liability equal to expectation damages minus past expenditures will induce performance (proposition 3). What about surprises? Distinguish three types: good, bad, and very bad news. Good news means a profitable contract: The value of performance for the promisee exceeds the promisor's past and remaining costs. In figure 8.4, news is good at time t when past costs equal 40, future costs equal 40, and the value of performance is 100. Bad news means an unprofitable contract that is worth completing. The value of performance for the promisee exceeds the remaining costs, but not the sum of remaining and past costs. In figure 8.4, news is bad at time t if past costs equal 40 and remaining costs equal 61. *Very* bad news means a contract that is not worth completing: the remaining costs of performance exceed its value for the promisee. News is very bad at time t if remaining costs equal 101.

Efficiency requires the promisor to perform if news is good or bad, and not to perform if news is very bad. Setting liability for breach equal to expectation damages causes the promisor to internalize the benefits of performance as required by efficiency. Consequently, expectation damages cause promisor to perform in

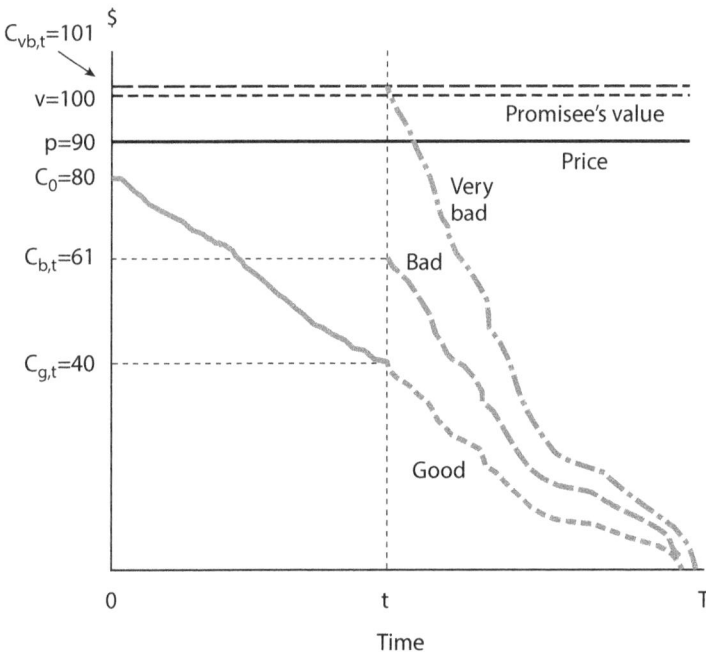

FIGURE 8.4. Good, Bad, and Very Bad News

response to good or bad news, and not to perform in response to very bad news. If liability at time t in figure 8.4 equals 100, then promisor performs as long as remaining costs do not exceed 100, and does not perform otherwise.

While expectation damages provide efficient incentives to the promisor, lower damages do not. Specifically, setting liability equal to expectation damages minus past expenditures on performance causes the promisor not to perform in response to bad news, even though efficiency requires performing. In our example, if liability at time t equals 100–40, then promisor does not perform as long as remaining costs exceed 60.

Bad news is problematic for promisor's incentives in decreasing liability contracts, but *very* bad news is unproblematic. A decreasing liability contract causes promisor to respond to very bad news by not performing, just as efficiency requires.

Liability for expectation damages minus past expenditures on performance provides efficient incentives for a promisor who receives either good or very bad news, and inefficient incentives for a promisor who receives bad news. If the probability of bad news is high, then decreasing liability contracts undermine the promisor's incentives for efficient behavior. (An adjustment in the contract might correct for this problem.[12]) If the probability of bad news is small, however, then deducting past expenditures from liability runs little risk of undermining the promisor's incentives.

In figure 8.3, 20 is the amount by which future costs can exceed original expected costs without affecting promisor's decision to perform—the margin for error without harmful incentive effects. If the margin for error remains roughly constant in *absolute* size as performance progresses, then the margin for error increases as a *proportion* of expected remaining costs. To illustrate, a margin for error of 20 equals 20/80 or 25 percent at time 0, and it equals 20/40 or 50 percent at time t.

These observations yield our fourth proposition:

Proposition 4: Assume that liability equals expectation damages minus past expenditures. Also make certain reasonable assumptions about the probability of errors in predictions. Then the longer the contract progresses as predicted, the lower the probability of breach.

Proposition 4 implies that the probability density in the problematic area for promisor's incentives decreases as the contract progresses as predicted.[13]

Having explained the problem of bad news, we return to the question of why we recommend a decreasing liability contract in which the nonperforming

---

[12] If the parties feel that bad news is likely, they might prefer to stipulate a deduction equal to *half* of past costs, instead of all past costs.

[13] An implication of proposition 4 that we do not investigate here is that, under certain assumptions, the optimal contract not only provides for decreasing liability with time, but would also specify that liability decreases at an increasing rate. For practical reasons, such complicated liability schedules are unlikely to be used.

party pays expectation damages minus past costs. Past costs are the best deduction for two practical reasons. First, past costs provide sufficient margin for error so that the promisor seldom receives such bad news that he does not perform when efficiency requires performance. The promisor who has sunk costs in the project usually has sufficient incentives to perform, even without internalizing the full cost of nonperformance. Second, past costs are relatively easy to observe and verify, which is why these terms figure frequently in everyday contracts or legal rules applied to them. Instead of adjusting the deduction for past costs, fundamentally different principles of deduction are easy to imagine, but they are usually susceptible to practical or theoretical objections.[14]

F. Progress Payment Contracts and Timing of Payments

Progress payments contracts are used in a variety of contractual settings involving interdependence between the parties, in which the assistance of the promisee is required, and that assistance is unobservable and unverifiable. Examples include making a movie, building a computer program to a buyer's specifications, retaining an attorney in complex litigation, or complex construction projects.[15] Progress payments can protect the assistance interest in much the same way as decreasing liability contracts. For any decreasing liability contract, there exists a progress payment contract with materially equivalent incentives for promisor's performance and promisee's assistance, and vice versa. To make the two kinds of contracts materially equivalent, two conditions should be satisfied. First, the progress payment should approximately equal the costs incurred. Legal disputes provide evidence that such contracts are common.[16] Second, the progress payment should be nonrecoverable.[17]

---

[14] An appealing alternative awards damages slightly above *future* costs, not *past* costs, so the promisor always has an incentive to complete performance. In reality, however, future costs are more speculative and manipulable than past costs. The practical advantages strongly favor past costs rather than future costs.

[15] Victor Goldberg analyzes various complex contracts with some of these features. See VICTOR P. GOLDBERG, *The Net Profit Puzzle*, 97 COLUM. L. REV. 524 (1998).

[16] In legal disputes over progress payments, the parties often agree that the contract entitles seller to receive progress payments equal to costs incurred, but the parties dispute over their extent. To illustrate, in *U.S. v. Taber Metals Holding, Inc.*, 341 F. 3d 843 (8th Cir. 2003), a government contractor with liquidity problems requested progress payments on "pro forma invoices," that is, on invoices to pay for goods that as yet were undelivered. The court "accepted as true, indeed, as undisputed . . . that under the applicable procurement regulations progress payments may only be based upon current obligations (incurred costs)." Instead of requiring progress payments for actual costs, some progress payment contracts liquidate the costs. One form of liquidation requires buyer to pay a fixed percent of actual costs. For example, in *Rumsfeld v. Freedom NY, Inc.*, 329 F. 3d 1320 (Fed. Cir. 2003), the government agreed to "make progress payments in the amount of 95 percent of incurred costs."

[17] The progress payment may be nonrecoverable by law, as when the contract allows Seller to terminate without breaching. Progress payment may be nonrecoverable in fact, as when seller is bankrupt or buyer bears prohibitive transaction costs of recovery. The legal cases provide ample

Here is an example of materially identical contracts with one cast as a decreasing liability contract and the other cast as a progress payment contract. The project occurs in two phases, with Seller incurring costs of 40 in the first phase and 40 in the second phase. Buyer receives no benefit from the first phase and benefits of 100 from the second phase. The contract price is 90, so Seller and Buyer each expect to gain 10 from completion. The two kinds of contracts can be constructed to have the same material consequences if the contract is terminated after completion of its first phase.

In a decreasing liability contract, Buyer makes an upfront payment of 90. If Seller terminates after phase 1, Seller incurs cost of 40 and faces liability of 100 minus costs incurred of 40. Seller's net payoff under a decreasing liability contract equals $+90 - 40 - (100 - 40) = -10$.

In the equivalent progress payment contract, Buyer makes a nonrefundable progress payment of 40 after phase 1. If Seller terminates after phase 1, Seller keeps the progress payment and pays liability of 10. Thus Seller's net payoff is -10 under a progress payment contract: $+40 - 40 - 10$.

It is easy to show that when Seller terminates after the first phase, Buyer's net payoff is -30 under either the decreasing liability contract or the progress payment contract.[18] Termination causes a loss to both parties that is shared between them. It is also easy to see that if Seller completes the first and second phases, Buyer and Seller each have a net payoff of 10 under either contract.[19] While the form of the two contracts is different, the net payoffs are the same.

G. Renegotiation

How does the possibility for renegotiation affect decreasing liability contracts? Two reasons typically cause parties to renegotiate a contract. First, when

---

evidence where seller's bankruptcy makes progress payments nonrecoverable in fact. Buyer who anticipates seller's termination for reason of bankruptcy may attempt to withhold progress payments owed under the contract as setoff for expectation damages. Seller may counterclaim that withholding progress payments triggered bankruptcy. See *Johnson v. All-State Construction Inc.*, 329 F. 3d 848 (Fed. Cir. 2003).

[18] Under a decreasing liability contract, if Seller breaches after the first phase Buyer loses the 90 he paid upfront and receives 100–40 in damages, for a net loss of 30. Under the equivalent progress payment contract, Seller's breach after the first phase causes Buyer to receive 10 in damages after a first phase payment of 40, for a net loss of 30.

[19] At the end of the second phase, Seller has incurred costs of 80 and Buyer has received performance valued at 100. Under a decreasing liability contract, the Buyer pays upfront the contract price of 90. Under a progress payment contract, after completion the Buyer pays the second progress payment of 40 plus a completion bonus of 10. The only difference between the two contracts is the timing of payments. This difference is easily eliminated by modifying the terms in one of the contracts. The timing of payment makes no difference to our analysis so long as Buyer's obligation to pay depends *only* on time. To illustrate, Buyer in example 1 could pay Developer upfront with a bond of 90 that pays off at time T. Using a bond shifts Buyer's payment in time and leaves the other features of the contract unchanged, including its incentive effects.

circumstances change, modifying the contract can avoid inefficient behavior. Efficiency-increasing modifications increase the contract's expected value. Second, when bargaining power changes, one of the parties may demand modification to redistribute the contract's value. Demands for redistributive modifications slow performance, distort the parties' incentives, and decrease the contract's expected value.

Decreasing liability contracts do not usually increase the likelihood of distributive modifications.[20] The situation is different, however, when promisor receives "bad news," because promisor will not perform under a decreasing liability contract, even though performance is efficient. Under a decreasing liability contract, bad news gives promisor a credible threat of nonperformance that can be used against the promisee.[21] The possibility of renegotiation and modification ameliorates this problem. Instead of actually breaching, promisor can credibly threaten to breach unless promisee agrees to modify the contract's terms and pay the promisor more. The parties can presumably agree on terms that give each of them a share of the surplus from performing rather than not performing. Courts should enforce such a value-increasing modification.[22] The possibility of renegotiation makes decreasing liability contracts more attractive by reducing the probability of inefficient nonperformance.

The preceding discussion concerns rational behavior and credible threats. How do irrational behavior and incredible threats affect the desirability of decreasing liability contracts? Choosing the action with higher net costs is ordinarily irrational, but people sometimes do it.[23] A threat is effective, whether rational or not, if the hearer believes that the speaker may act on it. The speaker is presumably more likely to act if the threatened action costs him less. Consequently, promisor's threat against promisee is presumably more effective if the threatened action costs the promisor less.

A decreasing liability contract can change the cost of acting on an irrational threat. Assume that nonperformance costs the promisor 50 and performing costs him 40. Since the promisor loses 10 from nonperforming, the promisor's

---

[20] If events unfold as anticipated, promisor finds that performing is cheaper at each phase than not performing, so the promise to perform is credible and a threat not to perform is incredible. Also, promisee finds that assisting is cheaper than not assisting, so a threat not to assist is incredible.

[21] Cf. IAN AYRES & KRISTIN MADISON, *Threatening Inefficient Performance of Injunctions and Contracts.* 148 U. PA. L. REV. 45 (2000).

[22] For an argument that courts should enforce modifications when the threat of breach by the promisor is credible, even if made under circumstances considered by prevailing contract law as "duress," see OREN BAR-GILL & OMRI BEN-SHAHAR, *The Law of Duress and the Economics of Credible Threats,* 33 J. LEGAL STUD. 391 (2004).

[23] For example, experiments in behavioral economics show that people will often reduce their own objective payoffs to prevent someone else from gaining an unfair advantage. ERNST FEHR & SIMON GACHTER, *Altruistic Punishment in Humans,* 415 NATURE 137-140 (2002). As another example, a repeat player may undertake the more costly action in a particular situation to gain the future advantage of a reputation for toughness. The repeat player's local irrationality is globally rational.

threat not to perform is incredible. Still, the promisor may be irrational, and this threat may be effective. Presumably the threat would be even more effective if nonperformance causes the promisor to lose 5 rather than 10. With these observations in mind, compare the effectiveness of promisor's threats in constant and decreasing liability contracts. In terms of figure 8.1, a constant liability contract is a point on the 45° line, and a decreasing liability contract would be represented by downward movement along the 45° line. Lower liability makes the threat of nonperformance less costly for the promisor, thereby increasing the effectiveness of such a threat. Similarly, lower damages make the threat of nonassistance more costly for the promisee, decreasing the effectiveness of such a threat. To summarize: starting from any constant liability level, decreasing liability below that level increases the effectiveness of the promisor's threat not to perform and decreases the effectiveness of the promisee's threat not to assist.

H. Identifying Contracts in Which Efficiency Requires Decreasing Liability

We recommend that transaction lawyers use decreasing liability contracts for phased contracts wherein both parties need incentives to increase the contract's value by unobservable and unverifiable means.

One way to affect the promisee's incentives is limiting liability to reliance damages or to any other measure of damages that is below expectation damages.[24] Reducing liability below expectation damages is generally inferior to decreasing liability for phased contracts in which the optimal damage schedule is dynamic. We will elaborate on the two factors that determine the magnitude of the advantage of decreasing liability: the changing benefits of improving the promisee's incentives and the changing costs of undermining the promisor's incentives.

1. IMPROVING THE INCENTIVES OF THE PROMISEE

The promisee can often assist performance and take precaution against breach in various ways. Sometimes courts recognize the importance of assistance by the recipient of performance, and even imply principles resembling comparative fault or contractual duties of cooperation. To the extent that these efforts to assist are unobservable or unverifiable, however, a legal duty to perform them is unenforceable, regardless of whether the duty is stipulated in the contract or inferred from a legal doctrine such as contributory or comparative fault. In such circumstances, however, undercompensation gives the promisee an incentive to assist, and the incentive increases as damages decrease. In example 1 undercompensation gives Buyer an incentive to help Developer to obtain building

---

[24] For the argument that reliance damages supply better incentives to the promisee to cooperate than expectation damages or liquidated damages, see YEON-KOO CHE & TAI-YEONG CHUNG, *Contract Damages and Cooperative Investment,* 30 RAND J. ECON. 84 (1999).

permits and reveal information necessary for performance after the contract was made, even if the efforts are unobservable or unverifiable. This is a typical situation across a wide category of cases in which promisee's assistance in performing the contract could prevent a breach or reduce its likelihood.

Here are some forms of promisee's assistance that are difficult to observe or verify.

Example 3: Developing a Computer Program. Programmer promises Buyer to develop a computer program adapted to Buyer's idiosyncratic needs. Developing the program requires intensive, costly cooperation between them. Programmer breaches the contract by failing to develop the program as promised. Programmer argues that if Buyer had cooperated, Programmer would not have breached the contract. Since most efforts by Buyer to cooperate, or the lack thereof, are unverifiable, Programmer cannot invoke any kind of defense based on Buyer's noncooperation.

Expectation damages in example 3 do not give Buyer strong incentives for expensive cooperation. The only effective way to provide Buyer with strong incentives to cooperate is to undercompensate him significantly if Programmer breaches the contract. Deducting past expenditure from expectation damages produces this outcome. Realizing all that in advance, the parties may adopt a decreasing liability contract.

Now we turn to an example of revealing information at the performance stage.

Example 4: Revealing Information Necessary for Performance. Developer promises to construct a building for Buyer. After partially performing, Developer encounters difficulties in completing performance owing to geological obstacles to construction. As a result, Developer breaches the contract. Buyer easily could have acquired information concerning those obstacles, but refrained from doing so. Buyer's lack of effort is unobservable and unverifiable. Had Buyer acquired the information and disclosed it to Developer, Developer would not have made the contract and breached it.[25]

Expectation damages from breach in example 4 give Buyer no incentive to acquire or disclose information concerning geological difficulties. The situation changes when damages decrease below the expectation level. Each reduction in damages gives Buyer stronger incentives to acquire and disclose the information. Foreseeing these facts, the parties might recognize that a decreasing liability contract improves incentives relative to a constant liability contract.

Finally, we turn to an example of misunderstandings.

Example 5: Clarifying Misunderstandings. Seller mistakenly renders defective or delayed performance, thus breaching the contract. Buyer knew or

---

[25] For discussion of a similar example under a comparative fault defense, see ARIEL PORAT, *A Comparative Fault Defense in Contract Law*, 107 MICH. L. REV. 1397, 1400 (2009).

could easily have known about Seller's misunderstanding, but Buyer did not take any steps to prevent it. Had Buyer clarified the misunderstanding, Seller would not have breached the contract. Proving that a misunderstanding caused Seller's breach, or that Buyer knew or could easily have known about Seller's misunderstanding, is difficult or impossible.[26]

By assumption, stipulating a duty by Buyer to clarify misunderstandings as in example 5 is ineffective. Undercompensating Buyer, however, would encourage him to prevent misunderstandings.

2. UNDERMINING THE EFFICIENT INCENTIVES OF THE PROMISOR

By our definitions, news is "bad" (but not *very* bad) when the value of performance exceeds its future costs, but the value of performance is moderately less (but not grossly less) than the total of past and future costs of performance. Decreasing liability distorts the promisor's incentives when news is bad. Thus, a *low* probability that the cost of performance modestly exceeds its value favors decreasing liability contracts. Here are some factors that produce this result.

LENGTH OF PERFORMANCE

When the time needed for performance is short, the risk that costs of performance will exceed its value is typically low. In these circumstances, a decreasing liability contract is a good way to induce unverifiable assistance in performance by the promisee.

STABLE MARKETS

Performance often requires the promisor to purchase inputs. Stable markets for inputs reduce the probability of bad news. To illustrate, when the price and supply of working materials and manpower is predictable, decreasing liability contracts pose little risk of creating incentives for inefficient breach. Conversely, unstable markets for inputs create risk that an increase in costs will cause promisor to breach inefficiently.

In some circumstances, the parties can solve the problem of unstable markets for inputs without abandoning the advantages of a decreasing liability contract. To solve the problem, the promisee may assume the risk of market fluctuations. Buyer might agree to reimburse seller for an increase in the cost of construction materials.[27] In these circumstances, the risk that input costs will increase need not prevent the parties from adopting a decreasing liability contract.

---

[26] For discussion of a similar example under a comparative fault defense, see PORAT, *id.*, at 1399.

[27] A stipulation in the contract, which burdens the promisee with any increase in the cost of performance, would create a moral hazard problem with regard to the promisor's incentives to reduce costs of performance. In the context of the present discussion, however, we assume that the market fluctuations which increase costs of performance could not be affected by the parties to the contract.

The risk that a decreasing liability contract will cause inefficient breach relates to the time pattern of market fluctuations. News of rising costs is more likely to cause promisor's breach when received in an early phase, because more inputs remain to be purchased. When breach occurs early enough so that promisor has made little or no expenditures, the deductibility of expenditures makes little or no difference to liability. Consequently, early receipt of bad news does not cause a significant difference in decreasing liability contracts as compared to constant liability contracts.

Conversely, news of rising costs is less likely to cause promisor's breach when received in a later phase. Because few inputs remain to be purchased at this stage, late receipt of bad news is unlikely to cause inefficient breach of a decreasing liability contract.

The greatest risk that a decreasing liability contract will cause inefficient breach occurs when the promisor receives bad news in the middle phases of the contact. When drafting the contract, the parties should keep this possibility in mind when they consider the time pattern in the contract's phases in relation to possible market fluctuations.

We have discussed the potential problem that unstable input prices pose for decreasing liability contracts. A similar problem concerns unstable output prices. When output prices are unstable, a third party may appear and offer Seller more than Buyer promised to pay in the contract. To illustrate by our first example, Developer might get a bid from a third party during performance that he can accept only if he defaults on the original contract with Buyer.

The third party presents Developer with an opportunity that is realizable only by breaching the existing contract. The cost of performing, rather than breaching, then includes both the cost of inputs and the lost opportunity. Consequently, the analysis of unstable input and output prices is essentially the same. When the output price is predictable, decreasing liability contracts pose little risk of creating incentives for inefficient breach. Conversely, unstable output markets create risk that an increase in output prices will cause promisor to breach inefficiently. As with unstable input prices, the parties can solve the problem of unstable output prices without abandoning the advantages of a decreasing liability contract by the promisee assuming the risk. Buyer might agree to reimburse Seller for loss of an opportunity to sell to a third party.

CORRELATED COSTS AND VALUE OF PERFORMANCE

The cost of performance and its value are sometimes correlated. The correlation often exists because an increase in production costs causes an increase in the product's value. To illustrate, an increase in the cost of construction may increase the value of the existing stock of buildings.

Consider the consequences for a contract stipulating liability equal to expectation damages minus actual costs. As long as expectation damages increase by the same amount as remaining costs, the former offset the latter, so the change in prices does not induce promisor to breach. Therefore, as long as the value of performance increases by at least as much as the remaining costs of performance, the decreasing liability contract does not create a problem of inefficient breach. In these circumstances, the parties can stipulate decreasing liability without fear that price changes will cause inefficient breach.

THE PROMISOR'S INEFFICIENT INVESTMENT IN PERFORMANCE
In our model, the promisor must make expenditures in each phase of performance in order to go on to the next phase. Our model assumes that expenditures in each phase are binary—either expenditures are sufficient to go to the next phase, or expenditures are insufficient and the promisor cannot perform. Our model allows no time-shifting of expenditures on performance. The real world, however, usually permits some time shifting. In most phased contracts, higher expenditures in a later phase can make up for lower expenditures in an earlier phase. Also, in the real world, higher expenditures in any phase often increase the probability of completing performance later.

A less tractable and more realistic model than ours would allow a flexible time pattern of expenditures on performance. We do not construct such a model, but we mention a new problem to be encountered. In a constant liability contract with expectation damages, promisor internalizes 100 percent of the costs of breach, regardless of when it occurs. However, in a decreasing liability contract, the promisor internalizes a variable percentage of the costs of breach, depending on when it occurs. With a flexible time pattern of expenditures on performance, a decreasing liability contract may enable the promisor to shift expected costs to the promisee by shifting expenditures forward in time. The promisor who expects to gain from shifting expenditures forward in time will not take account of negative effects on the promisee, which are the reduction in damages promisee expects to receive in the event that promisor breaches early in the contract.[28] (Even in these circumstances, however, a contract specifying *decreasing liquidated damages* might solve the problem.[29])

---

[28] To illustrate, assume the contract in example 1 stipulates that Developer who breaches at time t pays expectation damages $V = 100$ minus expenditures on partial performance C_t. If Developer breaches at time t after expenditures of 40, Developer's liability equals 60. Consequently, breach at time t results in Developer's total costs of $40 + 60 = 100$. Now assume that technology changes and allows Developer to shift costs of 30 from after time t to before time t. Consequently, breach at time t results in Developer's total costs of $70 + 30 = 100$. Since Developer's costs of breach are constant regardless of whether or not he shifts costs forward in time, he will decide whether or not to make the shift purely on the basis of whether his costs of performance rise or fall. Thus he will shifts costs forward in time if he saves 1 in costs of performance.

When he shifts costs forward in time, however, Buyer's damages from breach fall by much more than 1. Specifically, Buyer's damages from Developer's breach at time t fall from 60 to 30. If the probability of breach is significant, shifting costs forward in time is inefficient, but Developer gains an advantage by doing so.

[29] Instead of stipulating that breaching promisor can deduct *actual* expenditures, the contract might stipulate the exact deduction in dollars allowed after breach at each phase. The parties might

LITIGATION COSTS

We will briefly discuss litigation costs. In any decreasing liability contract, the promisor's liability for breach decreases with time, so promisee's recovery also decreases with time. In the decreasing liability schedule that we recommend, the promisee's recovery equals promisee's value of performance minus promisor's costs. As performance approaches completion, the promisee's recovery approaches the promisee's value of performance minus the promisor's cost of performance, which is the value created by the contract. Our recommended decreasing liability schedule thus gives a credible threat to sue throughout the contract's life so long as the contract's value exceeds litigation costs. If, however, plaintiff's costs of litigation exceed the contract's value, then a threat by the promisee to sue the nonperforming promisor would no longer be credible and the contract becomes ineffective. If the parties foresee that these circumstances are likely, they would gain by making a different contract in which damages decrease at a slower rate.

In figure 8.3, the promisee's damages decrease from 100 at time 0 to 20 at time T. Promisee has a credible threat to sue for nonperformance throughout the contract's life so long as his litigation costs do not exceed 20. Assume, however, that the promisee's cost of litigation exceeds 20 and equals, say, 30. When damages decrease below 30, the credibility of a threat by promisee to sue the promisor for nonperformance disappears. Foreseeing this eventuality, the parties could stipulate that the loser pays the winner's litigation costs, or the parties could stipulate a liability schedule that decreases more slowly so that damages always exceed 30.

I. Conclusion

The economic analysis of contracts clarified debates over alternative liability rules, especially by demonstrating that ideal expectation damages cause promisor to internalize the cost of breach to the promisee. Relying on this insight, most law and economics scholars have commended expectation damages as more efficient than any alternative. This conclusion, however, loses sight of the promisee's incentives to assist the promisor's performance. The standard argument for expectation damages fails for contracts in which the promisee's unverifiable assistance significantly affects performance. In these circumstances, efficient incentives for both parties require promisee to assign the right to expectation damages to a third party (the anti-insurer). In the absence of such an

---

try to liquidate damages equal to expectation damages minus *optimal* expenditure, regardless of *actual* expenditures. Liquidated decreasing liability requires a great deal of information. Also, it may not solve the problem of time-shifting to lower the probability of breach, as opposed to time-shifting to lower the cost of performance.

assignment, reducing liability below the level of expectation damages usually increases efficiency. To be precise, reducing liability below expectation damages increases efficiency when the promisor's last dollar spent on performing increases the contract's value less than the promisee's first dollar spent on assisting.

For this reason, we advocate reducing damages below the expectation level whenever promisee's unverifiable assistance significantly affects performance. While such a reduction can typically be achieved through either reliance or restitution damages, we do not advocate them. Instead, we advocate a damage measure whose justification relates directly to the goal of improving the promisee's incentives to assist the promisor. For phased contracts, the promisor's remaining costs of performance ordinarily decrease as each phase is completed. Consequently, the level of liability required to induce performance also decreases. A contract that stipulates decreasing liability can provide sufficient incentives for the promisor to perform, while motivating the promisee to assist.

To implement such a contract, we recommend deducting past expenditure on incomplete performance, either actual or stipulated, from liability. (We omit the related question of deducting from liability other losses suffered by the breaching promisor.[30]) The justification for this form of decreasing liability over possible alternatives is practical—it produces good incentives by using variables that parties have experience writing into contracts and courts have experience adjudicating.

Decreasing liability, or its material equivalence through progress payments, is the most practical way for a phased contract to motivate a promisee whose assistance is unobservable or unverifiable. If transaction lawyers appreciate the problem of promisee's unverifiable assistance, they will understand better when to use progress payments and how to set their magnitude and timing. Transaction lawyers may sometimes find that switching language from "progress payments" to "decreasing liability" increases the contract's clarity. In addition, if courts understand the purpose of decreasing liability and progress payments, they will interpret and enforce contracts better. Perhaps the decreasing liability contract will become so common in the future that courts will adopt it as the default rule for damages in some phased contracts.

---

[30] Thus, the promisor could suffer reliance losses, lost profits, or nonlegal sanctions imposed by third parties. Like expenditures on phases of performance, the presence of such losses decreases the level of liability required to induce a promisor to perform, so a case could be made for deducting these losses from liability. For making this argument with respect to nonlegal sanctions, see *infra* chapter 11.

Restitution and Positive Externalities

The third claim in this book is that the law should compensate for unrequested benefits more often in order to induce people to provide more of them.

Suppose that your neighbor intentionally broke some boards on your fence in order to get a better view from his porch. Under current law, your neighbor must compensate you for the resulting harm. Alternatively, suppose that vandals broke some boards on your fence and your neighbor repaired it. Your neighbor, who wanted to keep the dogs from ruining your flowers, did not obtain your consent because you were unreachable while traveling abroad. When you return, your neighbor asks for a modest reimbursement for his costs. Under current law, you are not obliged to reimburse your neighbor, even though you benefited from his work and obtaining your consent in advance was impossible.

For most people, it is obvious why the wrongdoer who damaged the fence should compensate the victim, while it is much less obvious whether or not the benefactor who repaired the fence should recover his costs. Most people take for granted that the two cases are completely different from each other, and they are indeed different in law. The first case concerns tort law, which is about liability for causing harm. The second case concerns restitution law, which is about liability for benefits received.

Although they appear different, costs and benefits are the same in economics but for their sign. Causing harm raises much the same incentive problems as receiving benefits. Efficiency requires that injurers (and in bilateral precaution cases, injurers and victims alike) internalize the harms they cause (or wrongfully cause). Tort liability makes injurers internalize the harm that they cause, regardless of whether or not the parties could bargain or make agreements in advance. Similarly, efficiency requires that benefactors (and in bilateral precaution cases, benefactors and beneficiaries alike) internalize the benefits that they create. In most circumstances, the benefactor and the beneficiary can bargain together and agree on a price for providing benefits, so restitution law is unnecessary. In other circumstances that preclude bargaining, however, restitution can enable benefactors to internalize the benefits that they create. When the parties cannot reach agreements due to high transaction costs, restitution law should internalize positive externalities in order to maximize social benefits.

Such is the logic of economics. Given the symmetry of benefits and costs, you might expect the scope of tort liability to resemble the scope of restitution. In fact, the two bodies of law differ markedly in scope. Tort liability encompasses many harms and restitution encompasses few benefits. The law is much more willing to allow victims to recover for harms they suffered from injurers than to allow benefactors to recover for unrequested benefits they conferred upon recipients.

Can we reconcile economic symmetry and legal asymmetry in the scope of liability for harms and benefits? Chapter 9 (A Public Goods Theory of Restitution) argues that economics justifies some legal asymmetry, but less than in current law. The duty of restitution should be expanded so that beneficiaries are liable for more unrequested benefits than under current law. With an expanded duty of restitution, many public goods that are never produced due to high transaction costs will be privately supplied. The expanded duty of restitution, however, should stop far short of the scope of liability for causing harm. Causing harm is sufficiently different from causing benefits to justify a significant difference in scope between the law of torts and the law of restitution.

Chapter 10 (Liability Externalities and Mandatory Choices) deals with mixed situations when an activity produces negative and positive externalities. Injurers who create both negative and positive externalities are charged for the former by law and not credited for the latter. Here too, the law responds more to negative than to positive externalities. Ignoring positive externalities creates social costs that some changes in tort law might avoid.

Chapter 11 (The Relationship Between Nonlegal Sanctions and Damages) turns to nonlegal sanctions imposed on injurers and breaching parties, and indicates that they often create positive externalities. Chapter 11 explains how nonlegal sanctions should affect the amount of damages awarded by courts in tort and contract cases.

A Public Goods Theory of Restitution

hy do public places have so much litter and so few roses? The law has a lot to do with it. Someone who picks up litter on the sidewalk or plants roses in public view benefits others. The law seldom rewards an individual who creates an unrequested benefit for others. So private production of public goods is deficient.

To understand the problem, consider some examples where law gives or withholds rewards for unrequested benefits to others.

Example 1: Heirs to Estate. Five heirs will divide equally the estate of a deceased person. A debtor owes 20 to the estate. One of the heirs sues the debtor on behalf of the estate and the estate wins 20. Each heir's share of the 20 is 4. The heir who brought suit spent 15 on the case. She asks each of the heirs to pay an equal share of it. They refuse, so she sues each of them for 3 and wins. Her net gain from suing the debtor and the heirs is 1. (Her share of the cost of the suit against the debtor was 3 and her share of the estate's gain was 4.)

Example 1 is a "common fund" case in the law of restitution. A beneficiary of a common fund who acts to increase its value can recover a share of his or her costs from other beneficiaries, even if they refused to support these efforts on behalf of the common fund.[1] Like example 1, a class action lawsuit is also a type of common fund. At the culmination of a class action, the court rewards the initiator of a suit that benefits a large group of plaintiffs.

Here is another example where law rewards someone who creates an unrequested benefit for others.

Example 2: Co-Ownership of Parking Lot. The five residents of an apartment building jointly own the building's parking lot. The parking lot has substandard lighting that endangers its users at night. One of the owners installs a

---

[1] The Restatement Third, Restitution and Unjust Enrichment § 30 (2010) allows recovery in cases where "the recipient obtains a benefit in money," thereby substantially broadening the common-funds category of cases. For examples of suits brought by an heir against his or her co-heirs, see the Restatement Third, Restitution and Unjust Enrichment § 29, illustrations 23-25, and 2 George E. Palmer, The Law of Restitution §§ 6.1, 10.7 (1978).

light at her own expense, at a cost of 15. Each of the owners benefits from the light by 4, for a total gain of 20. The person who installed the light asks each of the others to contribute 3 to its costs. When they refuse, she sues each of them for a share of her costs and wins. Her net gain is 1.

Example 2 is a co-ownership or joint ownership case in the law of restitution. In these cases, a co-owner incurs expenses to maintain or protect co-owned property. The law of restitution allows a co-owner of property who increases its value to recover a share of the cost of doing so from the other owners.[2]

By contrast, with a small change in the facts of example 2, the law withholds a reward from the creator of unrequested benefits:

Example 3: Separate Ownership of Parking Spaces. The facts are the same as in example 2, except the parking spaces are separately owned. Consequently, the person who installed the light loses her suit and her net loss is 11.

In example 3 the parking spaces are owned separately, not jointly owned as in example 2. To establish a duty of restitution in example 3, the case law and commentary require a "proximity of interests," "nexus of interests," or "closeness of interests" among the parties.[3] Proximity can arise from a contractual relationship, but the parties in example 3 have none. Probably the circumstances as described in the example do not constitute "proximity of interests." If the resident who installed the light foresaw a net loss of 11, she probably would not have done it.

Here is another example where the parties apparently lack "proximity of interests":

Example 4: Polluted Stream. A polluted stream runs through five private properties. The upstream owner pays 15 to install equipment that purifies the stream's water. Each of the properties increases in value by 4, for a total gain of 20. The upstream owner asks downstream owners to share the costs of the purification equipment. They refuse to pay, so he sues each of them for 3 and loses. His net loss is 11.[4]

---

[2] 2 PALMER, *supra* note 1, § 10.7(c); DANIEL FRIEDMANN, *Unjust Enrichment, Pursuance of Self-Interest, and the Limits of Free Riding,* 36 LOY. L.A. L. REV. 831, 856–58 (2003).

[3] The RESTATEMENT THIRD, RESTITUTION AND UNJUST ENRICHMENT § 26 cmt. a. (2010) ("In either case, payment confers a benefit on the recipient because of the way the parties' interests and obligations are intertwined. . . . The claimant's expenditure must have been necessary to protect an interest in property, and there must be a nexus of interests. . . .").

[4] A variation of this example is when the pollution is created by a tortfeasor, and A incurs costs, stops the pollution, and thereby creates benefits to him and to other victims. See ARIEL PORAT, *Private Production of Public Goods: Liability for Unrequested Benefits,* 108 MICH. L. REV. 189, 205-7 (2009). Another interesting scenario is when several actors are obliged by law to prevent harm to a potential victim, but only one of them acts, thereby benefiting the other actors by discharging them from their obligations to act. For very illuminating discussion of that latter scenario, see ASSAF JACOB, *Dilution of Liability and Multiple Tortfeasors in the Context of Liability for*

Finally, the parties in our next example certainly lack "proximity of interests" in law, so there is no duty of restitution:

Example 5: The Garden. A homeowner converts his front yard into a rose garden at a cost of 20. His many neighbors can see the rose garden. The rose garden causes the property of its owner to rise in value by 15. His neighbors' properties also increase in value by 10. The owner of the rose garden tries and fails to convince his neighbors to pay him 8 for constructing it. The owner sues his neighbors for contribution to its costs and loses. His net loss is 5.

In each of the preceding examples, the benefactor's act conveys a benefit to everyone in a group. Economists refer to such an act as "supplying a public good" (more on public goods later). The law of restitution encourages the private production of public goods in special cases by holding the recipients liable for unrequested benefits. Specifically, the private production of unrequested public goods creates a right to restitution in special cases involving a common fund or joint ownership, but not in most other cases.[5] The duty of restitution is limited to a small fraction of unrequested benefits. A person who voluntarily picks up litter in a public place or plants roses that benefit others does not have a right to restitution from the recipients of the public good created.

Expanding the right of restitution to situations like example 5 poses many practical problems. If implemented wrongly, the result could be a nightmare. Instead of increasing social welfare, the burden of having to pay for unrequested benefits could discourage private ownership of property susceptible to such duties. Conversely, confining the right of restitution precludes the production of many public goods at great loss to society.

We will develop the "public goods theory of restitution." It applies when one person's act creates unrequested benefits for two or more people. We use the public goods theory of restitution to explain the existing law of restitution for unrequested benefits, and then we develop the case for an expanded duty of restitution (EDR). We advocate expanding the right to restitution in order to increase the private supply of public goods, but doing so cautiously in light of practical obstacles. Liability for receiving unrequested benefits should be broader than current law, but it still should be far narrower than liability for causing harm.

Unrequested Precautions, 108 MICH. L. REV. FIRST IMPRESSIONS 12 (2009). Available at: http://www.michiganlawreview.org/assets/pdfs/108/jacob.pdf; ALON HAREL & ASSAF JACOB, *An Economic Rationale for the Legal Treatment of Omission in Tort Law: The Principle of Salience*, 3 THEORETICAL INQ. L. 413 (2002).

[5] For a full account of the categories of cases where prevailing restitution law imposes liability for the conferral of unrequested benefits, see PORAT, *id.*, at 195-8.

A. Unrequested Benefits under Prevailing Law

A review of the law[6] suggests four necessary conditions for imposing a duty of restitution on a recipient of unrequested benefits. First, before conferring the benefit, agreement in advance must be impractical or impossible. Whenever a consensual transaction is feasible, this path must be taken and the path of restitution is closed. Thus the law channels activity into a voluntary agreement where possible, and the law sometimes allows restitution where voluntary agreement was impossible.[7]

In economics, an agreement is a "transaction" and the obstacles to it are "transaction costs." The first reason for restitution is that transaction costs preclude agreeing in advance. Examples 1–4 involve only five people. The transaction costs of bargaining among five people are not very high, but they increase sharply with the number of recipients. The justification for a legal duty of restitution in examples 1–4 would strengthen if the examples were modified to increase the number of recipients.

Second, the benefactor must create the benefit primarily to pursue his own interests.[8] This condition prevents sellers from making a business of supplying unrequested benefits to collect payments from others. Thus a lighting company could not take the initiative to install a light in the parking lot in example 3 and then demand restitution from the residents, without their prior agreement.[9]

---

[6] PORAT, *id.*, at 195-8.

[7] For a comprehensive account of the reasons for the rarity of restitution duties for unrequested benefits, see SAUL LEVMORE, *Explaining Restitution*, 71 VA. L. REV. 65 (1985). Bar-Gill & Bebchuk explain why a market operating under a restitution rule, where sellers provide goods and services without buyers' consent but are entitled to recover the value of the benefits, will probably not survive. OREN BAR-GILL & LUCIAN ARYE BEBCHUK, *Consent and Exchange* 39 J. LEGAL STUD. 357 (2010). Their argument is limited to situations in which transaction costs are low and consensual exchange is possible. For an innovative explanation of why a duty of restitution is so rare, see GIUSEPPE DARI-MATTIACCI, *Negative Liability*, 38 J. LEGAL STUD. 21 (2009). Dari-Mattiacci argues, *inter alia*, that under a rule of negligence, it is sufficient for the law to have one sanction at its disposal, since in equilibrium, there is no negligence and the sanction is never implemented. In contrast, in benefit cases, the "sanction," or, more accurately, the subsidy, should be implemented again and again, whenever a benefit is created by one person for another person. For a nonefficiency explanation for the rarity of a duty of restitution for unrequested benefits, see SCOTT HERSHOVITZ, *Two Models of Tort (and Takings)*, 92 VA. L. REV. 1147 (2006).

[8] Rescue cases are an exception: See PORAT, *supra* note 4, at 195-8. The second condition makes the cases for which a duty of restitution applies "self-interested intervention," which are often contrasted with "emergency intervention," a term which is ascribed to rescue cases. See the RESTATEMENT THIRD, RESTITUTION AND UNJUST ENRICHMENT §§ 20-21 (1981).

[9] Assume that in example 1, the deceased woman's heirs are her mature children and not her husband. If the husband sues the debtor of his deceased wife's estate entirely for the benefit of their children, not for his own benefit or at the estate's request, he probably cannot recover legal costs from his children.

(This condition often prevents an altruist from obtaining legal compensation for generosity to others.[10])

Third, the benefactor must protect or preserve existing entitlements, not create new ones. This requirement reflects the law's preference for maintaining the status quo over a broader principle of improving wellbeing.[11] Thus the heirs in example 1 had a right to money owed to the estate and the lawsuit vindicated this right. In contrast, the property owners in example 4 apparently do not have a right to an unpolluted stream. The owner who installed the purification equipment arguably created a new benefit, rather than protecting or preserving an existing entitlement.

Fourth and last, both the case law and commentary suggest an additional condition for recovery of unrequested benefits: "proximity of interests," "nexus of interests" or "closeness of interests" between the parties involved.[12]

We agree fully with the first condition for a duty of restitution: high transaction costs of voluntary exchange. In financing public goods, agreement is preferable to coercion for reasons of economy and liberty. However, we do not agree with the necessity of the other conditions. Together, they preclude a market in unrequested benefits. The second condition precludes such a market by requiring that the benefactor act primarily for his own benefit. This condition is analogous to forbidding a farmer from selling potatoes unless he grows them primarily for his own consumption.

The third condition—protecting existing entitlement, not creating new benefits—gets the relationship between entitlements and benefits wrong. The purpose of liability for unrequested benefits is to provide incentives for their creation. The creation of public goods creates benefits for the owners of existing entitlements, such as the separate owners of parking spaces in example 3, the owners of land along the stream in example 4, and the neighbors who view the roses in example 5. Higher benefits often increase the value of entitlements such as ownership of real estate, so liability for unrequested benefits could serve entitlements not only by preserving their value but also by increasing it. The third condition is analogous to refusing to register a patent because it creates a new benefit rather than protecting an existing entitlement.

As to the fourth and last condition, terms like "proximity of interests" suggest easy bargaining among the parties. The EDR proposed by us, however, is certainly not limited to cases where bargaining is easy. On the contrary, the main appeal of the proposed duty of restitution derives from the parties'

---

[10] Altruists are limited to recovering the cost of saving someone's life, health or property in an emergency. See *supra* note 8.

[11] Some categories of cases where a duty of restitution applies do not strictly comply with this condition. See PORAT, *supra* note 4, at 195-8.

[12] *Supra* note 3 and accompanying text.

inability to regulate their relationship through contract due to high transaction costs. We advocate retaining condition one and replacing conditions two, three and four with ones that we develop from the public goods theory of restitution.

B. A Private Production of Public Goods Theory

The law of restitution could be the legal framework for the private supply of public goods, analogous to the way property law is the legal framework for the private supply of private goods. A defining characteristic of a pubic good in economics is "nonexclusion." Thus none of the heirs in example 1 can be excluded from the benefits of collecting the estate's debt, none of the residents in examples 2–3 can be excluded from the benefits of lighting the parking lot, none of the homeowners in example 4 can be excluded from the benefits of purifying the stream, and none of the neighbors in example 5 can be excluded from the benefits of the rose garden.

Absent legal intervention, each beneficiary of a public good can enjoy it regardless of whether or not he pays its supplier. Consequently people refuse to share in the costs of producing a public good—they "free-ride." To overcome the free-rider problem, the law sometimes imposes a duty on the beneficiaries of a public good to reimburse its private supplier. Liability for unrequested benefits thus increases the private supply of public goods.

We explained the law's four necessary conditions of liability for unrequested benefits. The first condition concerns the transaction costs of voluntary exchange. When transaction costs are low, voluntary exchange assures that everyone expects to benefit, which economists call a "Pareto improvement." ("Pareto efficiency" refers to the exhaustion of opportunities for Pareto improvements.) When transaction costs are high, exchanges that would benefit everyone are blocked.

The law of restitution ideally should allow private parties to make Pareto improvements through involuntary exchanges. This fact points to a necessary condition for financing the private supply of public goods through restitution: everyone should benefit. Specifically, the benefit conferred on each person should exceed his liability for costs incurred. To achieve this result, we favor the liability formula "cost incurred plus a fraction of net benefits."

The requirement of Pareto improvement for the private supply of public goods is far more difficult to satisfy than the usual requirements for the government supply of public goods. Public projects often apply cost-benefit analysis, according to which the benefits to the project's winners must exceed the costs to the project's losers. Thus the benefits from creating a new park financed by public money must exceed its cost to taxpayers. When the benefits exceed the costs in aggregate, many individuals find that their benefits exceed their costs, and some find that their costs exceed their benefits. That is why most projects justified by cost-benefit analysis are not Pareto improvements. In our view, the law of restitution should secure the private supply of public goods when everyone benefits, whereas public law should secure the public supply of public goods when many benefit and some lose. We favor limiting the EDR to Pareto improvements, not extending it to cost-benefit improvements.

According to the public goods theory of restitution, the purpose of liability for unrequested, nonexcludable benefits is to enhance the welfare of the beneficiaries by overcoming bargaining failures. Preclusive transaction costs and a Pareto improvement should be necessary conditions for liability for unrequested benefits. The law should abandon the requirements that the benefactor creates the benefit primarily to pursue his own interests, that the benefactor protects an existing entitlement, and that proximity of interests exists between the parties. Restricting liability for unrequested benefits to Pareto improvements makes sense in terms of economic efficiency. It also makes sense in terms of liberty and autonomy.[13]

Examples 1–4 involve nonexclusion of five recipients. With five recipients, voluntary negotiations might solve the problem. As the number of nonexcluded recipients increases, as in example 5, voluntary negotiations are unlikely to succeed. As the number of nonexcluded recipients becomes larger, the good becomes less private and more public. The more public the good, the worse is the problem of free-riding and the greater the need for restitution law.

We explained how public goods theory revises the law's necessary conditions of liability for an unrequested benefit. Public goods theory also clarifies and amends the basis for calculating liability. In current law, restitution for unrequested benefits is based on the costs incurred by the benefactor, not the benefits conveyed to the recipients. The second condition in prevailing law for restitution—the benefactor must create the benefit primarily to pursue his own interests—implies that the benefactor is one of the recipients. Thus, under current law, the benefactor who receives restitution gains by being a recipient, as in examples 1 and 2 where the benefactor gains 1 and so do the beneficiaries.

To encourage the private supply of public goods, the law should allow the benefactor to gain more than other recipients. The benefactor might recover his costs incurred and a fraction of the benefits conveyed, with the remaining fraction going to the other recipients.[14]

The existing law of restitution provides no basis for a private business of supplying public goods. A private business of restitution is self-defeating under current law because, according to the second necessary condition for restitution, the benefactor primarily motivated by the right to restitution cannot

---

[13] For the autonomy argument against EDR, and for a response, see PORAT, *supra* note 4, at 215-7.

[14] If the basis of restitution is benefits conveyed, then each recipient gains nothing from someone else supplying the public good.

receive it. In order to create a private market for public goods, benefactors primarily motivated by the right to restitution must be allowed to retain some of the benefits they created. Therefore, the basis of restitution must include a fraction of benefits conferred, not merely costs incurred. A firm that merely recovered its costs would never enjoy profits. To gain the advantages of a private market in public goods, the law of restitution must allow professional benefactors to receive benefits exceeding their costs.

C. Implementation

1. VALUATION

A large economics literature identifies fundamental problems in the supply of public goods that affect an EDR. One problem concerns "preference revelation." With private goods, the price that a buyer pays reveals information about its subjective value to him. With public goods, no one buys it, so no one reveals his subjective value of the good. The problem of "preference revelation" is to find out how much a public good is worth to someone who does not buy it.

If this problem is unsolved, benefits might be overvalued, in which case some people who appear to benefit from the project would be harmed by it. Overvaluation is a practical problem when identifying Pareto improvements.[15] To illustrate, return to example 5, in which the owner expects a benefit of 15 from constructing a garden at a cost of 20 and neighbors expect a benefit of 10. Change the numbers. Assume that the actual benefit to neighbors is 4, but the court evaluates it as 10. With the court's numbers, a right of restitution for benefits conferred will cause the owner to build a garden that costs more than its value, and the neighbors will pay more for it than they gain.

To avoid overvaluation, the courts should adopt as a practical principle that liability in restitution should not exceed the recipient's indisputable benefit. Sometimes the cost incurred is clear, and the benefits conveyed are certainly larger than the cost incurred, but saying how much larger is difficult. In these circumstances, the recipient's share of the costs incurred can benchmark the indisputable benefit.

Two mechanisms could be used to reduce the risk of overvalution of benefits. The first mechanism is *licensing*. If there is a large risk of overvaluation, the law should allow an EDR only with prior government authorization. Thus the certification of a class action can be regarded as a court license to produce an unrequested benefit. The second mechanism is *voting*. Conditioning the

---

[15] LEVMORE, *supra* note 7, at 69-72 (1985) (claiming that the law may be seen as normally disallowing restitution claims because of valuation difficulties); see also HANOCH DAGAN, THE LAW AND ETHICS OF RESTITUTION 139-48 (2004) (discussing the recipient's subjective devaluation of the conferred benefit).

application of an EDR on recipients' advance vote in favor of production of the benefits could reduce the risk of overvaluation. [16]

Another practical problem concerns *liquidity*. When a recipient receives a nonmonetary benefit and is required to pay for its market value, he may find himself—because of a lack of liquidity—in a position that is worse than the position he would have occupied had he not been conferred the unrequested benefit.[17] Thus, if the recipient is a property owner and the benefit she receives is an increase in her property's market value, obliging her to compensate the benefactor for this benefit might force her to take a loan, sell the land, or use other resources differently from how she would prefer. This would create a burden for her that, if ignored, would lead to overvaluation of her benefits.

To solve the problem, restitution could be delayed until monetary profits materialize from the sale of the property. To secure the benefactor's interest, a lien could be placed on the enhanced property.[18] A market would then likely develop in which firms purchase the liens from benefactors who receive immediate payment.

2. COMPETITION

Another practical problem concerns competition to supply the public good. Recall the five heirs in example 1 who stand to benefit from a lawsuit against the estate's debtor. Assume that the heir who initiated the suit retains a lawyer. Any one of the other heirs can also retain a lawyer and proceed. Suppose two

---

[16] One version of this mechanism would be that recipients vote unanimously in favor of paying for the unrequested benefits as a condition for applying the EDR. This version of the voting mechanism would eliminate the risk of overvaluation completely. It could be practical, however, only in cases of a relatively small number of recipients. Alternatively, a supermajority vote requirement (e.g., three-quarters or two-thirds of recipients) or even a simple majority could be required. Under this version, since a greater proportion of the recipients would be required to obligate all recipients to pay for the unrequested benefits, the total risk of overvaluation would be reduced. The problem with the voting mechanism, however, is that it could trigger a free-riding problem, in that there would be the risk of recipients' making their vote conditional on their paying less than others to the benefactor. A secret vote could presumably mitigate this problem, but it could be objectionable on other grounds.

[17] See DAGAN, *supra* note 15, at 141 (describing the duty of restitution for unrequested benefits as an obligation to exchange money for nonmonetary values without an opportunity to refuse the exchange). For another articulation, see LEVMORE, *supra* note 7, at 74-79, who detaches the misvaluation argument from another argument, according to which even if the recipient is required to pay no more than the value of the benefit, because people's decisions to spend money depend on their wealth, a duty of restitution might force some recipients to spend their money in a way that deviates from their preferences. Levmore calls this latter argument the "Wealth Dependency" argument.

[18] 1 PALMER, *supra* note 1, § 1.5(a) (explaining how equitable lien is used to protect plaintiff rights); The RESTATEMENT THIRD, RESTITUTION AND UNJUST ENRICHMENT § 26 cmt. a (2010) ("If the claimant has made expenditures to protect an interest in common property . . . the basic requirement that a liability in restitution not prejudice an innocent recipient . . . is implicitly observed by giving a remedy by equitable lien or subrogation, rather than by money judgement").

heirs independently sue. If only one of them is entitled to recover costs, which one is it? If both of them are entitled to recover their costs, how does the court prevent legal expenses from exceeding their value to the heirs? Similarly, assume that one of the heirs sues and another heir insists that he could have sued at lower cost. Should the court use the actual or alternative cost of the suit when calculating restitution?

This coordination problem exists under current law, but it is a minor problem that parties usually solve by communication among themselves. An EDR will worsen the problem by increasing the potential number of competing benefactors, but it should remain minor.[19]

3. PUBLIC VS. PRIVATE PRODUCTION

Suppose that the government or a private benefactor can supply a public good. Who should supply it? The private supply of public goods is usually best when the change is a Pareto improvement (benefits some people without harming anyone), which is the condition under which we would acknowledge a right to restitution. In these circumstances, private beneficiaries can supply public goods better than public officials for three reasons. First, the law of restitution ideally aligns the benefactor's self-interest with the public interest, which is easier when the change is a Pareto improvement than when it is not. The political process and bureaucratic public agencies are notoriously weak at aligning the interests of officials and the public. Second, individuals often possess better information than government offcials about Pareto improvements from public goods, so individuals can act more flexibly and discerningly. In examples 1–5, the benefactor is closer to the facts than any official. Third, restitution causes the recipients to pay the costs, not the taxpayers. Sometimes this is a preferable solution for society with respect to distributional considerations. In example 5 the owner who builds the rose garden probably possesses better information than the government about its value and cost, he can probably build it at lower cost than the government, and he can only receive recovery from the recipients, not from taxpayers.[20]

---

[19] Absent cooperation, the courts can proceed pragmatically by restricting recovery to reasonable costs and a portion of the indisputable benefit created. In measuring the reasonable costs and the indisputable benefit, alternative options of production could be taken into account. In particular, the possibility that somebody else, or even the benefactor himself, could have produced, at lower cost, an alternative benefit that would have been greater than that actually produced or created, should be considered. Thus, if more than one person can produce the benefit, each of the potential producers should be certain enough before acting that he can do so in the most efficient way. Alternatively, when there are many potential benefactors, a licensing mechanism can be used. See *supra* text accompanying note 16. In class actions, a parallel question arises when there are many candidates for the class action plaintiff and only one can be chosen.

[20] For more extensive discussion of the division of private and public provision of public goods, see PORAT, *supra* note 4, at 217-222.

To better understand the latter point, compare public goods created by the government with public goods privately created under an EDR. The typical public good created by government is a cost-benefit improvement, which involves conflicts of interest and shifts income distributions in ways that need to be resolved politically, especially because public supply usually means tax financing. Conversely, restitution under the EDR requires payment by recipients exclusively, it avoids most conflicts of interest by benefiting everyone, and it has negligible distributional consequences.

4. ENFORCEMENT

Another objection that could be raised against expanding the duty of restitution is high enforcement costs.[21] Enforcement costs increase when the benefits spread nonuniformly across many recipients. Thus an EDR would not be justified in example 5 (the garden) if there were hundreds of neighbors with small, unequal benefits. In contrast, when the group of recipients is tightly defined and the benefits uniformly high as in examples 3–4, enforcement costs should not preclude restitution. In any case, if the benefactor bears the cost of enforcing recipients' duty of restitution, he would decide whether or not supplying the public good is worth the enforcement costs.

5. ALTERNATIVE MECHANISMS

Sometimes altruism and social norms produce local public goods with no need to invoke a right of restitution, especially in close-knit communities and among repeat-players with long-term relationships. A classic example is the landowners in Shasta County, California, who shared the costs of fences according to informal norms.[22] They did not need restitution law to encourage cooperation and overcome a free-riding problem. When altruism or social norms produce the same results as restitution, the law is unnecessary, although it is also unharmful.[23]

Sometimes people organize in a way that makes the EDR redundant. One such organization is a condominium. Another is a "business improvement district" (BID). A BID is a public-private partnership in which property and business owners of a defined area elect to make a collective contribution to

---

[21] *Cf.* Donald Wittman, *Liability for Harm or Restitution for Benefit?* 13 J. Legal Stud. 57 (1984) (arguing that the choice between encouraging actors to create benefits by sanctions and by subsidies should depend to a great extent on the litigation costs entailed in each method).

[22] Robert C. Ellickson, Order without Law: How Neighbors Settle Disputes 65-76 (1991).

[23] In special circumstances, a law can "crowd out" social norms, in which case applying restitution law could be harmful. See Bruno S. Frey, *A Constitution for Knaves Crowds Out Civic Virtues,* 107 The Economic Journal 1043 (1997).

the maintenance, development, and promotion of their commercial district.[24] The existence of condominiums and BIDs does not imply that people who choose *not* to live in one also reject the EDR. Although preferring not to live in condominiums or BIDs, many beneficiaries of an EDR will want to receive its benefits. An EDR would provide recipients with an ad hoc solution, which is often more suited to their needs and preferences than an institutional solution.

D. Benefits vs. Harms—an Aside

Under tort law, injurers often impose risks unilaterally on potential victims without getting their consent and subsequently bear liability from accidents. Tort victims ideally receive perfect compensation, so injurers internalize the harm that they cause (or wrongfully cause) and their incentives are efficient. Unilateral risk creation by injurers coupled with internalization of victims' harm (or wrongful harm) is a central feature of tort law.[25] Similarly, restitution law allows benefactors to confer benefits unilaterally on recipients, but, unlike tort law, benefactors are typically not entitled to recover for costs incurred or benefits conveyed. Consequently, incentives are inefficient and many public goods whose benefits exceed their costs are not produced.

While injurers are allowed to act unilaterally and force transactions on victims (impose a risk and compensate for the harm), benefactors are not allowed to do the same (confer a benefit and get recovery). We have argued that the duty of restitution for unrequested benefits should be expanded so that benefactors can force transactions on their beneficiaries. Nevertheless, the right of restitution should be smaller in scope compared to the entitlement of injurers to impose risk on others.

To understand why, contrast a world in which law prevents unilateral creation of benefits or harms. In this world, injurers need permission from *all* victims in order to impose risks on them. The law we are imagining, unlike

---

[24] BIDs require legislative authorization from the local government. They typically provide services such as street and sidewalk maintenance, public-safety officers, park and open-space maintenance, marketing, capital improvements, and various development projects. The services provided by BIDs supplement the services already provided by the local government. BIDs are funded through special assessments collected from the property owners in the defined boundaries of the district. Like a property tax, the assessment is levied on the property owners who can, if the property lease allows, pass it on to their tenants. For further details, see the websites of The Los Angeles Downtown Center Business Improvement District, http://www.downtownla.com, and the Downtown DC BID, http://www.downtowndc.org.

[25] For an insightful discussion of the symmetries and asymmetries between harm cases and benefit cases, and for the argument that many of the impediments to recognition of liability for benefits in general do not exist in the area of intellectual property, see WENDY J. GORDON, *Of Harms and Benefits: Torts, Restitution, and Intellectual Property*, 21 J. LEGAL STUDIES 449 (1992).

actual accident law, absolutely bars injurers from unilaterally imposing risk on their victims. Under this imagined law, injurers need unanimity among victims before subjecting them to risk. In such a world, each victim enjoys veto power over the risky activity, so there is a severe *holdout* problem. The parallel situation in restitution law denies benefactors who act unilaterally any means of forcing beneficiaries to pay for the public goods the benefactors create. The latter description, however, applies to the real world of law as it actually is. In this world, there is a severe *free-riding* problem.

In a world in which law prevents unilateral creation of benefits or harms, harm cases have a holdout problem, and benefit cases have a free-riding problem. The holdout problem with respect to harms is a greater impediment to efficiency than the free-rider problem with respect to benefits.[26] With holdout, it is enough that one would refuse to cooperate to disallow the imposition of risk.[27] A unanimity requirement for imposing risks on others is intolerable, not merely inefficient. A unanimity rule for harm cases would paralyze activities and enterprises. In contrast, the absence of a restitution rule for benefit cases does not paralyze the private production of public goods, because some people will still cooperate to create such benefits;[28] in fact, instances of private creation of public goods are not that rare. The absence of a restitution rule to encourage production of public goods is inefficient, not intolerable.

E. Conclusion

A duty of restitution for unrequested benefits to several recipients finances the private provision of public goods. The duty is sharply restricted in scope under current law, and we favor expanding its scope. An expanded duty of restitution (EDR) should enable recovery under two conditions: Transaction costs

---

[26] See LLOYD COHEN, *Holdouts and Free Riders*, 20 J. LEGAL STUD. 351 (1991) (comparing holdout and free-riding and indicating that sometimes free-riding is a more severe obstacle to efficiency than holdout).

[27] For a further elaboration on the holdout vs. free-riding issue, see PORAT, *supra* note 4, at 198-205.

[28] See ROBERT NOZICK, THE NATURE OF RATIONALITY, 50-55 (1993) (arguing that rational actors would cooperate and not free ride); ERNST FEHR & URS FISCHBACHER, *Why Social Preferences Matter—The Impact of Non-Selfish Motives on Competition, Cooperation and Incentives*, 112 ECON. J. 478 (2002) (arguing that identification with the group can also prevent free-riding); DAVID M. KREPS et al., *Rational Cooperation in the Finitely Repeated Prisoners' Dilemma*, 27 J. ECON. THEORY 245 (1982) (arguing that repeat players will tend not to free-ride); DAPHNA LEWINSOHN-ZAMIR, *Consumer Preferences, Citizen Preferences, and the Provision of Public Goods*, 108 YALE L.J. 377 (1998) (arguing that the main reason for people's reluctance to take part in financing public goods is not their desire to free-ride but, rather, their belief that others will do so); GARY J. MILLER, *The Impact of Economics on Contemporary Political Science*, 35 J. ECON. LIT. 1173, 1179-83 (1997) (describing experiments that show that the free-riding problem does not always preclude cooperation).

preclude the benefactor from obtaining consent of the recipients in advance, and each of the recipients indisputably benefits more than his share of the costs (Pareto improvement). We would eliminate the current legal requirements that the benefactor's act preserve existing entitlements, with no provision for creation of new goods; that the benefactor act primarily for his own gain independent of his recovery under restitution law; and that those conferring and receiving the benefit have a proximity of interests. The benefactor's recovery should equal costs incurred plus a fraction of the benefits conveyed.

We recommend applying the EDR to a defined set of cases when the market, the government, or the parties through consensual transactions are incapable of creating the benefit in question themselves. Furthermore, the risk of overvaluation of the benefits must be low, and the costs of enforcing the EDR cannot be too high. The most suitable cases for EDR would be those in which the value of the recipients' property increases monetarily.

Liability Externalities
and Mandatory Choices

"Externality" usually means costs and benefits conveyed to others that market prices do not capture. When markets fail to capture the cost of harm that one actor causes to another, liability law often improves the situation by making injurers compensate victims. Sometimes, however, liability law leaves significant costs externalized. "Liability externality" is our phrase for costs and benefits conveyed to others that market prices do not capture and liability law does not correct. In these circumstances, adjusting liability can improve incentives, as in this example.

> *Example 1: Liability Externality.* A driver negligently breaks a pedestrian's leg, and a doctor negligently breaks his patient's leg in a separate accident. The seriousness of injury, pain, treatment, and course of recovery are identical for both victims. According to prevailing law, the driver and doctor are both liable for the same damages. Driving usually costs society more than drivers pay (negative externality), and doctoring usually benefits patients more than they pay for their care (positive externality). Does efficiency require adjusting damages in light of externalities, so the driver pays more and the doctor pays less?

Damages are the same under legal principles in example 1, but not under economic principles. Law should discourage activities with negative liability externalities. A tax on these activities will discourage them. Many jurisdictions tax driving, but we know of no jurisdiction that calibrates the tax according to the risk that drivers impose on others. In the absence of a tax on risk, private law should ideally discourage driving by increasing liability beyond full compensation.

Unlike pedestrians and drivers, patients contract with doctors for treatment and willingly submit to the risk of harm. If medical markets worked perfectly, contracts would internalize all marginal costs and benefits, so liability law would not need to encourage or discourage doctoring. In reality, medical markets are imperfect and doctors convey more positive than negative externalities on their patients. Law should encourage activities with positive externalities. Doctoring is not subsidized in the U.S. except for the poor. Reducing liability for doctors would encourage activities that need encouragement.

Asking courts to use private law to discourage driving and encourage doctoring in light of externalities possibly asks too much. Judges appropriately take a narrower view of their role in law-making than legislators. There is, however, a special class of liability externalities that judges can address better than legislators. These are the externalities created by liability law itself.

In the case of drivers, the prevailing rule of liability is a negligence rule. Negligence rules generally externalize the risk of engaging in an activity when it is done with reasonable care. Thus a negligence rule for road accidents creates an incentive to restrain reckless driving and it creates no incentives to restrain excessive driving. As long as a person drives safely, he does not bear the cost of the risk that driving more miles imposes on others. *Non*-negligent drivers impose risk on pedestrians without being liable for it. Courts created this liability externality by adopting a rule of negligence: They understand it better than legislators, and they should respond appropriately by adjusting damages upward.

The activity level externality of driving is well understood by law and economics scholars. In the case of medical malpractice, a negligence rule creates a pervasive externality that is not so well understood. Doctors often have to choose the best treatment among available alternatives. Liability for making the wrong choice often threatens the doctor with a risk that exceeds the risk he created toward his patient, as in this example.

Example 2: Least Risky Alternative. An obstetrician must decide whether to deliver a baby in difficult circumstances by vaginal or Caesarean birth. The choice is mandatory because she must deliver a baby by one means or the other. Vaginal birth imposes the unavoidable risk of one type of harm to baby and mother of 200 with probability .10 (expected harm of 20). Caesarean birth avoids the risk of this type of harm. However, Caesarean birth imposes the unavoidable risk of a different harm of 300 with probability .10 (expected harm of 30). Vaginal birth avoids the risk of this type of harm. The obstetrician, who should choose vaginal birth, mistakenly chooses Caesarean birth and the harm materializes. A court applies a negligence rule to these facts and finds the obstetrician liable. How much damages should the patient receive?

The patient actually suffered harm of 300 from Caesarean birth. But for the negligent choice of Caesarean birth, this type of harm would have been 0. By applying legal principles, courts are likely to find that the doctor's negligent choice caused the harm of 300, and therefore the doctor owes damages equal to the patient's actual harm of 300.

Economic principles yield a different result. To give the doctor efficient incentives to choose, the doctor's risk of liability for the negligent choice should equal the resulting increase in the patient's risk of harm. Caesarean birth, which is the negligent alternative, imposed a risk of harm to the patient of 300 with probability .10. Vaginal birth, which is the least risky alternative, imposed a risk of harm to the patient of 200 with probability .10. The doctor's negligent choice increased the patient's risk of harm by 10 (from an expected harm of 20 to an expected harm of 30). The law should correspondingly increase the doctor's liability risk from a negligent choice by 10. A wrongful choice materializes in harm and liability with probability .10. Therefore, damages of 100 will increase the doctor's liability risk by 10. Applying economic principles, courts would award damages equal to 100. Later we will explain why legal rules produce the wrong economic result in many cases.

Medical professionals allege that high damages for tort liability in the U.S. cause too few doctors to specialize in obstetrics.[1] This allegation implies that doctors cannot fully recoup liability through higher fees. Applying this assumption to example 2, damages of 300 make the obstetrician's practice relatively unprofitable, which would discourage medical students from specializing in obstetrics.

The court in example 2 can verify whether or not the obstetrician chose the right method of delivery and the court can impose liability for making the wrong choice. In a more common situation described in example 3, the court cannot verify the right method of delivery in the circumstances. Instead, the court can assess whether the actual method chosen was executed negligently or non-negligently.

Example 3: Negligent Execution of a Mandatory Choice. An obstetrician must decide whether to deliver a baby by vaginal or Caesarean birth. The obstetrician's fees and profits are the same, but the doctor's liability costs are different. In vaginal delivery the obstetrician makes a mistake with probability .10 that causes harm of 200, so the patient's risk is 20. The doctor's probability of liability when he causes harm is 1. The doctor's liability internalizes the full harm of 200 from an accident. In Caesarean delivery the obstetrician makes a mistake with probability .10 that causes harm of 300, so the patient's risk is 30. The doctor's probability of liability when he causes harm is .5. On average, the doctor's liability externalizes half of the harm of 300, or 150. So the doctor delivers by Caesarean to reduce his liability, even though vaginal delivery is safer for patients.

---

[1] Pamela Robinson et al., *The Impact of Medical Legal Risk on Obstetrician Gynecologist Supply*, 105 Obstetrics & Gynecology 1296 (2005); Michelle M. Mello & Carly N. Kelly, *Effects of a Professional Liability Crisis on Residents' Practice Decisions*, 105 Obstetrics & Gynecology 1287 (2005).

Given that other costs and benefits are roughly equal, economic principles require the doctor to deliver by the least risky alternative, which is vaginal. However, the doctor's expected liability is higher for vaginal than Caesarean delivery in example 3. A self-interested doctor chooses Caesarean delivery to lower his liability costs, which is more risky for the patient. The difference in the private decision maker's costs drives the choice between the alternatives.

To provide socially efficient incentives, the doctor's liability risk must be lowest for the choice with the least accident risk for patients. The law can accomplish this in two ways. First, equalizing the actor's externalized harm between mandatory alternatives will make the least risky alternative for society into the least risky alternative for the doctor. In example 3, the external harm is 150 for Caesarean delivery and 0 for vaginal delivery. To equalize the external harm, the court can subtract 150 from liability for vaginal delivery of 200, which makes liability fall from 200 to 50. Now the doctor faces expected liability of $50 \times .1 = 5$ for vaginal delivery, and he faces expected liability of $300 \times .1 \times .5 = 15$ for Caesarean delivery. Therefore the doctor reduces his expected liability by choosing vaginal delivery over Caesarean delivery.

Second, instead of equalizing the externality, the court could make the doctor internalize it. The doctor is found liable in half the cases where Caesarean delivery causes harm. Doubling damages would offset the error in finding liability. So doubling liability from 300 to 600 makes the doctor internalize the expected harm from Caesarean delivery.

Internalizing the externality and equalizing the externality provide the same incentive to make the best mandatory choice. Note, however, that internalizing the externality makes the activity less profitable for the actor than equalizing it.[2]

Below, we develop the general theory of liability externalities as illustrated in example 1, and apply it to mandatory choices as illustrated in examples 2 and 3. We also identify suitable circumstances for applying our theory, given limited information available to courts. When externalities are positive, liability should decrease below the harm caused by the actor's negligence in order to encourage the underlying activity. We propose that legislatures give courts the choice of lowering tort damages for doctors in certain circumstances and we suggest how to do so for mandatory choices.[3]

---

[2] Internalizing the externality adds an additional burden on the activity. The expected value of the additional burden in example 3 is 150, conditional on harm materializing. Equalizing the externality reduces the burden on the activity. The reduction in the burden in example 3 is 150, conditional on harm materializing.

[3] For a recent proposal to reduce doctors' liability by allowing medical care providers to self-regulate, see RONEN AVRAHAM, *Private Regulation*, 34 HARVARD JOURNAL OF LAW & PUBLIC POLICY 543 (2011).

A. Liability Externalities

According to the standard economic analysis of law, a rule of strict liability with perfect compensation causes injurers to internalize the risk that they impose on others. The precaution and activity levels of injurers, consequently, are efficient. The conclusion is different, however, for a negligence rule. A negligence rule gives actors an incentive to escape liability by satisfying the legal standard of care. Having escaped liability, careful actors engage in too many harmful activities.

For drivers, the legal standard concerns how carefully people drive, not how much they drive. Since careful drivers escape liability most of the time, they externalize part of the risk of harming others, which makes them drive too much.[4] For doctors, the legal standard concerns their choice of treatment and their skill in carrying it out. Like drivers, careful doctors satisfy the legal standard and escape liability most of the time.

For careful physicians, unlike careful drivers, escaping liability does not cause them to doctor too much. Doctors and patients have a contractual relationship. Patients agree to submit to the risk that their doctor will accidentally and non-negligently harm them. If these contracts approached the economic ideal of perfect competition, prices would capture all of the benefits and costs, including risks of injury. Instead of perfect competition, however, medical markets have administered prices and quantities. Doctors often create benefits for patients that exceed their fees in total and at the margin.

A negligence rule, however, does not actually allow careful actors to escape liability in all circumstances. Courts sometimes make mistakes in applying the duty of care and hold careful actors liable. Like courts, normally careful actors occasionally make mistakes and harm others. Whether due to court or personal error, even normally careful actors bear some of the risk associated with their activity. Higher damages, consequently, reduce the incentive of careful actors to engage in the activity. In the case of drivers, higher damages will increase auto insurance premiums and drivers will respond by driving less and buying fewer cars. In the case of doctors, higher damages will cause them to perform fewer treatments that risk liability and discourage them from specializing in

---

[4] Negligent drivers, as well, drive too much for the same reason, but they pay for a higher fraction of the harm they cause relative to careful drivers. Even if drivers create some positive externalities, the negative externalities they create are much greater. A careful empirical study concludes that a tax on driving to cover the negative externalities from accident risk would exceed $2,000 per car in regions with high traffic density. In California the total tax revenue would exceed the sum of the current corporate and personal income tax. See AARON EDLIN & PANIAR KARACA-MANDIC, *The Accident Externality from Driving*, 114 JOURNAL OF POLITICAL ECONOMY 931 (2006).

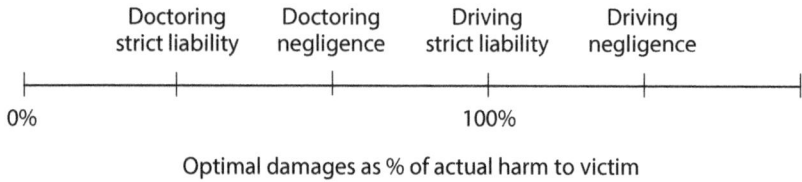

FIGURE 10.1. Optimal Damages for Drivers and Doctors

fields with high liability risk. Lowering damages will decrease these undesirable effects and benefit patients.[5]

Figure 10.1 depicts these observations about driving and doctoring. The horizontal line represents optimal damages as a percentage of full compensation. For activities like driving, incentives are optimal under a rule of strict liability when damages equal 100 percent of the victim's harm. For a negligence rule, however, incentives for drivers' activity are optimal when damages exceed 100 percent of the victim's actual harm. For activities with positive externalities like some medical specialties, incentives are optimal when damages are less than 100 percent of the victim's actual harm. For these activities, optimal damages fall as the rule of liability shifts from negligence to strict liability.

Empirical studies show that courts tend to award higher damages in medical malpractice cases than in road accident cases. When researchers controlled for injury severity, amount of reported economic damages, and other factors, malpractice awards remained approximately three times larger than injury awards in automobile cases.[6] Furthermore, in cases of wrongful death, the median award in malpractice trials was $876,000, while the median award in automobile trials was $318,000.[7] This data, however, requires cautious

---

[5] Tom Baker argues that doctors, health care providers, and medical malpractice insurers pay much less than necessary to cover the true social costs of doctors' wrongdoing. See Tom Baker, The Medical Malpractice Myth (2005). If the external costs discussed by Baker exceed the external benefits of doctoring, then incentives exist for too many people to become doctors. This chapter does not compare the negative and positive liability externalities of doctors in general. Rather, we assume that there are several fields of medicine wherein the positive externalities exceed the negative externalities. For example, much research supports the argument that positive externalities exceed negative externalities in obstetrics. See *infra* note 23. Liability law biases doctors against specializing in these fields.

[6] A. Chin & M. Peterson, *Deep Pockets, Empty Pockets: Who Wins in Cook County Jury Trials*, The Rand Institute for Civil Justice, Pub. Num. R-3249-ICJ 36 (1985). The median award was $201,000 and the mean was $1,057,000. When outlier awards were excluded, the mean was $432,000. Fully 15 percent of malpractice awards exceeded $1 million.

[7] Thomas H. Cohen & Steven K. Smith, *Civil Trial Cases and Verdicts in Large Counties* (2001); Bureau of Justice Statistics (2004). Available at: http://bjs.ojp.usdoj.gov/index.cfm?ty =pbdetail&iid=559.

interpretation.[8] Turning from econometrics to raw statistics, plaintiffs have lower success rates[9] and higher awards in medical malpractice cases, compared to automobile cases or tort cases in general.[10]

"Liability externality" refers to costs and benefits conveyed to others that market prices do not capture and liability law does not correct. Given liability

---

[8] The discrepancy between tort awards overall and malpractice awards is likely due, in large part, to differences in how malpractice cases are selected for trial. See NEIL VIDMAR, *Pap and Circumstance: What Jury Verdict Statistics Can Tell Us About Jury Behavior and the Tort System*, 28 SUFFOLK U. L. REV. 1205, 1212-1222 (1994). Other differences could also explain the discrepancy: Automobile cases often involve multiple plaintiffs, the driver and passengers of the second car, but usually a single defendant, the allegedly negligent driver of the first car. Malpractice cases, however, typically involve a single plaintiff, the injured patient, and multiple defendants. Automobile cases may involve contributory negligence, which is not claimed as often in malpractice cases. Medical malpractice lawyers tend to be specialists who carefully screen cases and invest heavily in experts, whereas generalist lawyers who often call few or no experts tend to litigate automobile cases. See FRANK M. MCCLELLAN, MEDICAL MALPRACTICE: LAW TACTICS AND ETHICS 45-62 (1994); PAUL C. WEILER, MEDICAL MALPRACTICE ON TRIAL 19-26 (1991). The crux of the matter is that "juries hear very different cases in medical and automobile negligence trials and decide them under different legal standards." VIDMAR, *id.*, at 1222.

[9] The overall win rate for medical malpractice plaintiffs (27 percent) was about half of that found among plaintiffs in all tort trials (52 percent). See THOMAS H. COHEN, *Medical Malpractice Trials and Verdicts in Large Counties, 2001*, CIVIL JUSTICE DATA BRIEF, BUREAU OF JUSTICE STATISTICS (2004) at http://bjs.ojp.usdoj.gov/content/pub/pdf/mmtvlc01.pdf; COHEN & SMITH, *supra* note 7, at 1. See also NEIL VIDMAR, MEDICAL MALPRACTICE AND THE AMERICAN JURY: CONFRONTING THE MYTHS ABOUT JURY INCOMPETENCE, DEEP POCKETS AND OUTRAGEOUS DAMAGE AWARDS 39 (1997). For comparison, in automobile negligence trials, plaintiffs prevailed in 61.2 percent of the trials. COHEN & SMITH, *id.*

[10] In general tort cases, the median verdict, including punitive damages, was $51,000. BRIAN J. OSTROM et al., *A Step above Anecdote: A Profile of the Civil Jury in the 1990's*, 79 JUDICATURE 233, 238 (1996). The mean award was much higher, at $408,000. The discrepancy between median and mean was produced by some very large awards. When the top and bottom 5 percent of these outlier awards were excluded, the mean was $160,000. Medical malpractice cases, however, had substantially higher awards. *Id.* See also COHEN, MEDICAL MALPRACTICE TRIALS, *supra* note 8 (The median award of $425,000 in medical malpractice trials was nearly 16 times greater than the overall median award of $27,000 in all tort trials). The Rand Corporation studies indicated that even when juries considered injury severity, medical malpractice plaintiffs and product liability plaintiffs received awards several times greater than those received by automobile injury plaintiffs. AUDREY CHIN & MARK A. PETERSON, DEEP POCKETS, EMPTY POCKETS: WHO WINS IN COOK COUNTY JURY TRIALS (1985). Randall Bovbjerg and his colleagues found that the expected awards for automobile cases are only two-thirds those for malpractice cases (0.66 as compared to 1.00); or, conversely, malpractice scores half again higher. RANDALL R. BOVBJERG et al., *Juries and Justice: Are Malpractice and Other Personal Injuries Created Equal?* 54 LAW & CONTEMP. PROBS. 5, 25 (1991). Almost one out of every four medical malpractice awards exceeded $1 million. In contrast, the mean and median awards in automobile and premises liability cases were much lower. NEIL VIDMAR, *The Performance of the American Civil Jury: an Empirical Perspective*, 40 ARIZ. L. REV. 849, 876 (1998). However, punitive damages remain rare in medical malpractice jury trials. From 1992 to 2001, 1 to 4 percent of plaintiff winners in medical malpractice jury trials received punitive damages. COHEN, *Medical Malpractice Trials, supra* note 9; see also MARC GALANTER, *Real World Torts: An Antidote to Anecdote*, 55 MD. L. REV. 1093, 1134, 1138 (1996).

externalities, adjusting damages can improve incentives. When liability externalities are negative, as with driving, increasing damages above full compensation improves incentives for the activity by discouraging it. Thus if drivers are liable for, say, 50 percent of the accidents that not driving would eliminate, they will drive too much. Increasing the damages when they are found liable to, say, 150 percent will discourage driving as required for efficiency. Conversely, when liability externalities are positive, as with doctoring in certain fields, decreasing damages below full compensation improves incentives for the activity by encouraging it. If doctors get paid for, say, 50 percent of the benefits that they create for their patients, then they will doctor too little. Decreasing the damages when they are found liable to, say, 25 percent will encourage doctoring as required for efficiency.

While improving incentives for the activity, these adjustments can distort the incentives for precaution. Increasing the damages of drivers when they are found liable to, say, 150 percent could induce them to avoid liability by excessively cautious driving. Similarly, decreasing the damages of doctors when they are found liable to, say, 25 percent could make them risk liability by insufficiently cautious doctoring. A tradeoff exists between precautions and activity level.[11] We think that improving incentives for an activity often dominates

---

[11] To formulate the tradeoff mathematically, consider an activity that benefits other people, and also imposes risks on them. The activity creates benefits of b for other people and imposes risk of harm h on them with probability p. Thus the marginal net benefit to others is $b - ph$. Because of a market transaction, the actor receives the market price m. Liability law requires the actor to pay damages d with probability q. Thus the actor's expected net benefit equals $m - qd$. The variables labeled here as b, q, d, p, and h may be interpreted as marginal values. To internalize marginal net benefits, the actor's expected net payoff must equal the net social benefit of the activity to others at the margin:

$$m - qd = b - ph \qquad (1)$$

Solving for d yields the level of damages d^* that internalizes social costs:

$$d^* = \quad (1/q) \qquad [ph - \qquad (b-m)] \qquad (2)$$

reciprocal   expected   price
of enforcement   harm   externality error

Applied to automobile accidents, the injurer and victim are usually strangers, so they do not negotiate a price before driving: $m = 0$. Drivers do not convey benefits to their potential victims: $b = 0$. Equation (2) reduces to $d^* = (p/q)h$. Damages internalize the externality when $d = (p/q)h$. To illustrate, if drivers expect to be liable 33 percent of the time, then damages must equal 300 percent of the actual harm in order to internalize the risk of harm to others.

Applied to medicine, doctors receive a price m that encompasses some, but not all, of the benefits to the patient, so $m < b$. This price externality causes optimal damages d^* to decrease below 100 percent of the actual harm h. With a negligence rule, doctors are liable for some, but not all, accidents: $q < p$. This fact, according to Equation 2, causes damages d^* to increase above 100 percent of the actual harm h.

Less care by the injurer increases the probability of an accident. Assume that less care also increases the probability that the victim can prove negligence and recover damages. These

worsening incentives for precaution. In the case of mandatory choices, our next topic, improving incentives for the activity also improves incentives for some forms of precaution.

B. Mandatory Choices

Providers of services are usually free to choose whether or not to serve a particular client.[12] Once the actor commits to providing the service, however, he faces mandatory choices. Mandatory choices usually arise from a relationship created by contract. For some mandatory choices, each of the alternatives imposes risks on others.[13] Doctors must choose among treatments, each of which risks harming the patient—such as the choice of how to deliver a baby, whether or not to operate, or whether or not to administer a particular drug. The same problem of mandatory choice with unavoidable risks arises in various fiduciary relationships: between a client and bank, an investor and the firm's board of directors, or a client and his attorney.

Our discussion of example 2 explained how liability affects the obstetrician's choice between vaginal and Caesarean delivery. Figure 10.2 imbeds this mandatory choice in some decisions that precede and follow it. Before choosing, the obstetrician must prepare to make the choice, which involves examining the patient and ordering tests. Much earlier in the sequence, the medical student must decide whether or not to specialize in obstetrics. Finally, after making the mandatory choice, the obstetrician must carry it out, either carefully or negligently. We will analyze the connection between these decisions and tort liability.

1. THE LEAST HARMFUL ALTERNATIVE

A general principle of tort law holds a person liable for damages equal to the harm caused by his negligence. For mandatory choices, courts apply this principle inconsistently. In example 2, the actor did not cause the mandatory choice that he must make on behalf of the patient. Given the mandatory choice, risk of

---

assumptions imply Craswell's Paradox: With the multiplier, the optimal sanction is less when wrongdoing is worse. By definition the multiplier equals the reciprocal of the enforcement error, and, by assumption, worse wrongdoing is more likely to be detected, so worse wrongdoing must result in a lower sanction. RICHARD CRASWELL, *Deterrence and Damages: The Multiplier Principle and Its Alternatives*, 97 MICH. L. REV. 2185 (1999).

[12] Law sometimes requires a professional to provide a service. For example, according to the Emergency Medical Treatment and Active Labor Act 42 U.S.C. 1395dd (1998), hospitals have an obligation to provide examination and treatment for emergency medical conditions. For a claim that common law should recognize a duty of "medical rescue" on the part of doctors and other health care professionals, see KEVIN WILLIAMS, *Medical Samaritans: Is There a Duty to Treat?* 21 OXFORD J. LEGAL STUD. 393 (2001).

[13] ARIEL PORAT, *The Many Faces of Negligence*, 4 THEORETICAL INQ. L. 105, 121-4 (2003).

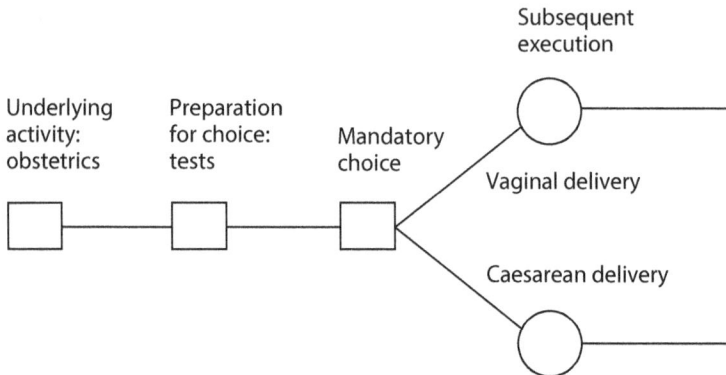

FIGURE 10.2. Acts Preceding and Following a Mandatory Choice

harm at the level caused by the least harmful alternative was unavoidable. The actor's faulty choice caused additional risk of harm, equal to the patient's actual risk minus the risk from the least harmful alternative. In example 2, the additional risk is $30 - 20 = 10$. Because the risk associated with the actor's choice materialized, the actual harm equaled 300. In setting damages, the court might want to subtract the unavoidable risk from the actual harm, resulting in damages of 280.[14] Or the court might want to award 100, in order to make the actor bear the incremental risk of his wrong choice.

The principles of positive law, however, do not allow the court to subtract anything as long as the risks of the faulty choice and the risks of the least harmful choice do not overlap. To illustrate nonoverlapping risks, vaginal delivery is more likely to cause uterine prolapse, whereas Caesarean birth carries risks associated with surgery. If the obstetrician wrongfully chooses Caesarean delivery and the mother suffers harm in surgery, the principles of positive law do not allow a deduction for avoiding the risk of uterine prolapse.

The principles of economics favor a different conclusion from positive law. The obstetrician's faulty choice increased one risk by 30 and reduced another risk by 20, thus causing additional risk of 10. This is true even though the risks do not overlap. In order to make the doctor internalize the social costs of his wrong choice, he could be held liable for imposing risk of 10, whether or not the risk materialized. Tort law, however, imposes liability for materialized harm, not for exposure to risk. Harm materializes with probability .10. Liability of 100 for materialized harm has the same incentive effects as liability of 10 for

---

[14] An award of 280 is analogical to probabilistic recovery awarded by some courts for lost chances of recovery. See ARIEL PORAT AND ALEX STEIN, TORT LIABILITY UNDER UNCERTAINTY 73-76, 101-129 (2001).

exposure to risk.[15] The socially efficient level of damages for materialized harm equals 100 in this example.

Notice that our rule differs from a rule of probabilistic recovery. A probabilistic recovery principle mandates imposing liability on a defendant for the harm suffered by the plaintiff multiplied by the probability that the harm was caused by the defendant's wrongdoing.[16] Some courts apply the principle in medical malpractice cases in which the doctor's negligence diminished the plaintiff's chances of recovery. Consider the patient who arrives at the hospital with 30 percent odds of recovery, but because his disease is not diagnosed by the doctor in time, his chances drop to zero. The patient brings a tort action against the doctor. The patient would lose if the preponderance of evidence standard were applied, because the probability that the doctor caused the harm is lower than 50 percent. The court might apply a probabilistic recovery rule, which would result in the doctor bearing liability for 30 percent of the patient's harm.[17]

Under a probabilistic recovery rule damages in example 2 should be 280. The reason is simple: The patient suffered harm of 300. But for the doctor's negligence the patient would have suffered either no harm or harm of 200. The probability of the latter is .1. Therefore, 200x.1 should be deducted from the actual harm of 300 suffered by the patient. Conversely, under our rule, liability should be for 100. Liability for 100—not for 280—will make the doctor internalize the true risk he created by his negligence.

Our rule is motivated not by the uncertainty of the case (which is the motivation for a probabilistic recovery rule), but by the presence of positive externalities. In example 2 the doctor's negligent choice caused both negative and positive effects: He increased one risk by 30 (negative externality) and he also decreased another risk by 20 (positive externality). Prevailing tort law makes the doctor internalize the negative effects by imposing liability on him when harm materializes, but the positive effects remain externalized. As a result, the doctor bears more than the net risk created by his negligence. We suggest correcting this distortion by crediting the doctor with the positive externalities he created through his negligence and reducing his liability accordingly.

To formalize this argument, let A denote the reasonable choice that risks harm h_a with probability p_a. Let B denote the unreasonable choice that risks harm h_b with probability p_b. The expected harm from the least harmful

---

[15] For simplicity, we also assume that actors are risk-neutral.

[16] PORAT & STEIN, *supra* note 14, at 116-29 (2001).

[17] In this context, the principle is known as the "lost chances of recovery principle." See, e.g., *Herskovits v. Group Health Coop. of Puget Sound* 664 P. 2d 474 (Wash. 1983); *Perez v. Las Vegas Med. Ctr.* 805 P.2d 589, 592 (Nev. 1991). For support for the principle, see JOSEPH H. KING, JR., *Causation, Valuation, and Chance in Personal Injury Torts Involving Pre-Existing Conditions and Future Consequences*, 90 YALE L.J. 1353 (1981). The market share liability doctrine is another application of a probabilistic recovery rule. PORAT & STEIN, *supra* note 14, *id.*

alternative equals $p_a h_a$, and the expected harm from the chosen alternative equals $p_b h_b$. Deducting the former from the latter yields $p_b h_b - p_a h_a$, which indicates the additional risk from choosing the wrong alternative. Instead of liability for risk, the court imposes liability for realized harm. To find the level of liability for realized harm that is equivalent to liability for additional risk, multiply the preceding difference by $1/p_b$, which yields $h_b - p_a h_a / p_b$.

We have explained that when the risks from a mandatory choice do not overlap, legal principles would not allow subtracting from the victim's actual harm a fraction that reflects the *risk* of the least harmful alternative. When the mandatory choice imposes unavoidable *harm* rather than risk, however, the court has no difficulty subtracting the least harmful alternative when computing damages. To illustrate, modify example 2 and assume that vaginal delivery causes harm of 200 to mother with certainty, and Caesarean delivery causes her different harm of 300 with certainty. Courts would note that, but for the actor's negligence, harm would have been 200 rather than 300, so the negligent choice caused harm of 100. When a mandatory choice results in certain harm, the "but for" test of causation requires subtracting the least harmful alternative for the victim from the victim's actual harm.

The same conclusion applies in another set of circumstances as illustrated by a modification of example 2. Assume that two alternative procedures, A or B, benefit the patient equally and cost the doctor the same. Each procedure risks the same harm to the patient's *left* leg—harm of 200 with probability .1. Since the risk to the left leg is the same for both procedures, we call it *overlapping*. Procedure A poses no risk to the patient's *right* leg, and procedure B poses a risk to the patient's *right* leg—harm of 100 with probability .1. Since the risk to the right leg only occurs with procedure B, we call it *nonoverlapping*.

The doctor negligently chooses procedure B and the patient suffers total harm of 200 to his left leg and 100 to his right leg. The doctor's negligent choice did not change the overlapping risk to the left leg. The doctor's wrong choice, however, increased the nonoverlapping risk to the right leg. Under appropriate application of causation law,[18] liability for making the wrong choice will be imposed on the doctor only for the harm to the right leg. By this reasoning, the doctor's liability equals 100, although the patient suffered harm of 300.

Another variation concerns nonoverlapping harm to different people. In example 2 assume that the risk to the mother is identical under both procedures, whereas Caesarean delivery poses additional risk on the baby. By assumption, the risks to mother by both methods of delivery overlap, while the risks to baby are separate. If the obstetrician delivers by Caesarean and harm materializes,

---

[18] GUIDO CALABRESI, *Concerning Cause and the Law of Torts: An Essay for Harry Kalven, Jr.*, 43 U. CHI. L. REV. 69 (1976).

mother suffers loss of 200 and baby suffers loss of 100. Baby is entitled to damages of 100 while mother is entitled to no damages.[19]

We have explained that economic principles require that damages for a negligent mandatory choice make the injurer bear a liability risk equal to the incremental risk of his wrongful choice. However, legal principles of causation require courts to allow this only when the least harmful choice is certain or overlapping, not when it is probabilistic and not overlapping.[20]

Failing to reduce damages has three negative consequences, as represented from left to right in figure 10.2.

First, it discourages medical students from specializing in obstetrics. Even though in theory doctors could shift the additional liability to their patients, in fact doctors cannot fully recoup liability through higher fees.[21]

---

[19] If vaginal delivery risks harm of 200 with probability .1 to mother, and Caesarean delivery risks harm of 300 with probability .1 to baby, and the doctor wrongfully chose Caesarean and harm materialized, the risks do not overlap and the doctor will pay damages of 300, not 100. But this should not come as a surprise to tort law scholars who know that positive externalities to one person (e.g., the mother) do not affect the victim's right to compensation (e.g., the baby). Efficiency would mandate liability of 100 in all such cases.

[20] Arlen and MacLeod argued that doctor's liability should equal the difference between the patient's expected benefits from optimal treatment and the patient's actual benefit from the erroneous treatment that he received. Assuming underenforcement, that difference should be divided by the probability that the doctor is found liable when negligent. See JENNIFER ARLEN & W. BENTLEY MACLEOD, *Malpractice Liability for Physicians and Managed Care Organizations*, 78 NY U. L. REV. 1929, 1984-5 (2003). Those authors, however, did not distinguish between certain harms and uncertain risks, overlapping and nonoverlapping risk, and risks to same patient or different patients.

The idea developed here with respect to mandatory choices has a wider scope. In general, when a wrongful act creates risks but at the same time reduces other risks, either to the victim or to third parties, liability should be reduced, reflecting the net rather than gross risks which the wrongful behavior created. Especially when applied to reduced risks to third parties, the argument invites strong opposition from corrective justice scholars. See ARIEL PORAT, *Offsetting Risks*, 106 MICH. L. REV. 243 (2008).

[21] MELLO & KELLY, *supra* note 1. On the inability of doctors to pass higher insurance costs along to patients, see PETER EISLER, JULIE APPLEBY & MARTIN KASINDORF, *Hype Outraces Facts in Malpractice Debate*, USA TODAY (3/5/2003), available at: http://www.usatoday.com/news/nation/2003-03-04-malpractice-cover_x.htm. (Claiming that the cause of this inability is the limitations on reimbursements made by managed care insurers, Medicare and Medicaid); BAKER, *supra* note 5, at 64-65 (Admitting that ". . . physicians have little or no ability to raise prices in response to increased costs. When a malpractice insurance crisis hits, the burden falls disproportionately on physicians in high-risk specialties and locations, who cannot raise their prices in response"). It is worth mentioning that medical practice has negative externalities as well due to the fact that many patients who sustain injury as a result of negligence do not sue. See BAKER, *id.*; A. RUSSELL LOCALIO et al., *Relations Between Malpractice Claims and Adverse Events Due to Negligence: Results of the Harvard Medical Practice Study III*, 325 NEW ENG. J. MED. 245 (1991); DAVID M STUDDERT et al., *Negligence Care and Malpractice Claiming Behavior in Utah and Colorado*, 38 MED. CARE 250 (2000). Other research by Studdert points to the costly litigation in these cases which might discourage patients from suing. See DAVID M. STUDDERT et al., *Claims, Errors, and Compensation Payments in Medical Malpractice Litigation*, 354 NEW ENG. J. MED. 2024 (2006).

Second, it causes too many tests in preparing to choose a procedure. To illustrate by example 2, when negligent obstetricians are liable for 300, obstetricians order more tests than if they were liable for 100.[22]

Third, it causes obstetricians who face mandatory choices to choose the alternative that reduces the risk of liability and not the risk of harm. This fact might explain the high number of Caesarean deliveries compared to vaginal deliveries. In general, when liability for negligence is larger, the incentives of doctors to escape the risk of liability by practicing defensive medicine are stronger.[23]

The preceding analysis assumed a mandatory choice between two alternatives, but the results change only modestly when there is a mandatory choice among continuous alternatives. Assume that the mandatory choice involves alternatives that run continuously from the least risky alternative to increasingly risky alternatives. Somewhere along this continuum is the boundary between negligent and non-negligent behavior. As the injurer's behavior approaches this boundary, the risk of injury increases continuously, whereas the expected liability jumps discontinuously at the boundary. The jump occurs so long as the court awards compensation for the victim's actual harm without subtracting damages that reflect the least harmful alternative. An earlier chapter explained how this discontinuity affects behavior.[24]

---

[22] The reason for that is the possibility of courts' and doctors' errors in determining whether the doctor satisfied the standard of care. In principle, courts could solve the problem by imposing strict liability on obstetricians for the full harm that resulted from either choice. Strict liability would discourage obstetrics by making obstetricians pay much more than the social costs of their activities. Indeed, non-negligent obstetricians would have to pay for the risks caused by the pregnancy of their patients.

[23] Caesarean delivery rates in the United States rose from 4.5 per 100 births in 1965 to 24.1 per 100 in 1986. A. R. LOCALIO, A. G. LAWTHERS, J. M. BENGTSON et al., *Relationship Between Malpractice Claims and Cesarean Delivery*, 269 JAMA 366 (1993). In response to the growing concerns in the 1980s about the rising Caesarean rate, the U.S. Department of Health and Human Services established decreasing the Caesarean rate as one of the Healthy People Year 2000 objectives. U.S. DEPARTMENT OF HEALTH AND HUMAN SERVICES, PUBLIC HEALTH SERVICE, *Healthy People 2000: National health promotion and disease prevention objectives* (1990).

A reason for high Caesarian rates may be found in the malpractice crisis. The practice of obstetrics is experiencing growing claims rates and now fields more malpractice claims than any other specialty. ROGER A. ROSENBLATT et al., *Why Do Physicians Stop Practicing Obstetrics? The Impact of Malpractice Claims*, 76 OBSTETRICS & GYNECOLOGY 245, 249 (1990).

Fear of being sued if complications arise in a vaginal delivery has contributed to the rising number of Caesarean sections. See ELIZABETH SWIRE FALKER, *The Medical Malpractice Crisis in Obstetrics: A Gestalt Approach to Reform*, 4 CARDOZO WOMEN'S L.J. 1, 15 (1998). Studies examined the impact of malpractice risk on Caesarean deliveries and found that a "systematic relationship between the rate of Cesarean surgical procedures and malpractice claim frequency exists." MICHAEL DALY, *Attacking Defensive Medicine Through The Utilization of Practice Parameters*, 16 J. LEG. MED. 101, 105 (1995).

[24] For the discontinuity and its behavioral consequences see *supra* chapter 1.

2. DISGORGEMENT

Faced with a mandatory choice, a self-interested injurer will choose the alternative whose net benefit is higher for him, even if his choice excessively increases the risks to the victim. If the injurer must disgorge his savings each time he chooses the more risky alternative, he will have an incentive to choose the less risky alternative. To illustrate, assume that the obstetrician's fee in example 2 is the same for Caesarean and vaginal delivery, but vaginal delivery costs the doctor 1 more than Caesarean delivery. The obstetrician thus gains 1 each time he negligently chooses Caesarean delivery. If the obstetrician were required to disgorge his gain every time he negligently chooses Caesarean delivery, then he would have efficient incentives. If, however, the disgorgement takes place only when the obstetrician negligently chooses Caesarean delivery and harm materializes, then deterring wrongdoing requires increasing damages to reflect the obstetrician's gain in the cases where he negligently chooses Caesarean delivery and harm did not materialize. In our example, the obstetrician expects to pay damages when harm materializes, which occurs in 10 percent of Caesarean deliveries. Damages of 10 for materialized harm will cause the obstetrician's expected liability to equal his expected gain from negligence, so he expects to disgorge his gain from wrongdoing.

Alternatively, the injurer can cut costs by reducing efforts to verify which alternative is the least risky alternative. Spending less on preparing to choose increases the probability of making the wrong choice. To illustrate, assume that the obstetrician saves 1 by refraining from making costly tests to decide how to deliver the baby, and the lack of a test causes the obstetrician to choose the more risky alternative.

We coin the phrase "Disgorgement Damages for Risk of Accidents" (DDA) to refer to damages that make the negligent injurer's expected liability equal to his expected gains from negligence. For mandatory choices these gains include the difference between the injurer's costs of executing the two alternative procedures. These gains also include the untaken precautions that should have been taken in the course of preparation as the actor evaluated alternatives. The DDA generally equals or exceeds the actual gain in the case where the harm materializes. In the preceding examples, DDA equals the gain multiplied by the reciprocal of the probability of liability.[25]

---

[25] Here is a mathematical formulation. We will derive this result for a case where the alternative procedures have different costs for the injurer. Let a_A and a_B represent the cost of alternative acts to the actor. Assume that act a_B involves more costs than act a_A. As before, m is the price paid to the actor, q is the probability of liability, and d is damages. Disgorgement damages $d_A^{'}$ equalize the net costs of each act to the actor:

$$[m_B - a_B - q_B d_B] = [m_A a_A q_A d_A^{'}].$$

Since DDA exactly offsets the expected gain from making the wrong choice, DDA is the lowest level of damages that cause self-interested actors to behave non-negligently. Moving from left to right in figure 10.2 reveals an advantage and a disadvantage of DDA. For activities with positive externalities, DDA has the advantage of encouraging more of the underlying activity than any alternative damage measure that deters negligence. DDA, however, is likely to give the injurer deficient incentives to prepare for the mandatory choice. The preparations are often nonverifiable, so the gains included in the DDA exclude them. Applied to example 2, DDA gives the obstetrician the required incentive to choose vaginal delivery, and DDA encourages medical students to become obstetricians, but DDA is likely to give insufficient incentives for testing before deciding on the method of delivery. To illustrate the latter effect by example 2, under DDA the doctor is likely not to take tests that cost him more than 1, even though the expected harm from making the wrong choice is 10.

Another problem with DDA arises in cases where an ordinarily careful actor's attention lapses and he causes harm. Under prevailing law a lapse of attention that causes harm is considered negligence and triggers liability. Typically, the injurer gains nothing from lapsing, which implies that DDA equals zero. To avoid DDA of zero, the court would have to find someone liable who saved costs from the doctor's untaken precaution. Thus overwork or inferior working conditions could cause an obstetrician to lapse. Perhaps the doctor's employer overworked the doctor and caused the lapse, or perhaps the doctor's employer provided inferior working conditions that caused the lapse. Courts could apply DDA to the employer's gains from overworking the doctor or providing inferior working conditions.[26]

Rearranging terms yields a formula for disgorgement damages:

$$d'_A = \frac{1}{q_A}q_B d_B + \frac{1}{q_A}[(m_A - m_B) + (a_B - a_A)].$$

Under the simplifying assumptions that $d_B = 0$ and $m_A = m_B$, the preceding equation reduces to the proposition that damages equal the reciprocal of the probability of harm multiplied by the gain from negligence:

$$d'_A = \underset{\substack{\text{gain from} \\ \text{negligence}}}{\frac{1}{q_A}(a_B - a_A)}.$$

[26] Saul Levmore raised the possibility of using a multiplier in restitution cases but rejected it as impractical. Even though Levmore has not explicitly discussed accident cases, his analysis can be applied to them. SAUL LEVMORE, *Probabilistic Recoveries, Restitution, and Recurring Wrongs*, 19 J. LEGAL STUD. 691, 713.

A mechanical application of the DDA could end up with liability which is higher than liability for the entire harm. That could create a moral hazard. Suppose gains from untaken precautions are 1, probability of harm is .1, and harm, if materialized, is 5 in half of the cases, and 25 in the rest of the cases. Mechanical application of the DDA would impose liability on the injurer for 10,

3. EQUALIZING EXTERNALITIES

Think of liability as having two components: the baseline of liability for harm resulting from the right choice, plus the increase in liability for making the wrong choice. The increase in liability for making the wrong choice is the incremental liability, which can be used to control the mandatory choice. The baseline of liability can be used to control other behaviors: engaging in the underlying activity, preparing to choose and executing the choice. In section A of this chapter, we assumed the baseline to be zero. Now we explore under what circumstance it should be positive.

As we have shown, disgorgement damages (DDA) provide the lowest liability for a mandatory choice that still gives an incentive to make the right choice. As long as the difference in liability for each of the choices equals or exceeds DDA, the actor has incentives to make the right choice. In figure 10.3, the point on the line labeled "mandatory choice" graphically demonstrates our reasoning that liability at least as large as DDA provides efficient incentives for the mandatory choice.

Now consider how the baseline of liability affects the first choice depicted in figure 10.2—engaging in the underlying activity. The incentive to engage in the underlying activity depends on the level of liability imposed. A higher baseline discourages engaging in the activity, and a lower baseline encourages it. The lowest baseline for damages provides the strongest incentives to engage in the activity. If the activity has more positive than negative externalities, as with specializing in obstetrics, then the most efficient incentives to engage in the underlying activity require the lowest baseline for damages,[27] which is zero.[28] Figure 10.3 depicts this by placing "activity level" at zero on the damages line.

Now consider how liability for the wrong mandatory choice affects the act that immediately precedes it in figure 10.2, namely preparing to choose. The difference in liability determines how much the actor stands to lose from making the wrong choice. When the actor stands to lose more from the wrong choice, he has a stronger incentive to prepare to choose. Damages exceeding DDA are required for efficient incentives to prepare to choose. Specifically, incentives to prepare are efficient when the difference in liability equals the difference in

---

regardless of whether the materialized harm is 25 or 5. That could provide incentives for victims to bring upon themselves harm of 5, and get compensation of 10. See LEVMORE, *id.* To avoid moral hazard we suggest applying the DDA in a different way: Impose liability according to the ratio between gains and expected harm. In the latter example the ratio between gains and expected harm is 1/3. Therefore, if harm of 5 materializes liability will be for 1.66, and if harm of 25 materializes liability will be for 8.33. The expected liability of the injurer in this example will be exactly 1 and the moral hazard problem completely avoided.

[27] Note that setting the liability difference and baseline in a discrete choice corresponds to setting the marginal and average liability in a continuous choice.

[28] We assume that the baseline cannot be negative.

0   DDA   Equalization   Internalization

├──────────────┼──────────────┼──────────────┼──────────────

(Activity   (Mandatory   (Preparing   (Execution
level)   choice)   to choose)   of choice)

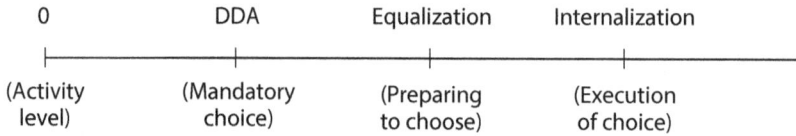

FIGURE 10.3. Damages and Optimal Incentives for Different Choices

social costs between the alternatives. Figure 10.3 illustrates this conclusion by our placement of "equalization" to the right of DDA on the damages line.

We apply these principles to example 2, where vaginal birth risks harm of 200 with probability .10 (expected harm of 20), and Caesarean birth risks harm of 300 with probability .10 (expected harm of 30). For efficient incentives to prepare to choose and to make the right choice, the difference in expected liability must equal the difference in expected harm, which is 10. If liability is imposed for materialized harm and not exposure to risk, the difference in liability must be 100. Assume the *difference* in liability for materialized harm equals 100: Then, making the wrong choice increases liability by 100 as compared to making the right choice. Now consider the *baseline*, which refers to liability for harm when making the right choice. The baseline could be 200, which implies damages of 200 and 300 for harm from vaginal and Caesarean birth, respectively. Or the baseline could be 50, which implies damages of 50 and 150, respectively. Or the baseline could be 0, which implies damages of 0 and 100, respectively. Since the underlying activity in example 2 has beneficial externalities, damages for making the wrong mandatory choice should be computed by starting with a baseline of 0 and adding the difference in harm to the victim, so liability for materialized harm in Caesarean birth should equal 100. This is equivalent to starting with the actual harm to the victim (300) and subtracting the least harmful alternative (200).

We summarize these results in a general principle. The *Equalization Principle* is the principle that the difference in expected social harm between mandatory alternatives should equal the difference in the actor's liability. The Equalization Principle provides socially efficient incentives to prepare to choose and to make the right choice. Since the Equalization Principle concerns the difference in liability and not the baseline, the latter can be adjusted for the best incentives to engage in the underlying activity, in a way that can be formulated mathematically.[29]

---

[29] We formalize the Equalization Principle by using the same notation as before, where the mandatory choice is between A and B. The following expressions give the externalities for the two acts:

$$FOR\ ACT\ A:\ q_A d_A - p_A h_A + b_A - m_A$$
$$FOR\ ACT\ B:\ q_B d_B - p_B h_B + b_B - m_B.$$

$$\underbrace{liability}_{externality} \qquad \underbrace{price}_{externality}$$

Now we turn to the fourth choice in figure 10.2—execution of a mandatory choice. Expected liability must equal the expected harm of faulty execution in order to provide perfectly efficient incentives for proper execution of the procedure. Figure 10.3 depicts this equivalence by placing "execution of choice" at the "internalization" point on the damages line.

To illustrate by example 3, the obstetrician makes a mistake in executing vaginal delivery with probability .10 that causes harm of 200, and the probability of liability is 1. In Caesarean delivery the obstetrician makes a mistake with probability .10 that causes harm of 300, and the probability of liability is .5. Since the probability of liability is .5 for the harm caused by faulty Caesarean delivery, the harm is externalized half of the time. To overcome this distortion, set liability equal to 200 percent of the harm from faulty Caesarean delivery. Now the obstetrician is liable for 100 percent of the expected harm from faulty vaginal or Caesarean delivery, as required to internalize the social costs of negligent execution.

Figure 10.3 summarizes the tradeoffs in incentives for the four choices when setting liability, assuming that the activity has more positive than negative externalities. Incentives for the activity level are best when liability equals zero. To provide efficient incentives for making the right mandatory choice, damages must increase at least to the disgorgement level (DDA). Increasing damages to the equalization level will provide efficient incentives for preparing to make the mandatory choice and for making it. To provide incentives for executing the mandatory choice, damages must increase to the internalization level.

C. Uncertainty about the Right Choice and Application

Thus far we have assumed that courts have accurate information about the private and social costs of the relevant acts.[30] In fact courts seldom possess complete information about the alternatives faced by the actors. Even so, courts

---

The Equalization Principle requires equating the externality for the two acts:

$$(q_A d_A - p_A h_A) + (b_A - m_A) = (q_B d_B - p_B h_B) + (b_B - m_B)$$

For an application of the preceding equation, assume the consumer pays for the benefit he receives, or $b_A = m_A$ and $b_B = m_B$. The equation reduces to

$$(q_A d_A - p_A h_A) = (q_B d_B - p_B h_B)$$

This equation states that the difference between expected liability and social harm for act A equals the difference between expected liability and social harm for act B.

[30] When we applied the Least Harmful Alternative Principle to example 2, we assumed that courts could verify that the unavoidable risks of vaginal delivery were 20 while the risks of Caesarean were 30. When we discussed disgorgement damages for accidents (DDA), we assumed that courts could verify the gains to the doctor from choosing Caesarean and the probability of the resulting harm. Similarly, when we applied the Equalization Principle to example 3 we assumed that courts can verify the risks of negligent execution of each alternative, as well as the level of externality associated with each of the underlying activities.

can often conclude that negligence caused harm. For those cases we propose that in certain areas where positive externalities are high or mandatory choices are common, legislatures give courts several options for setting damages. Legislatures might authorize courts to award damages of 25 percent, 50 percent, 75 percent 100 percent, 125 percent or 150 percent of the plaintiff's harm. Legislation could allow courts to award damages as guided by the underlying externalities. For driving, liability might equal, say 150 percent. When two automobiles collide, part of the damages ideally would be paid to the state.[31] For immunization from diseases, liability might equal, say, 75 percent.[32]

For mandatory choices with positive externalities in the underlying activity, such as obstetrics, courts should be allowed to choose damages below 100 percent. The exact choice should depend on the court's information, and the incentive effects explained in this chapter. If the actor saved money by untaken precautions, the court might want to give damages that approximate disgorgement for accidents. Application of DDA requires information about the gain of the injurer from untaken precautions and information about the probability of the injurer's liability. In example 2, DDA requires information on both the doctor's gain from her negligence (which is 1) and the probability of holding her liable when she behaves negligently (which is .10). Disgorgement damages should be a relatively low percentage of the victim's harm, say 25 percent. Disgorgement damages are especially attractive if the court has little concern with incentives to prepare for the mandatory choice or to execute it.

Alternatively, the court might want to set damages by deducting a fraction that reflects the risk of the least harmful alternative. This approach requires verifying the harm, the risk of the chosen alternative and the risk of the least harmful alternative. When the court cannot verify the two latter values precisely, it might roughly estimate the magnitudes. To illustrate, suppose the court in example 2 finds out that the risk from Caesarean delivery was between 30 and 40, whereas the risk from vaginal delivery was between 10 and 20. The court should reduce damages by at least 25 percent.[33]

---

[31] If a car strikes a pedestrian, damages of, say, 150 percent will discourage driving and hence correct for the negative externality. This is true whether or not the pedestrian gets all of the damages. If one car strikes another car, damages of 150 percent paid to the victim will redistribute money from negligent to non-negligent driver. It will discourage negligent driving and encourage non-negligent driving. The state should take, say, half of the damages in order to discourage non-negligent driving.

[32] Since immunization also creates benefits for people who do not receive the vaccine, which constitute positive externalities. See STEVE P. CALANDRILLO, *Vanishing Vaccinations: Why Are So Many Americans Opting Out of Vaccinating Their Children?* 37 U. MICH. J. L. REFORM 353, 419-420 (2004). AMY B. MONAHAN, *The Promise and Peril of Ownership Society Health Care Policy*, 80 TUL. L. REV. 777, 833-834 (2006).

[33] The most favorable assumption for the plaintiff is that the risk associated with Caesarean was 40 and that for vaginal delivery was 10; thus liability should be for $(40 - 10)/40 \times H$.

Finally, if the court can verify the extent of the external harm from two alternatives in a mandatory choice, it may want to set damages to equalize the externalities. When the court cannot determine the exact expected harm of each alternative, it could use rough estimates. Assume that the court in example 3 can verify the range of risks associated with Caesarean delivery. Instead of specifying exact expected harm at 20, the court verifies that the expected harm is at least 20 and no more than 30. If the rate of externalization of Caesarean accidental harms is 50 percent, courts could safely assume that expected harm of at least 10 was externalized when the doctor chose Caesarean. Therefore courts could award damages for the full harm when the doctor chose Caesarean, and reduce damages when the doctor chose vaginal delivery. The rate of the reduction should reflect the minimum expected harm that Caesarean externalizes. Thus, in our case, if courts could assume that the expected harm of vaginal delivery is, say, also 20 to 30, they could safely reduce liability for accidental harm caused during vaginal delivery by 33 percent. That would result in reduction of expected liability for vaginal delivery by no more than 10. Of course, in a scenario involving these circumstances the court could reduce damages even further depending on the level of the positive externality of the underlying activity and the risk of eroding incentives to execute the alternative chosen by the doctor.

By using numbers, the preceding discussion suggests a level of precision that courts can seldom achieve. In fact we favor simple rules with modest information requirements that respond to the contours set out in the principles we advocate. As long as the simple rules respond to liability externalities and mandatory choices, many doctors will pay less.

D. Conclusion

Liability externality has various possible remedies. Since Pigou, the standard prescription taxes negative externalities and subsidizes positive externalities.[34] In principle taxes and subsidies are the best solution to externalities whenever private bargains cannot solve the problem. In practice, however, the scope and direction of taxes and subsidies have more to do with interest group politics than economic efficiency. Given practical limits on controlling externalities by taxes and subsidies, liability law might be adjusted for better results. This is especially true for those externalities that courts can easily understand because they arise from the liability system itself, such as the activity level problem.

Several dimensions of liability law could be adjusted in principle: the rule of liability (strict liability versus negligence), the standard of care, the standard and burden of proof, and the level of damages. Recently Jeong-Yoo Kim argued

[34] ARTHUR CECIL PIGOU, THE ECONOMICS OF WELFARE (1932).

that negligence is generally a better rule than strict liability when the activity involves positive externalities unrelated to the accident. Kim observes that a negligence rule places a smaller burden of liability on the activity, which is desirable when it has positive externalities.[35] Similarly, Keith Hylton argued that a strict liability rule is suitable only when the external costs of the activity exceed the external benefits by a substantial amount, whereas a negligence rule is better when the external costs and external benefits are roughly the same.[36]

Another possibility is adjusting the legal standard of care under a liability rule. A lower standard of care for activities with positive externalities reduces expected liability and thus increases incentives to engage in the activity, whereas a higher standard of care has the opposite effect. Similarly, increasing the standard of proof reduces the injurer's expected liability and thus increases incentives to engage in the activity, while shifting the burden of proof to the defendant has the opposite effect.

Instead of these possibilities, we focus on adjusting damages to remedy liability externalities. Adjusting damages could be regarded as a supplement or an alternative to the other possibilities. Compared to the alternatives, adjusting damages has distinct advantages. We believe that a full exploration of all the alternatives would lead to the conclusion that the principles developed in the discussion here are easier for courts to understand and to apply accurately than the alternatives.

Our suggestions in this chapter could be criticized as undermining one of the major goals of tort law, which is compensation. Here is how to defend our focus on incentives rather than compensation. Full compensation through tort law is detrimental to potential victims when they benefit from the underlying activity. Excessive liability for childbirth discourages doctors from specializing in obstetrics and encourages them to engage in defensive medicine, which makes patients suffer. Given these facts, the potential victims may prefer to provide for compensation by other means than tort law, such as social or private insurance.

---

[35] JEONG-YOO KIM, *Strict liability Versus Negligence When the Injurer's Activity Involves Positive Externalities*, 22 EUROPEAN JOURNAL OF LAW AND ECONOMICS 95 (2006). See also MARK GEISTFELD, *Should Enterprise Liability Replace the Rule of Strict Liability for Abnormally Dangerous Activities?* 45 UCLA L. REV. 611, 653 (1998) (arguing that with positive externalities strict liability is undesirable as a means of reducing risks relative to negligence).

[36] KEITH N. HYLTON, *A Missing Markets Theory of Tort Law*, 90 Nw. U. L. REV. 977, 984 (1996).

The Relationship between Nonlegal
Sanctions and Damages

driver has a moral and a legal obligation to drive carefully, and a contractor has a moral and a legal obligation to keep his promises. As with driving and contracting, social and legal norms often regulate the same behavior. A wrongdoer who violates the norm may suffer a nonlegal sanction such as damage to reputation, and he may suffer a legal sanction such as liability. When morality and private law align, the total sanction suffered by the wrongdoer equals the nonlegal sanction plus damages. This fact poses a question that remains mostly unexplored in legal theory. Courts typically set damages to compensate the victim. Should courts deduct the nonlegal sanction suffered by the wrongdoer from compensatory damages owed to the victim?[1] We provide the answer for a legal system that seeks to minimize social costs.

When legal and social norms align, the wrong committed by the defendant harms the plaintiff and triggers nonlegal sanctions that harm the wrongdoer. Besides harming the wrongdoer, nonlegal sanctions typically benefit other people by informing, protecting, or transferring business to them. Thus damaging the wrongdoer's reputation alerts potential victims to avoid him, boycotting a wrongdoer may transfer business to his competitors, and these nonlegal sanctions protect potential victims by deterring other wrongdoers.

In simple economic models of liability, incentives are best when the damages equal the net social costs of the act that triggered liability. This is true in

---

[1] The growing literature on social norms has largely overlooked the interaction between damages and nonlegal sanctions. For an exception that considers this interaction, see LISA BERNSTEIN, *Private Commercial Law in the Cotton Industry: Creating Cooperation Through Rules, Norms, and Institutions*, 99 MICH. L. REV. 1724 (2001). For a discussion of the differences in the incentives of legal and nonlegal sanctions for breach of contract, see DAVID CHARNY, *Nonlegal Sanctions in Commercial Relationships*, 104 HARV. L. REV. 375, 400-3 (1990). For the relationship between criminal punishment and nonlegal sanctions, see DAN M. KAHAN & ERIC POSNER, *Shaming White-Collar Criminals: A Proposal for Reform of the Federal Sentencing Guidelines*, 42 J. L. ECON. 365 (1999). For a thorough analysis of the way tort law should be adjusted to coordinate with already existing criminal, nonlegal or regulatory sanctions, see KYLE D. LOGUE, *Coordinating Sanctions in Tort*, 31 CARDOZO L. REV. 2313 (2010).

almost all models of strict liability and most models of negligence. By focusing on the most important elements of social costs and benefits, we reduce a long list to three:

(1) plaintiff's harm from the wrong, plus
(2) defendant's harm from the nonlegal sanctions, minus
(3) other peoples' benefit from the nonlegal sanctions.

This chapter considers whether wrongdoers internalize each of the three elements.

Liability for compensatory damages ideally makes the wrongdoer internalize the plaintiff's harm, which is the first of the three elements. The wrongdoer necessarily bears the harm that he suffers from nonlegal sanctions, which is the second element. The third element, however, creates a problem for the wrongdoer's incentives. The wrongdoer typically externalizes the benefits to other people caused by bringing nonlegal sanctions on himself. Externalization of the third element overdeters unintentional wrongdoing.

To avoid overdeterrence, the state could subsidize wrongdoers. A more practical alternative is for courts to reduce the wrongdoer's liability. We will argue that courts should award compensatory damages minus the benefits of the nonlegal sanction. We call this damage measure "ideal net damages" because damages computed in this way are ideal for wrongdoers' incentives. Courts should award ideal net damages in the typical case where nonlegal sanctions benefit other people. Courts should award compensatory damages in the atypical case where nonlegal sanctions do not benefit anyone—they are a dead-weight loss.

After analyzing wrongdoers' incentives, we next consider victims' incentives. Victims can typically reduce the expected harm from accidents and breach of contract. Compensatory damages typically erode victims' incentives to reduce expected harm.[2] Unlike damages, however, nonlegal sanctions typically do not compensate victims. By substituting nonlegal sanctions for damages, courts can improve victims' incentives to reduce harm. If courts must award damages to victims, then a reduction in their amount typically improves victims' incentives. Consequently, deducting the benefit of the nonlegal sanction from compensatory damages typically improves victims' incentives.

Having made these theoretical arguments about injurers' and victims' incentives, we turn to a practical issue. Courts that attempt to minimize social costs by awarding ideal net damages will often have difficulty determining the extent of the benefits of the nonlegal sanction. Instead of deducting *benefits* from the compensatory damages owed to the victim, practical considerations commend courts to deduct the *burden* of the nonlegal sanction on the wrongdoer. We call this damage measure *practical net damages*. Implementing this proposal,

---

[2] See *supra* chapter 6.

which makes modest demands on courts, would significantly reduce the damages awarded in many cases.

In principle, social efficiency in contracts or torts requires eliminating all externalities by adjusting damages for third party effects. Unlike nonlegal sanctions, many third party effects are small, unmeasurable, episodic, or offsetting (the benefits equal the costs). Courts, consequently, should not attempt to deduct most third party effects. In contrast, third party effects of nonlegal sanctions are large, measurable, endemic, and not offsetting. Courts should deduct the burden of nonlegal sanctions from damages when the nonlegal sanction benefits third parties.

The preceding analysis assumes that courts do not influence nonlegal sanctions, except possibly by announcing liability. In fact, courts can often influence the form and size of nonlegal sanctions. Courts should substitute nonlegal sanctions that create or transfer value for sanctions that destroy value. When true reports of sleazy practices harm a business's reputation, the loss of reputation creates value by alerting gullible buyers and transfers value to competing businesses. In contrast, when false rumors harm a business's reputation, the loss of reputation destroys value by deflecting transactions to higher cost providers. Liability for damages destroys value by eroding the victim's incentives to take precaution against accidents and to assist the promisor in performing a contract. In crafting sanctions, courts should substitute against sanctions that destroy value and favor sanctions that create or transfer it.

A. Wrongdoer's Incentives When Nonlegal Sanctions Are Dead-Weight Losses

Here are two examples where nonlegal sanctions are dead-weight losses.

Example 1: Sexual Harassment I. A man who owns a small company flirts with a female employee. He mistakes her politeness for encouragement and, consequently, acts improperly. His improper act is the tort of sexual harassment, but not a crime. As news of the event spreads, the owner's friends and associates become angry with him. The owner suffers a loss of reputation that he values at $25. The owner's loss of reputation does not benefit anyone. The employee sues and the court finds that damages of $100 will perfectly compensate the victim. Should the court award damages of $100 or $75?

Example 2: Sharp Dealing I. A company aggressively interprets a contract with a supplier and eventually breaches it. When the supplier sues, the court finds that damages of $100 will perfectly compensate the victim for breach. Although consumers who buy from the company are not at risk, the news of the court's finding makes some of them angry and they boycott the company, which causes it to lose $25 in profits. The market is so competitive that the boycott does not measurably harm consumers or benefit other sellers.[3] Should the court award damages of $100 or $75?

If the law's goal is compensating victims, then damages should equal $100 in both examples. Alternatively, if the law's goal is deterring wrongdoers, then damages of $100 deter more than damages of $75. The economic analysis of private law, however, typically regards compensating victims or deterring wrongdoers as instrumental goals, behind which lies the goal of minimizing social costs. To minimize social costs, the wrongdoer should typically internalize the harm that he caused. In example 1, the owner caused $100 of harm to the employee and $25 of harm to himself from loss of reputation. In example 2, the company caused $100 of harm to the supplier and $25 of harm to itself from the boycott. By setting damages equal to $100 in both cases, the wrongdoer will face a total sanction of $125, which equals the total harm that he caused. Consequently, efficient deterrence requires the court to award perfectly compensatory damages in both cases, which equal $100.

Now we will formulate the conclusion of examples 1 and 2 more abstractly. Over the years, the economic analysis of law has developed simplified models of torts and contracts. Standard assumptions for beginning an analysis include risk-neutrality, zero litigation costs, no enforcement errors, one-shot transactions between the parties, and no "contracting around" the legal rule of liability. Also, the potential injurers and victims have sufficient information about damages and nonlegal sanctions to respond to them.

Two particular assumptions are especially significant in examples 1 and 2. First, we assume that reports of wrongdoing cause the loss of reputation, not court-imposed damages. The level of damages set by the courts does not influence the severity of the nonlegal sanction. Second, in example 1 we assume that loss of reputation harms the wrongdoer without affecting anyone else. For purposes of analysis example 1 assumes that shunning, shaming, criticizing, or disesteeming only affects its subject. Similarly, in example 2 we assume that the boycott harms the defendant without affecting anyone else. In both examples, the nonlegal sanction destroys value rather than transferring or creating it.

Bearing these assumptions in mind, we can formulate our general conclusion about these two examples.

Proposition 1: Assume that nonlegal sanctions are a dead-weight loss that fall on the wrongdoer. Under standard assumptions, the wrongdoer has efficient incentives to avoid causing harm when damages perfectly compensate the victim.

---

[3] We have these specific assumptions in mind: Consumers can shift costlessly to other sellers who continue earning zero profits, but the wrongdoer suffers a loss of reputation that raises his selling costs.

According to proposition 1, the goal of compensating victims aligns with the goal of deterring wrongdoers when the nonlegal sanction is a dead-weight loss. The next section changes this assumption and brings these goals into conflict.

B. Wrongdoer's Incentives When Nonlegal Sanctions Transfer or Create Value

We now consider the possibility that wrongdoing benefits some people other than the wrongdoer, by triggering a nonlegal sanction. In principle, every kind of benefit or cost is relevant when minimizing net social costs. In practice, courts may restrict consideration to the most important elements, as when they apply the doctrine of "proximate cause" to remove remote harms from damages. To keep the analysis manageable, we make our best guess for the typical case and reduce a long list of benefits and costs caused by nonlegal sanctions to three.

First, the nonlegal sanction may convey *information* about the wrongdoer that enables potential victims to escape injury. To illustrate, the owner's loss of reputation in example 1 may alert potential victims of sexual harassment to avoid him. In this example, conveying the information that the wrongdoer violated the norm *is* the loss of reputation that constitutes the nonlegal sanction. Similarly, the news that the company in example 2 aggressively interpreted a contract and breached it may enable other suppliers to avoid becoming victims. In this example, conveying the information that the wrongdoer violated the norm *causes* a boycott that is the nonlegal sanction.

Second, the nonlegal sanction may *advantage competitors* of the wrongdoer. To illustrate, with a small change in assumptions, the consumer boycott in example 2 that harms the defendant might benefit a competitor. Similarly, if the owner in example 1 competes with others for social status, then decreasing his social status by shunning, shaming, criticizing, or disesteeming may enhance other peoples' social status. Nonlegal sanctions often convey advantages to the wrongdoer's economic and social competitors.

Third, the imposition of a nonlegal sanction in a particular case may *deter* the wrongdoer or other potential wrongdoers from causing future injuries. Potential victims of sexual harassment in example 1 may benefit because the owner's loss of reputation deters other people from committing sexual harassment, and potential suppliers in example 2 may benefit because the boycott deters other companies from cheating on contracts.

Sanctions deter in two different ways. A norm is sometimes defined as an obligation backed by a sanction. A perfectly informed decision maker knows the probability and magnitude of the sanction. When a general practice determines the expected sanction faced by a wrongdoer, the news that a particular wrongdoer has been sanctioned usually confirms the general practice.

Confirming a general practice modestly increases its credibility, so deterrence increases modestly. In general, if potential wrongdoers believe that wrongdoing will be sanctioned as part of a general practice, then a particular person who brings a sanction on himself by doing wrong contributes modestly to deterring others.

In reality, however, people have imperfect information about general practices, and nonlegal sanctions may be more personal than general. Given these facts, publicizing someone's punishment, especially someone who is well known, can significantly change beliefs about the probability and magnitude of a sanction. Similarly, many psychological studies show that people especially respond to risks that materialize in concrete cases ("availability heuristic"). Publicizing someone's punishment can raise its salience in the minds of potential wrongdoers. For these reasons, nonlegal sanctions applied to a particular person, without any change in general practices, can significantly deter wrongdoing. In any case, the deterrence effect of the nonlegal sanction that a wrongdoer brings on himself counts as a *benefit* caused by his wrongdoing.[4]

We distinguished three types of benefit that can result when wrongdoing triggers a nonlegal sanction: transmitting information to potential victims, creating an advantage for the wrongdoer's competitors, and deterring future wrongdoing. These benefits are "external" in the sense that they accrue to people other than the wrongdoer. To illustrate each type, we will modify the preceding examples.

> *Example 3: Sexual Harassment II.* The man who owns a small company flirts with a female employee. He mistakes her politeness for encouragement and, consequently, acts improperly. In law his improper act is the tort of sexual harassment, but not a crime. As news of the event spreads, the owner suffers a loss of reputation that he values at $25. The owner's loss of reputation enables potential victims of his future misbehavior to avoid other uncompensated harms worth $40. The employee sues and the court finds that damages of $100 will perfectly compensate the victim. Should the court award damages of $100, $75, $60, or $35?

To find the answer by the shortest route, apply the general principle that efficient deterrence requires the court to set damages equal to the victim's harm ($100) minus the benefit to others ($40). By setting damages equal to $60, the court will cause the wrongdoer to internalize the external cost of his wrongdoing.

Here is an alternative route for calculation. In example 3, the wrongdoer caused harm of $100 to the employee, and the nonlegal sanction that he brought on himself caused a loss of $25 to himself, for a total cost of $125. However,

---

[4] Note that a nonlegal sanction could cause overdeterrence, which would count as a cost rather than a benefit.

the nonlegal sanction caused a benefit of $40 to others, so the net cost of his wrongdoing equals $85. Efficient incentives require the sum of the nonlegal and legal sanctions to equal $85. Since the wrongdoer suffers a nonlegal sanction of $25, the costs that remain externalized after the nonlegal sanction equal $60. Consequently, efficient incentives for the wrongdoer require the court to award damages of $60.

Setting damages above $60 could overdeter potential injurers. In this case, overdeterrence implies excessive precaution when flirting. The risk involved in flirting, which is an important social activity that presumably benefits the people who practice it, should not be increased above the level that minimizes social costs.

Having illustrated how nonlegal sanctions convey beneficial information, we modify example 2 to illustrate how nonlegal sanctions can benefit competitors of the wrongdoer.

Example 4: Sharp Dealing II. A company aggressively interprets a contract with a supplier and eventually breaches. When the supplier sues, the court finds that damages of $100 will perfectly compensate the victim for breach. Although consumers who buy from the company are not at risk, the news of the court's finding makes some of them angry and they boycott the company, which causes it to lose $25 in profits and its competitors to gain $25 in profits. Should the court award damages of $100 or $75?

To find the answer, apply the general principle that efficient deterrence requires the court to set damages equal to the victim's harm ($100) minus the benefit to others ($25).[5] Thus the court should ideally award net damages, which equal $75. Awarding more than $75 in damages would overdeter by prompting excessive precaution in contracts.

Example 3 illustrates how nonlegal sanctions convey beneficial information, and example 4 illustrates how nonlegal sanctions transfer value to competitors. Next we modify example 4 to illustrate how nonlegal sanctions deter.

Example 5: Sharp Dealing III. A company aggressively interprets a contract with a supplier and eventually breaches. When the supplier sues, the court finds that damages of $100 will perfectly compensate the victim for breach. Although consumers who buy from the company are not at risk, the news of the court's finding makes some of them angry and they boycott the company, which causes it to lose $25 in profits while its competitors gain $25 in profits. The fact that many consumers boycott sharp dealers has faded from

---

[5] Here is a more complete calculation that reaches the same conclusion. In example 4, the wrongdoer caused harm of $100 to the plaintiff, the boycott cost the wrongdoer $25, and the boycott benefited the wrongdoer's competitors by $25. Thus the net social cost equals $100. The wrongdoer internalizes the $25 cost of the boycott. Efficiency incentives require the wrongdoer to internalize another $75 in social costs, which is accomplished if the court should impose damages of $75.

the minds of some industry executives. Vivid reports of the boycott revive the memory and deter some executives from sharp dealing. If they had dealt sharply, they would have gained $5 and imposed a cost of $20 on their victims, for a net social loss of $15. Should the court award damages of $100, $75, $60, or some other number?

Again, apply the general principle that efficient deterrence requires the court to set damages equal to the victim's harm ($100) minus the benefit to others. Others benefit from the transfer ($25) and deterrence ($15). Deduct these benefits caused by the nonlegal sanction from the harm of $100 suffered by the plaintiff to obtain damages of $60.

Here is a longer explanation of the calculation. In example 5, the defendant caused harm of $100 to the plaintiff and deterred wrongdoing that carries a net social cost of $15. Thus, the net harm caused by the defendant's wrongdoing equals $85. The defendant also provoked a boycott that transferred $25 to the defendant's competitors, which does not increase or decrease total social costs. Efficient incentives require the sum of the nonlegal and legal sanctions to equal $85. The nonlegal sanction (boycott) costs the company $25, so damages should equal $60.[6]

Now we can state the generalization underlying all five examples with the help of some notation. A wrongdoer often brings a nonlegal sanction on himself. The *burden*, which we denote s_n, is the cost imposed on the wrongdoer by the nonlegal sanction. (We will not discuss cases where, instead of imposing a burden, the nonlegal sanction creates a *benefit* for the wrongdoer.[7]) In addition to the burden s_n, the nonlegal sanction may cause the *transfer* of value from the wrongdoer to other people, which we denote t. The nonlegal sanction may also *create* value for people other than the wrongdoer, which we denote v.[8] The net social cost of the nonlegal sanction equals $s_n - t - v$.

We assume that each dollar in cost that the nonlegal sanction imposes on the wrongdoer creates benefits for others. Let r denote the ratio of benefits for other people and costs to the wrongdoer: $r = (t + v)/s_n$. If the nonlegal sanction

---

[6] Notice that, contrary to the usual multiplier models, imperfect compensation of future victims by courts lowers the damages owed by the defendant in this case. For example, if future sharp dealing caused the uncompensated harm to increase from $20 to $25, then ideal net damages would fall from $60 to $55. This result occurs because the increase in uncompensated harm increases the gain from deterrence that occurs when committing the wrong triggers the nonlegal sanction. If, however, the uncompensated harm in future cases were linked to damages in this case, then the calculation requires another term to represent this effect. Many articles on tort law compute the adjustment in damages required when enforcement error allows some future wrongdoers to escape legal liability. See for example RICHARD CRASWELL, *Deterrence and Damages: The Multiplier Principle and its Alternatives*, 97 MICH. L. REV. 2185 (1999).

[7] To illustrate, the nonlegal sanction may benefit the wrongdoer when the wrongdoer's criminal subculture rewards wrongdoing.

[8] If the nonlegal sanction destroys value to third parties—which is atypical—v is assigned a negative value.

is a dead-weight loss, then $r = 0$. If the nonlegal sanction is a pure transfer from the wrongdoer to others, then $r = 1$. If the cost of the nonlegal sanction to the wrongdoer is less than the benefit transferred and created for others, then $r > 1$.

Now we can formulate a generalization.

> *Proposition 2*: Assume that the wrongdoer causes harm H to the victim, which causes the wrongdoer to suffer a nonlegal sanction s_n. The nonlegal sanction creates or transfers value to people other than the wrongdoer at the rate r. The wrongdoer has efficient incentives to avoid causing harm when damages D_w that he pays equal the harm H to the victim, minus the wrongdoer's loss from the nonlegal sanction s_n multiplied by the rate r at which the nonlegal sanction creates or transfers value to others: $D'_w = H - rs_n$.

In this calculation, the term r defines the fraction or multiple of the nonlegal sanction to deduct from damages in order to obtain the ideal measure of net damages.

In practice, courts aim to award compensatory damages, so they proceed as if $r = 0$. This practice would be justified if nonlegal sanctions were a dead-weight loss. In reality, however, nonlegal sanctions typically transfer and create value, so r almost always exceeds 0 and often exceeds 1. When r exceeds 0, proceeding as if $r = 0$ distorts the incentives of wrongdoers. Later we describe practical ways that courts can correct this distortion.

C. Victim's Incentives

Now we turn from the wrongdoer's incentives to the victim's incentives. A potential victim can often reduce the probability or magnitude of harm from a wrong. To illustrate, a promisee can help the promisor perform, rely less on the promise, or mitigate harm after breach. Similarly, a potential tort victim can reduce the activity that exposes him to risk, increase the care with which he does the risky activity, or search for the cheapest way to repair damage after it occurs. Finally, a property owner can locate and shield improvements to reduce their exposure to smoke, noise, or other nuisances.[9]

Liability law typically requires wrongdoers to compensate victims. In a traditional economic analysis, however, compensating victims typically erodes their incentives to reduce the probability or magnitude of harm. Arresting the erosion of victims' incentives requires reducing damages. In traditional economic models of torts, contracts, or property, reducing damages to zero typically solves the victim's incentive problem completely, whereas other solutions solve the problem incompletely.[10]

---

[9] See *supra* chapter 6.
[10] *Id.*

Extending economic analysis to encompass social norms changes the conclusion that ideal damages for victims' incentives are zero. The wrongdoer who harms the victim by violating a social norm may provoke a nonlegal sanction that destroys, transfers, or creates value. The victim can reduce the probability or magnitude of a nonlegal sanction by reducing the probability or magnitude of the harm that triggers it. Strictly speaking, efficient incentives require the victim to internalize these effects, which can be accomplished by adjusting damages up or down, depending on whether the nonlegal sanction creates or destroys value.

To explain the ideal adjustment, we turn to an example from contract law, which is a variation of one we presented in chapter 6.

Example 6: Construction of an Addition to Restaurant. Yvonne's prosperous restaurant needs enlarging, so she contracts with Xavier to build an addition that will be ready for use on September 1. To accommodate increased business in the addition, Yvonne needs to order more food than she can use in her original facility. Yvonne knows that events could prevent Xavier from completing construction on time, such as striking plumbers, recalcitrant city inspectors, or foul weather. Yvonne can reduce the probability of breach and the magnitude of the resulting harm in several ways. To reduce the probability of breach, Yvonne can give Xavier valuable information about the plumber's union and structural obstacles to renovating the building, and she can use her contacts in government to get the building inspection completed on time. To reduce the magnitude of the harm that breach will cause, she can restrain her food order. If breach occurs, she can mitigate damages by extending her hours of operation while also searching for other restaurants willing to buy the excess food.

Assume that Yvonne makes no effort to reduce the expected harm from breach, Xavier breaches, and the breach causes damage of $100. Xavier suffers a nonlegal sanction in the form of a boycott that costs him $20. The boycott transfers $15 to his competitors and creates $10 in benefits to others by deterring potential wrongdoers. What damages should the court award Yvonne?

Here we focus on Yvonne's incentives and ignore Xavier's incentives. Recall that Yvonne typically has incentives to minimize social costs when she internalizes the harm affected by her actions. The harm affected by her actions includes the harm that she suffers from breach. Full compensation makes Yvonne indifferent between performance and breach, so she externalizes the benefit from cooperating with Xavier. Contractual and legal devices can ameliorate this problem, but in practice they typically stop short of a solution.[11] To internalize

---

[11] See also ARIEL PORAT, *A Comparative Fault Defense in Contract Law*, 107 MICH. L. REV. 1397 (2009). In other chapters we discuss achieving efficient incentives through two contractual devices: anti-insurance and decreasing-liability contracts. See *supra* chapter 7 and chapter 8, respectively.

the harm that she suffers from breach, Yvonne must *not* receive compensation for the harm of $100 that she suffers.

Besides the harm that she suffers from breach, Yvonne's actions also affect the probability and magnitude of the nonlegal sanction, which costs Xavier $20 and benefits others by $25, for a net gain of $5. To internalize these values, Yvonne should receive damages of $5. Yvonne's incentives are most efficient when she receives no compensation for her own losses of $100 and she receives compensation of $5 for the net benefit of the nonlegal sanction to others.

Proposition 3 formulates precisely the generalization underlying this example.

Proposition 3: Assume that the wrongdoer causes harm H to the victim, which causes the wrongdoer to suffer a nonlegal sanction s_n. The nonlegal sanction creates or transfers value to people other than the wrongdoer at the rate r. By definition, the *net benefit of the nonlegal sanction* equals the difference between the value created or transferred to others and the cost to the wrongdoer. The victim has efficient incentives to reduce the probability and magnitude of the harm that he suffers when damages D_v that he receives equal the net benefit of the nonlegal sanction: $D_v^* = rs_n - s_n$.

In the absence of a nonlegal sanction ($s_n = 0$), proposition 3 implies the traditional conclusion that victims should receive no compensation ($D_v^* = 0$). In the presence of a nonlegal sanction ($s_n > 0$), proposition 3 implies that the victim should ideally receive damages equal to the net value created by the nonlegal sanction ($rs_n - s_n$).

Comparing propositions 2 and 3 reveals a tension between ideal incentives for wrongdoers and victims. Proposition 2 asserts that ideal incentives for the wrongdoer require him to pay damages equal to $H - rs_n$, whereas proposition 3 asserts that ideal incentives for the victim require him to receive damages equal to $rs_n - s_n$. Satisfying both conditions simultaneously is usually impossible. To illustrate by example 6, ideal damages from the standpoint of the injurer's incentives equal $75, whereas ideal damages considered in relation to the victim's incentives equal $5. To avoid this tradeoff and achieve the ideal for both actors simultaneously would require "decoupling," which means that the damages paid by the injurer do not equal the damages received by the victim.[12]

In this chapter we will not explore decoupling. Instead of aiming for ideal incentives, this chapter makes a practical proposal. The practical proposal is to deduct the *burden* of the nonlegal sanction on the injurer from compensatory damages. Now we want to explain why deducting the burden improves the victim's incentives in almost every case. In almost every case, damages are ordered as follows:

compensatory (H) > net practical ($H - s_n$) > victims' ideal ($rs_n - s_n$).

---

[12] The anti-insurance contract, *supra* chapter 7, imposes full liability on the promisor and allows no compensation to the promisee, thereby allowing decoupling at a level of 100 percent.

Given this ordering, deducting the burden of the nonlegal sanction from compensatory damages brings damages closer to the ideal for victims' incentives.[13] To illustrate by example 6, the victim's incentives improve by deducting the sanction's burden of $20 from compensatory damages of $100.[14]

We will summarize our conclusions from further analysis of example 6. Compensatory damages equal the harm Yvonne suffers from breach, or $100. Ideal net damages for Xavier's incentives equal Yvonne's harm minus the benefit of the nonlegal sanction, or $100 − $25 = $75. We advocate awarding practical net damages, which equal Yvonne's harm minus the burden of the nonlegal sanction on Xavier, or $100 − $20 = $80. Besides improving Xavier's incentives, reducing damages from $100 to $80 improves Yvonne's incentives. Reducing damages from $80 to $5 would improve Yvonne's incentives even more.[15] Once damages fall below $75, however, lowering damages to improve Yvonne's incentives worsens Xavier's incentives (assuming that the damages paid by Xavier equal the damages received by Yvonne). Given a tradeoff, we prefer to get incentives right for injurers rather than victims.

D. Optimizing the Nonlegal Sanction

The preceding analysis assumes that the court has no power to influence nonlegal sanctions. In reality, however, the court can sometimes affect nonlegal sanctions. To illustrate, in example 1 the court might increase the harm to the wrongdoer's reputation by a public condemnation in strong language. Or in example 2, the court might take steps to publicize its decision, to the point of expanding the scope of the boycott. In this section we explain how the court should exercise whatever control it possesses over nonlegal sanctions in order to minimize social costs.

First, the court should substitute as far as possible a nonlegal sanction that creates or transfers value for a nonlegal sanction that destroys value. For example, boycotts mostly transfer value, whereas shaming is probably close to a dead-weight loss. If boycotts transfer value and shaming destroys it, then social

---

[13] Note that if the value created by the nonlegal sanction exceeds net practical damages ($rs_n - s_n > H - s_n$), then the ideal damages for victim's incentives exceed net practical damages. In the most extreme case, the nonlegal sanction creates more value than the harm suffered by the victim ($rs_n - s_n > H$), so the victim should receive super-compensatory damages to induce the wrongdoer to harm him. This possible situation is very unlikely.

[14] Notice that if the nonlegal sanction benefited or harmed the victim, then the victim would already internalize that element of social benefit or cost, so our calculation of victim's incentives would be unaffected.

[15] Note that adjusting the numbers in the example could cause the ideal damages for Yvonne to fall below zero. If the net benefit of the nonlegal sanction were negative, then the ideal damages for Yvonne would be negative, which implies that she should ideally pay damages to someone else.

policy should favor boycotts over shaming. The court might encourage consumers to transfer business away from the wrongdoer rather than shaming him.

Second, the court should consider whether to substitute nonlegal sanctions for damages. To illustrate, instead of awarding damages to the plaintiff, the judge might blacken the defendant's reputation. How should courts decide whether to substitute nonlegal sanctions for damages? Consider increases in nonlegal sanctions that exactly offset decreases in damages, so the total sanction remains constant. Keeping the total sanction constant keeps the wrongdoers' incentives constant, so we can concentrate on victims' incentives.

As we have explained, reducing the damages paid to victims typically improves their incentives. Balanced against this gain is a potential loss. Whereas damages transfer value, nonlegal sanctions sometimes destroy value. To illustrate, the nonlegal sanction in example 1 is a dead-weight loss. When substituting nonlegal sanctions for damages with equal deterrence for injurers, the court must balance better incentives for victims against any losses from nonlegal sanctions. Thus lowering damages in example 1 motivates the victim to reduce the expected harm that she suffers from sexual harassment, and increasing the wrongdoer's loss of reputation may increase the dead-weight loss that is one effect of reputational sanctions.

Proposition 4 formulates this tradeoff.

Proposition 4. Assume the court can substitute the nonlegal sanction s_n for damages D, while keeping their sum constant. When substituting nonlegal sanctions for damages, minimizing costs requires the court to balance at the margin better incentives for victims against any losses from nonlegal sanctions.[16]

One implication of proposition 4 is that whenever the nonlegal sanction causes a net benefit rather than a net cost, the court should lower damages to achieve the ideal level for victims. To illustrate, the nonlegal sanction in

---

[16] We state this proposition in notation. Substituting s_n for D causes the victim to change his behavior y at a cost to him of wy. The change in his behavior changes the expected harm pH. We write the marginal social cost of the change as follows:

$$\left(w_v + \frac{\partial pH}{\partial y}\right)\frac{\partial y}{\partial D}$$

The nonlegal sanction, which occurs with probability p, causes net social costs to increase at the rate $(1 - r)$. A marginal substitution of s_n for D causes an expected increase in the net social loss at the rate $p(1 - r)$.

The court should substitute nonlegal sanctions sn for damages D so long as the reduction in social costs caused by improved victim's behavior exceeds the expected increase in the net social costs of the nonlegal sanction:

$$\left(w_v + \frac{\partial pH}{\partial y}\right)\frac{\partial y}{\partial D} \geq p(1 - r)$$

example 6 creates net benefits of 5, so ideal damages for victim's incentives equal 5. According to proposition 4, the court should substitute nonlegal sanctions for damages until damages fall to 5.

E. Implementing Net Damages

According to proposition 2, courts should deduct the benefits transferred or created by the nonlegal sanction from damages owed by the wrongdoer to the victim. In practice, however, these benefits are difficult for courts to evaluate. Precise valuations are sometimes unnecessary. Circumstances arise in which immeasurable benefits from the nonlegal sanction approximately offset immeasurable harms of the victim. To illustrate, a doctor's malpractice caused a patient to suffer emotional distress (as well as pecuniary losses). Emotional distress is a social cost that the doctor should pay in principle. When people learn about the doctor's negligence, patients may boycott the doctor. This boycott may deter malpractice by other doctors. Such deterrence is a social benefit that courts should deduct from the doctor's liability in principle. In practice, however, emotional distress and deterrence may be immeasurable. Instead of attempting to measure these values, the court might dismiss both as offsetting and similar in magnitude.

In more common circumstances, courts need a valuation. The benefits of the nonlegal sanction are often relatively hard to value, whereas the burden of the nonlegal sanction on the wrongdoer is relatively easy to value. To illustrate, the benefit of deterrence in the preceding example is hard to measure and the cost of the boycott to the doctor is relatively easy to measure. The doctor in the preceding example might be able to document that he lost profits from a patients' boycott by comparing his earnings in the year preceding the injury to his earnings in the following year. In general, monetizing the nonlegal sanction's burden on the injurer presents courts with a similar problem to monetizing the victim's harm.

Under certain circumstances, courts can justifiably deduct the measurable burden of the nonlegal sanction on the wrongdoer, rather than deducting the immeasurable benefit of the nonlegal sanction to others. Specifically, assume the court knows that the benefit exceeds the burden, and the court can measure the burden, but it cannot measure the benefit. Under these assumptions, the burden is the largest deduction that the court can justify, or the *maximum justifiable deduction*. In terms of our notation, if s_n is measurable and r exceeds 1 by an unknowable amount, then s_n is the maximum deduction justifiable by the facts known to the court.

Two facts typically establish that the benefit equals or exceeds the burden $(r \geq 1)$. First, the wrongdoer who suffers the nonlegal sanction usually competes economically or socially with others. For example, businesses compete for sales and people compete for prestige. Consequently, imposing the nonlegal sanction on the wrongdoer typically benefits competitors. In so far as competition approximates a zero sum game, the harm to the wrongdoer equals the benefit to competitors, so the nonlegal sanction approximates a transfer ($r = 1$).

The second fact concerns creating, not transferring, benefits. With most kinds of wrongs, the wrongdoer gains less than the victim loses. Preventing such a wrong causes a net social benefit. Nonlegal sanctions typically prevent future harms by deterring wrongdoers and providing potential victims with information needed to avoid being victimized. Preventing a wrong that would harm victims more than it would benefit the wrongdoer causes a net social benefit. The nonlegal sanction that prevents such wrongs creates social value ($r > 1$).

We have argued that the sum of value transferred and created typically equals or exceeds the burden of the nonlegal sanction, or $r \geq 1$. With such characteristic values of r, courts will typically reduce social costs by proceeding as if $r = 1$ and deducting the nonlegal sanction, rather than proceeding as if $r = 0$ and not deducting the nonlegal sanction.

Note that courts can typically measure the effects of the nonlegal sanction more accurately by bifurcating the trial. The first stage determines wrongdoing and possibly triggers the nonlegal sanction. The second stage determines damages. By postponing the determination of damages until the second stage, the court gets more time to observe the consequences of the nonlegal sanction that will be deducted from compensatory damages.

We conclude our discussion of implementation with a particular problem that can arise for courts. In so far as the victim must bring suit to trigger nonlegal sanctions, nonlegal sanctions suffer from the "victims' reporting problem." Specifically, the parties have an incentive to settle their dispute in order to avoid triggering the nonlegal sanction.[17] Frequently, however, settling the dispute will *not* avoid triggering the nonlegal sanction. For example, nonlegal sanctions may be triggered by committing the wrong, such as not performing a promise or causing an accident.[18] When committing the wrong triggers the nonlegal

---

[17] When a suit gains little for victims (no damages), they have little incentive to sue. When a suit costs wrongdoers heavily (triggers nonlegal sanction), they have a strong incentive to settle out of court. For example, wrongdoers and victims of crimes in medieval England settled out of court in order to deprive the King of the fine that he would collect at the conclusion of a successful prosecution. See DANIEL KLERMAN, *Settlement and the Decline of Private Prosecution in Thirteenth-Century England*, 19 LAW & HIST. REV. 1 (2001). The "victim's reporting problem" requires adjusting our model in ways that we do not discuss in this chapter. Like the King's fine, avoiding nonlegal sanctions motivates the settlements of suits.

[18] To illustrate, assume the promisor informs the promisee that he will not perform. In these circumstances, the promisor might offer to pay the promisee to release him from his promise. If the promisee's release would avoid the nonlegal sanction, then the victim's reporting problem exists. If instead the promisor would suffer the nonlegal sanction from nonperformance, regardless of whether or not the promisee released him, then the victim's reporting problem disappears.

sanction, the parties cannot avoid the nonlegal sanction by settling the dispute after the wrong was committed.

The trigger for nonlegal sanctions can be wrongs (a driver's negligence), harms resulting from wrongs (an automobile accident), or lawsuits (a suit for compensation from an accident).[19] Thus reckless driving is wrong, a resulting accident causes harm, and a lawsuit for damages may follow. The preceding discussion concerns nonlegal sanctions triggered by harm. Now consider nonlegal sanctions triggered by wrongs.

Assume that wrongdoing causes an accident in 10 percent of the cases and the harm from an accident equals 150, so the expected harm from wrongdoing equals 15. Also assume that wrongdoing always provokes a nonlegal sanction, and a nonlegal sanction causes third party benefits of 5. Thus the expected external net harm from wrongdoing is $15 - 5 = 10$. The wrongdoer internalizes this risk if his liability for an accident that materializes equals $150 - 50 = 100$. This calculation is generalizable into a formula.[20]

---

[19] There could also be cases where the harm triggers the nonlegal sanction, regardless of wrongdoing. For analyzing those situations, see LOGUE, *supra* note 1, at 2356-7.

[20] Assume a timeless world in which the probability that an act causes harm is independent of the probability that it provokes a nonlegal sanction.

H = the harm from an accident
p = probability that the act of wrongdoing causes harm H
q = probability that the act of wrongdoing causes a nonlegal sanction
s_n = burden of the nonlegal sanction on the injurer
t = transfer to third parties
v = value created for third parties
D = damages paid by injurer
D^* = optimal damages.

The expected net social cost is given by the formula

$$pH + q(s_n - t - v).$$

The injurer's expected cost is given by the formula

$$pD + qs_n.$$

Damages are optimal when the former equals the latter:

$$pD^* + qs_n = pH + q(s_n - t - v),$$

which implies

$$D^* = H - q/p\,(t + v).$$

In the preceding example in the text, $H = 150$, $q = 1$, $p = .1$, $t = 0$, and $v = 5$, so $D^* = 100$.

F. Setting the Legal Standard of Care

Our argument about deducting nonlegal sanctions, which we applied to setting damages, also applies to setting the legal standard of care. As with damages, the effect of the nonlegal sanction on the optimal legal standard of care depends on whether the nonlegal sanction destroys, transfers, or creates value. To see why, consider a numerical example. Assume that precautions of 100 eliminate accidents, the expected harm to accident victims is 75, and failing to take precautions triggers nonlegal sanctions that cost the injurer 75. If nonlegal sanctions are a dead-weight loss, then the 75 risk to injurers is a social cost just like the 75 risk to accident victims. Precautions of 100 thus eliminate social costs of 150: 75 in risk of accidents to victims, and 75 in risk of nonlegal sanctions to injurers. The legal standard of care should require the injurer to take precautions of 100 to avoid social costs of 150. Failure to take precaution costing 100 to avoid social harm of 150 should constitute negligence and trigger liability.

When setting the legal standard, ignoring the dead-weight burden of a nonlegal sanction is a mistake that raises social costs. If the court ignores the nonlegal sanction's dead-weight loss, it will weigh the cost of precaution of 100 against the harm of 75 to victims and conclude that failure to take precaution is not negligent. This is the wrong conclusion from the viewpoint of minimizing social costs. A self-interested injurer who foresees this mistake will realize that he will not be held liable for failing to take precaution. He will not spend 100 on precaution to avoid nonlegal sanctions costing 75. Because of the court's mistake, the injury will inflict social costs of 150 while at a cost of 100 in precaution it could have been prevented.

From the injurer's perspective, the expected harm to victims represents a risk to others, and the nonlegal sanction represents risk to himself. When setting the standard of care, the court should take account of both the risk to others and the injurer's self-risk. Ignoring the nonlegal sanction in this case is the mistake of ignoring self-risk discussed in chapter 2. The form of self-risk in chapter 2 is harm to the injurer from the accident, whereas the form of self-risk we deal with here is nonlegal sanctions imposed on the injurer.

When nonlegal sanctions impose dead-weight loss, their costs to the injurer are costs to society. What should happen to the legal standard when nonlegal sanctions transfer or create value, instead of destroying it? Modify the example by assuming that the nonlegal sanction of 75 is a pure transfer, not a dead-weight loss: the burden of 75 on the injurer is offset by a gain of 75 to third parties. Under this assumption, the failure to take precaution costing 100 causes social harm costing 75, so efficiency requires the injurer not to take precaution. If the court reasons correctly, it will conclude that the injurer was not negligent for failing to take precaution. If the injurer is not liable, then he will not spend 100 on precaution to avoid self-risk of 75. So no liability leads to efficient incentives.[21]

Finally, consider a case in which the nonlegal sanction produces net social benefits. Assume that the nonlegal sanction imposes a burden of 75 on the injurer and conveys a benefit of 85 to third parties. Thus the nonlegal sanction creates a net social benefit of 10. The difference between the victim's expected harm of 75 and the nonlegal sanction's net social benefit of $10 equals $65. When setting the legal standard, the court should ideally require the injurer to take precautions costing up to $65. In our specific example, the court ideally compares the cost of precaution of $100 against net social costs of $65 and finds no liability. (In practice the court can typically ignore the nonlegal sanction's net social benefit when it sets the legal standard of care or determines damages, as discussed above.)

What is the connection between the legal standard and damages? The effect of nonlegal sanctions often works in the opposite direction for legal standards and damages. If nonlegal sanctions destroy social value by imposing a dead-weight loss on injurers, this loss is a social cost just as much as the cost of accidents to victims. When setting the legal standard, courts should balance the injurer's cost of precaution against the harm to victims from accidents and the harm to injurers from the dead-weight loss of nonlegal sanctions. If nonlegal sanctions are dead-weight losses, then injurers already internalize them. What remains is for courts to make injurers internalize accidental harm to victims. When setting damages, courts should not deduct the dead-weight loss of social sanctions from the victim's harm. Thus the destruction of value by nonlegal sanctions increases the legal standard of care and does not decrease damages.

If wrongdoing triggers nonlegal sanctions and nonlegal sanctions create benefits for third parties, this is a social benefit from wrongdoing just as the risk of harm to victims is a social cost. When setting the legal standard, ideally courts should balance the injurer's cost of precaution against the harm to victims from accidents minus the net benefit of the nonlegal sanctions (which is the difference between the benefits to third parties and the burden to the injurer). Injurers do not enjoy the benefit of nonlegal sanctions. When setting damages, courts should deduct the benefit of social sanctions from the victim's harm. Thus the creation of value by nonlegal sanctions lowers the legal standard of care and decreases damages (although for practical reasons, as discussed above, courts should ignore the net benefit and proceed with the assumption that the nonlegal sanction transfers value). Table 11.1 summarizes these results.

If wrongdoing triggers nonlegal sanctions and nonlegal sanctions transfer value from injurers to third parties, the transfer is not a social benefit or a social

[21] If, however, the court mistakenly decides that the injurer who does not take precaution is liable, then the injurer who foresees this will spend 100 to avoid liability of 75 and the nonlegal sanction of 75. This is socially inefficient because the injurer spends 100 to avoid social costs of 75.

Table 11.1.
Effect of nonlegal sanctions on cost-minimizing legal standards and damages

Effect of nonlegal sanctions on social value	Legal standard	Damages
Destroy (dead weight loss)	Higher	None
Transfer (offsetting costs and benefits)	None	Lower
Create	Lower	Lower

cost. When setting the legal standard, courts should balance the injurer's cost of precaution against the harm to victims from accidents and ignore the transfer. When awarding damages, however, the courts should not ignore this transfer. The injurer bears the cost of nonlegal sanctions and does not enjoy the offsetting benefit to third parties. When setting damages, making the injurer internalize social costs requires courts to deduct the benefit of social sanctions to third parties from the victim's harm. Thus, when nonlegal sanctions transfer value, they should not affect the standard of care but should decrease damages.[22]

G. Conclusion

Modern courts largely ignore the interaction between their decisions and nonlegal sanctions. Instead of ignoring nonlegal sanctions, courts should take them into account in several ways. First, deducting nonlegal sanctions typically reduces social costs by improving the incentives of wrongdoers and victims. In many cases the deduction would significantly reduce damages, especially in close-knit communities and cyberspace—two venues where nonlegal sanctions observably work. The precise extent of the typical deduction is unknown because so little research measures nonlegal sanctions.[23]

Second, courts should consider substituting nonlegal sanctions for legal sanctions such as damages. Substitution of equivalents improves incentives

[22] This discussion assumes that making injurers internalize social costs reduces total social cost. As demonstrated in chapter 6, this is true under a rule of strict liability. This is also true under a rule of negligence, provided that the rule's application involves uncertainties about liability. However, increases in the level of damages above the net social costs have relatively little influence when the injurer feels confident that he can escape liability by satisfying the legal standard.

[23] We know of no empirical research measuring the benefit to other people from harming the reputation of wrongdoers. We know of little empirical research measuring the cost of harm to reputation. See JOHN LOTT, *An Attempt at Measuring the Total Monetary Penalty from Drug Convictions: The Importance of an Individual's Reputation*, 21 J. LEGAL STUD. 159 (1992); JONATHON M. KARPOFF & JOHN R. LOTT, JR., *The Reputational Penalty Firms Bear for Committing Criminal Fraud*, 36 J. L. & ECON. 757 (1993).

for victims and does not change them for injurers. Courts can improve the targeting of nonlegal sanctions by replacing rumors with authoritative determinations of facts. (Changes in court practices could further increase the information provided to citizens.[24]) The imprecision of nonlegal sanctions represents a practical obstacle to their invocation by courts. Perhaps courts can increase the precision of their influence on nonlegal sanctions by better calibrating the language for condemning wrongdoing.[25]

By reducing damages, our proposal undermines the legal goal of compensating victims. We live in an age of extensive private and public insurance. Many reformers believe that insurance provides more reliable and efficient compensation of victims than liability.[26] Like these reformers, we believe that the goal of compensation should diminish in importance for law as insurance expands. More complete insurance markets free liability law from the need to compensate victims, so liability law can minimize social costs by various means, including deducting nonlegal sanctions from damages.

---

[24] For example, instead of finding "liable" or "not liable," courts would find "liability proved," "liability disproved," or "liability unproved."

[25] For relevant empirical research, see CASS R. SUNSTEIN, DANIEL KAHNEMAN & DAVID SCHKADE, *Assessing Punitive Damages (with Notes on Cognition and Valuation in Law)*, 107 YALE L. J. 2071 (1998).

[26] Thus, Stephen Sugarman advocates replacing tort liability with social insurance. STEPHEN D. SUGARMAN, *Doing Away with Tort Law*, 73 CAL. L. REV. 558 (1985); STEPHEN D. SUGARMAN, DOING AWAY WITH PERSONAL INJURY LAW: NEW COMPENSATION MECHANISMS FOR VICTIMS, CONSUMERS, AND BUSINESS (1989).

Conclusion

his book makes three central claims, each developed in a separate part and each related to a different branch of private law. *First, to achieve efficiency under negligence law, all foreseeable risks should be included when setting standards of care and awarding damage.* In several important areas of law, however, courts disregard or miscalculate some risks, so standards of care misalign with liability for damages in important ways. Because of this misalignment, courts systematically exclude reduction in the injurer's risk to himself when considering the benefits of precaution by an injurer, so the legal standard of care is set too low. When an injurer breaches a statutory standard of care, courts that apply the doctrine of negligence per se allow recovery by victims in the foreground of the legislature's discussions, but no recovery by victims in the background of the legislature's discussion. Courts should allow recovery for both foreground and background harms, in order to give potential injurers efficient incentives to comply with the legal standard of care. When applying the doctrine of negligence to accidents caused by lapses, courts systematically deny an injurer the defense that self-monitoring was reasonable and the lapse was innocent. Courts should allow a lapse defense where feasible, especially for activities with external benefits such as doctoring. Finally, when several injurers contribute to harm and the court cannot observe how much harm each one caused, actual doctrines like proportional liability or no liability fail to create efficient incentives. A better approach would apply the novel principle of total liability for excessive harm.

Second, to achieve efficient contracts, the law should respond more to the promisee's incentives for cooperation and reliance. The problem of providing efficient incentives for the promisor and promisee in contract law is much the same as the problem of providing efficient incentives for the injurer and victim in tort law. Increasing the injurer's liability for the harm caused by an accident increases the injurer's incentives for care and decreases the victim's incentives for care. Similarly, increasing the promisor's liability for the harm caused by breach of a contract increases the promisor's incentives to perform and decreases the promisee's incentive to cooperate and restrain reliance. Anti-insurance supplies contract terms that ideally solve this incentive problem even when conduct is unverifiable. Promisee and promisor sign a contract to sell the promisee's right to compensation for breach to the "anti-insurer." Now the promisor has incentives to perform because he is liable to the anti-insurer for breach, and the promisee has incentives to cooperate and restrain reliance because she is uncompensated for breach.

Markets currently generate few contracts resembling anti-insurance, although that may change in the future.[1] Because anti-insurance is so rare, the doctrines of contract law should provide some solution that induces more efficient incentives for both promisor and promisee. Decreasing liability contracts offer such a solution for contracts whose performance occurs in phases, for instance construction of a building or participation in a joint venture to develop a new product. In a decreasing liability contract, the promisor's liability decreases as he completes more phases of the contract. Specifically, the promisor is liable for full compensation minus his expenditure on the contract's phases up to the time of breach. This liability schedule allocates enough losses to make the promisor want to complete the contract, and leaves the remaining costs of breach on the promisee, so the promisee cooperates and restrains reliance. Decreasing liability contracts exist under other names, and we believe that their use will spread once contractual parties understand better how to improve the promisee's incentive.

Third, the law should encourage unrequested benefits by making the beneficiaries compensate the benefactors more often, and by reducing the liability of injurers and breaching parties who externalize benefits. The law of restitution requires recipients to compensate benefactors for supplying unrequested benefits in limited circumstances such as "common funds." A public goods theory of restitution would allow benefactors to claim compensation from beneficiaries in more circumstances, provided that contracting is precluded. By extending the category of common funds, courts may allow recoveries at least in those cases with indisputable benefits for the beneficiaries. Development of this potentially revolutionary solution to the undersupply of public goods will require legislation, not just new court decisions.

Similarly, the law should encourage activities with undercompensated benefits by reducing the liability of benefactors to beneficiaries when accidents occur. Thus the injurer's ideal liability for an accident is the activity's *net harm*, which equals the victims' harm, minus the activity's external benefits, plus the activity's external costs. Courts can and should avail themselves of practical principles that reduce liability for activities with positive externalities and increase liability for activities with negative externalities, even though courts cannot and should not consider every type of benefit and harm when deciding liability in private law. A well documented pattern, in the U.S., is that doctors pay higher damages on average than drivers for causing similar harms. Ideally, physicians should pay lower damages on average than drivers for causing similar harm, because doctoring creates positive externalities and driving creates negative externalities. At a minimum, courts should remove this disparity.

---

[1] Profitable anti-insurance may require economics of scale, and first movers take the vast risk of never reaching an efficient scale. We hope that big consumer organizations such as Triple A will use anti-insurance first and others will follow them.

Going further, legislatures might enact laws instructing courts to allow less than 100 percent compensation for specific harms caused by activities with associated positive externalities, and more than 100 percent compensation for specific harms caused by activities that generate negative externalities.

Similarly, courts should ideally apply the net harm principle to damages that provoke nonlegal sanctions. When legal sanctions trigger nonlegal sanctions, the injurer's liability ideally equals the victim's harm minus the social benefits caused by the nonlegal sanctions. Legislatures should also consider instructing courts explicitly to adjust legal sanctions in light of nonlegal sanctions.

This book urges three main legal reforms. First, courts should remove misalignments in tort law. Second, when parties make contracts and courts interpret them, the terms should encourage the promisee to cooperate with performance and restrain reliance. Third, law should encourage acts that cause unrequested or undercompensated benefits by making the beneficiaries reward the benefactors, and by reducing the benefactor's liability for accidents. In short, private law should do a better job of promoting social welfare. That is our journey's destination. We hope you have enjoyed the trip.

Table of Cases

Table of Books and Articles

Subject Index

GPSR Authorized Representative: Easy Access System Europe - Mustamäe tee
50, 10621 Tallinn, Estonia, gpsr.requests@easproject.com